OECD Studies on Water

Water Governance in Cape Town, South Africa

OECD
BETTER POLICIES FOR BETTER LIVES

Please cite this publication as:
OECD (2021), *Water Governance in Cape Town, South Africa*, OECD Studies on Water, OECD Publishing, Paris, *https://doi.org/10.1787/a804bd7b-en*.

ISBN 978-92-64-67935-1 (print)
ISBN 978-92-64-33027-6 (pdf)

OECD Studies on Water
ISSN 2224-5073 (print)
ISSN 2224-5081 (online)

Photo credits: Cover © Ainhoa Sanchez/Volvo Ocean Race.

Corrigenda to publications may be found on line at: *www.oecd.org/about/publishing/corrigenda.htm*.

Preface

The OECD, the city of Cape Town, South Africa and the Western Cape Economic Development Partnership (EDP), are delighted to introduce the results of a year-long, bottom-up and inclusive policy dialogue on water governance, with over 80 stakeholders from public, private and non-profit sectors, and across all levels of government in South Africa.

The city of Cape Town has been particularly hard hit by the COVID-19 crisis, accounting for around 20% of total deaths in South Africa. One of the most important issues brought about by the pandemic was access to hygiene and sanitation, magnifying attention on inequalities in access to water quality services. In Cape Town, about 230,000 households living in informal settlements are more likely to be exposed to the virus than others. This is due to their difficulties in disposing of clean water and sanitation facilities. Looking ahead, megatrends such as climate change, urbanisation, and demographic change will only further exacerbate pressures on water resources and service delivery.

Lessons learned during the critical stages of Cape Town's 2016-18 water crisis were valuable to manage the short-term COVID-19 challenges. They were also key to help design long-term solutions towards greater water resilience. The water crisis triggered policy actions to cope with water scarcity issues, through risk assessments, communications and stakeholder engagement efforts, and regulatory changes. Indeed, in response to the pandemic, the city rolled out its water tanks programme to supply water to the most vulnerable communities in informal settlements.

Often – and the city of Cape Town is no exception – water crises are eye-openers to governance gaps, revealing challenges in relation to who does what, at which scale, how, when and why. As shown in the *OECD Principles on Water Governance*, policy responses to water-related challenges will only be viable if they are coherent, if stakeholders are properly engaged, if well-designed regulatory frameworks are in place, if there is adequate and accessible information, and if there are sufficient human and financial resources, as well as robust integrity and transparency frameworks in place.

The Cape Town water crisis opened a window of opportunity for new ideas to emerge, and to secure more acceptance and buy-in of reforms. But there is still room to do more. To meet current and future challenges, this report calls on the city of Cape Town to strengthen integrated basin governance and capacities at all levels of government; advance the water allocation reform; collect, generate and share accurate data; improve the financial sustainability of water and sanitation services; and facilitate peer-learning across service providers and stakeholders.

The OECD stands ready to continue to support Cape Town, working with all relevant stakeholders, in implementing these policy recommendations.

Ángel Gurría
OECD Secretary-General

Alderman Dan Plato
Executive Mayor
City of Cape Town, South Africa

Andrew Boraine
CEO
Western Cape Economic Development Partnership

Foreword

Water Governance in Cape Town adds to the rich compendium of country, region, city and thematic reviews published as part of the OECD Studies on Water over the past 15 years. This first OECD water policy dialogue at the local level contributes to expanding the global outreach of OECD's work adding to regional analyses of water governance in OECD countries (2011), Latin America and the Caribbean (2012), African Cities (2021) and Asia-Pacific (2020), as well as national water governance policy dialogues in Mexico (2013), The Netherlands (2014), Jordan (2015), Tunisia (2015), Brazil (2015 and 2017), Argentina (2019) and Peru (2021).

This report is an output of the OECD Programme on Water Security for Sustainable Development in Africa, launched in 2018 by the OECD Secretary-General Mr Ángel Gurría, the recipient of the 6th edition of the King Hassan II Great World Water Prize.

This report summarises the findings from a year-long bottom-up policy dialogue with more than 80 stakeholders in Cape Town and South Africa. It provides a diagnosis of key water governance challenges in Cape Town as well as policy recommendations to enhance more effective, efficient and inclusive water governance. The report argues that the water crisis in Cape Town presentedan opportunity for new ideas to emerge and for greater social and political acceptance of needed reforms. This analysis, and the underlying consultation process, are conceived as a first step to support better water policy design. This publication contributes to the work of the Regional Development Policy Committee (RDPC). It was approved by RDPC delegates via written procedure on 5 February 2021 under the cote CFE/RDPC(2021).

Acknowledgements

This report was prepared by the OECD Centre for Entrepreneurship, SMEs, Regions and Cities (CFE) led by Lamia Kamal-Chaoui, Director, as part of the Programme of Work and Budget of the Regional Development Policy Committee. This report is an output from the OECD Programme on *Water Security for Sustainable Development in Africa*, launched in 2018 by the OECD Secretary General and developed in cooperation with the Kingdom of Morocco and the World Water Council, as a follow-up to the 6th edition of the King Hassan II Great World Water Prize.

The report is the result of a year-long policy dialogue with more than 80 stakeholders from public, private and non-profit sectors and representatives from the city of Cape Town and across all levels of government in South Africa. Special thanks are extended to the Government of Flanders, Belgium for the financial support provided to carry out this policy dialogue.

Maria Salvetti, Water Economist and Policy Analyst in the OECD Water Governance Programme, drafted the report and co-ordinated the underlying policy dialogue with the support of Elisa Elliott Alonso, Junior Policy Analyst (Chapter 1), under the supervision of Aziza Akhmouch, Head of the Cities, Urban Policies and Sustainable Development Division in the CFE.Thanks are conveyed to OECD colleagues who provided valuable comments on the draft, especially Oriana Romano (Head of the Water Governance Programme), and Xavier Leflaive (Head of the Water and Adaptation Unit).

The OECD Secretariat is grateful for the excellent support and commitment from the city of Cape Town Water and Sanitation Department, in particular Michael Webster, Executive Director of Water and Waste, and Michael Killick, Director of Bulk Services, and from the Western Cape Economic Development Partnership, notably Selwyn Willoughby and Amanda Gcanga, both Programme Lead. Special thanks are also conveyed to John Dini from the Water Research Commission for his support and contribution.

Furthermore, the policy dialogue benefitted from insights from peer reviewers who contributed through their valuable expertise and country experience, participated in virtual missions and provided international best practices as well as guidance on the report, namely: Caroline Figuères, Strategic Advisor Water, Figuères Consultancy; Neil McLeod, Consultant; and Dr Koen Verbist, Programme Specialist, UNESCO.

As part of an inclusive and bottom-up consultation process, the draft report was shared for comments with more than 80 stakeholders from the city of Cape Town and South Africa (see Annex A) who were engaged throughout the policy dialogue via interviews and webinars. Earlier versions of this report were discussed with Cape Town authorities and stakeholders during two webinar held on 28 October 2020 and 28 January 2021, as well asat the 14th meeting of the OECD Water Governance Initiative (2-3 November 2020). Special thanks are conveyed to the following stakeholders, in particular for their written comments on earlier drafts: Patrick Mlilo and Makombe Tendayi from the National Department for Water and Sanitation; Melissa Lintnaar-Strauss from the Regional Office of the National Department for Water and Sanitation; John Dini from the Water Research Commission; Karen Shippey from the Department of Environmental Affairs and Development Planning of the Western Cape Government; Gail Cleaver-Christie, Jeanne Gouws and Andrew Turner from CapeNature; Michael Killick from the Water and Sanitation Department of the city of Cape Town; Rolfe Eberhard, consultant for the city of Cape Town; Selwyn Willoughby and

Amanda Gcanga from the Western Cape Economic Development Partnership; Chris Serjak from the United States Agency for International Development; Rob Uijterlinde from Dutch Water Authorities; Barbara Schreiner form the Water Integrity Network; Bernard Barraqué from CIRED-CNRS; and Claude Ménard from Paris University Panthéon-Sorbonne.

The report was submitted for approval by written procedure to the Regional Development Policy Committee on 5 February 2021 under the cote CFE/RDPC(2021)1. Special thanks are extended to Pilar Philip for preparing the report for publication and to Eleonore Morena for editing and formatting the report.

Table of contents

Tables

Figures

Boxes

Follow OECD Publications on:

http://twitter.com/OECD_Pubs

http://www.facebook.com/OECDPublications

http://www.linkedin.com/groups/OECD-Publications-4645871

http://www.youtube.com/oecdilibrary

OECD Alerts http://www.oecd.org/oecddirect/

Executive summary

While the COVID-19 virus has hit the Western Cape Province particularly hard with 270 691 cases and 10 731 deaths (20% of total deaths in South Africa) as of February 2021, located essentially in the city of Cape Town, the city administration has shown remarkable resilience in dealing with the pandemic, drawing extensively on lessons from past crises such as droughts. As in many other domains, COVID-19 has acted as a magnifying glass on pressing water challenges, amongst others stressing and widening existing inequalities in access to water and sanitation services in Cape Town's informal settlements; where 230 000 households rely on public water points and shared toilet facilities.

Lessons learned during the critical stages of Cape Town's 2016-18 water crisis were valuable for the city to manage the short-term COVID-19 implications and design long term solutions towards greater water resilience. At the beginning of 2018, the city of Cape Town was close to being the first city in the world to run out of water. Cape Town started experiencing drought in 2015, and water reservoirs reached critically low levels in 2017 and 2018. The intense hydrological drought attributable to the effects of climate change was exacerbated by anthropic factors such as rising urban population and competition among local water users, all placing enormous stress on limited resources. Without action, the 16 April 2018 was expected to be the day that Cape Town switched off its taps. Colloquially termed "Day Zero", this was defined as the point at which the dam levels were expected to fall to 13.5%, therefore requiring taps in the city of Cape Town to be shut off and citizens to fetch a daily 25 litres per person from communal water collection points. Though Day Zero was avoided by the joint efforts of all stakeholders, extreme events will continue to jeopardisewater scarcity in South Africa and Cape Town. In fact, it is estimated that, at the current rate, South Africa will experience a 17% water deficit by 2030 if no action is taken to respond to existing trends.

While exposing the city to serious vulnerability, the risk of a "Day Zero" triggered actions to cope with water scarcity issues. Institutional responses during the peak months of the drought between 2017 and 2018 included risk assessments, communications and stakeholder engagement efforts, and regulatory changes. The city council appointed a Water Resilience Task Team in May 2017 who designed a Water Resilience Plan outlining water supply augmentation targets. On the technical side, groundwater, reuse and, desalination were identified by city officials as potential techniques for supply augmentation. Cape Town's new Water Strategy, issued in 2019, aims specifically to turn Cape Town into a water sensitive city through the exploitation of diverse water resources, diversified infrastructure, making optimal use of stormwater and urban waterways for the purposes of flood control, aquifer recharge, water reuse and recreation, all based on sound ecological principles. Furthermore, the city has partnered with a number of public, private and/or, civil society entities to promote the improvement of freshwater quality and to manage water pollution.

Often – and the city of Cape Town is no exception – water crises are also eye-openers to governance gaps, revealing challenges in relation to who does what, at which scale, how, when and why, more than hydrological problems, which are often well-known. In the case of Cape Town, lessons learned from the water crisis management highlighted a series of governance gaps:

1. First, planning models, in which scenarios did not account for a drought event of such magnitude, had not been updated using the latest hydrology data available. It is likely that the potential effects of climate change on dam inflows had been underestimated since the plans used at the city, provincial and, national levels initially indicated that the city was water-secure until 2022. But it turned out that the city was more vulnerable than these plans indicated. While the severity of the

drought, a 1-in-590-year event, could not have been foreseen, resilience planning, including extensive use of climate change scenarios, might have helped to be better prepared.

2. Second, delayed water restriction decisions and enforcement, and a lack of leadership, amongst others, further aggravated water provision difficulties during the drought. Indeed, the city's exclusive reliance on traditional surface water sources made it more vulnerable in a context of much-reduced rainfall because when the drought hit, the city had limited ability to abstract water from alternative sources. Diversification of water supply through an optimised portfolio of grey and green infrastructure including water conservation measures, ground water abstraction, reuse and desalination, is needed and henceforth prioritised.
3. Third, the drought highlighted the absence of a holistic and effective water management policy. In 2019, with the objective to drive better resilience and preparedness to a future crisis, the city of Cape Town developed a Water Strategy aiming for a more holistic, integrated and multi-level approach to water management, in close coordination with the national government reconciliation strategy. The COVID-19 disruption may challenge implementation and delay the achievement of these goals, but is also an important testing ground for some lessons learned during the previous water crisis.

Crises, such as the one experienced by Cape Town, ften provide windows of opportunity for new ideas to emerge and create a social and political environment that is more conducive to making necessary reforms. Building on a year-long bottom-up policy dialogue with more than 80 stakeholders in Cape Town and South Africa, this report provides a diagnosis of key water governance challenges in Cape Town as well as policy recommendations to enhance more effectiveness, efficiency and inclusiveness in water management systems based on the OECD Principles on Water Governance. In particular, the report calls for:

- Strengthening integrated basin governance by establishing a single Catchment Management Agency covering the Western Cape Water Supply System territory and making better use of abstraction and pollution charges to fund water resources and conservation policies and mandates.
- Advancing the water allocation reform to better manage trade-offs across multiple users and revisiting water allocation regimes to face growing pressures on water resources and redress inequities in water use distribution. In that framework, cost-effective green solutions should also be prioritised to augment water yields in the Western Cape Water Supply System.
- Collecting, generating and sharing accurate data in order to drive better informed and evidence-based policies and decisions, especially with regard to water balance and water supply management in the Western Cape.
- Improving financial sustainability as well as technical and economic efficiency of water and sanitation services through developing an effective regulatory framework that incentivises utility performance. Indeed, service providers should not only approach cost recovery through increases in tariff levels, but should also seek efficiency gains as a priority. Moreover, thorough assessment and monitoring of all costs will help set up tariff calculations and levels that are sufficiently cost-reflective to drive long-term financial sustainability.
- Strengthening capacities at all levels of government including through more emphasis on capacity building in the National Water Strategy as well as through restoring and expanding mentoring programmes to attract and accompany water-related careers, students and professionals.
- Facilitating peer-learning and exchange of practices across water-related service providers and stakeholders would also contribute to further capacity development, stronger ownership and acceptance of decisions, and better policy implementation.
- Strengthening transparency, integrity and stakeholder engagement, through innovative open contracting models such as integrity pacts and e-procurement, and citizen engagement mechanisms to promote accountability and prevent corruption, political interference and their adverse effects.

1 Water security in Cape Town, South Africa

This chapter describes the stakes between water and the environment, water and the economy, and water and social inclusion in Cape Town. It then underlines how megatrends including climate change, economic growth, demographic changes and urbanisation are exacerbating water risks. Finally, it presents some key lessons learned from the water crisis, arguing that the drought resulted from multifaceted causes including reliance on vulnerable surface water resources, issues with data modelling and resource planning, or co-ordination and governance weaknesses. Nevertheless, the water crisis lessons are currently proving useful to manage the COVID-19 pandemic.

Setting the scene

South Africa is generally considered a water-scarce country due to its varying climatic conditions and increased demand for water resources (Box 1.1). Water scarcity is driven by recurrent droughts intensified by climatic variation. In addition, localised population growth and demographic changes coupled with high water consumption exert pressure on available resources and water balance between demand and supply. Although the country has a low level of renewable water resources of 900 m^3/capita/year (Food and Agriculture Organization of the United Nations, 2017[1]), it is estimated that South Africans consume about 237 litres of water per person per day. This is well above the world average of 173 litres per day (Minister of Human Settlements, Water and Sanitation, 2019[2]). South Africa's urban land expansion is the 11th largest urban expansion in the world and second greatest in Africa in absolute terms (Marron Institute of Urban Management, 2019[3]). With nearly a third of that expansion happening onto built-up rural areas and another 14% directly onto cultivated land, this rapid urbanisation is exacerbating flood risks. Many informal settlements in peripheral areas are on marginal land that is considered unsafe – around Cape Town, for instance, they are regularly exposed to flooding. Urban sprawl also has ecological consequences: 54% of South Africa's urban expansion in 2000-14 was onto habitats that sustain biodiversity and sequester carbon, such as forests, shrublands and especially grasslands. Water pollution is also a major issue in South Africa with 56% of the more than 1 150 wastewater treatment plants that are in poor and critical condition and need urgent rehabilitation and proper operation. Infrastructure is ageing with 57% of the asset being depreciated and needing renewal (DWS, 2019[4]). This situation generates water quality issues in areas where effluents are discharged.

Box 1.1. Key water data for South Africa

South Africa is the southernmost country of the African continent. With a surface area of over 1.22 million kilometres^2 (FAO, 2016[5]) and a total population of 58 558 270 inhabitants (World Bank, 2019[6]) growing at a current annual rate of 1.3% (World Bank, 2019[7]), it is one of the biggest countries in Africa, both in terms of surface area as well as population. It is also the second-largest economy in Africa, with a total expected GDP of USD 711 billion in 2020 in purchasing power parity (PPP) (IMF, 2020[8]) and a gross domestic product (GDP) per capita of USD 11 900 in 2020 in PPP (IMF, 2020[8]).

Though South Africa is considered a semi-arid country with an average annual rainfall of 495 mm, due to its vast surface area and geographical location, rainfall can vary widely from less than 100 mm/year in the west to approximately 500 mm/year in the east. Three different climate zones can be distinguished (FAO, 2016[5]):

- The eastern parts of the country, which are summer rainfall areas with annual precipitation of 500 mm and more.
- The central and western parts of the great plateau, which are semi-arid to arid and are characterised by late summer rains, varying from less than 100 mm/year to approximately 500 mm/year.
- The Cape Fold Mountains and the area between them and the sea have a winter rainfall season in the west and rainfall throughout the year in the more south-easterly parts. Annual precipitation in this region varies from about 300 mm to more than 900 mm. Situated in this climactic region, the Western Cape, where Cape Town is located, enjoys a Mediterranean climate and winter rainfall, as opposed to the rest of the country which experiences summer rainfall.

In 2019, South Africa used about 10 200 million m^3 of water a year from its major dams (DWS, 2019[9]). According to the National Water and Sanitation Master Plan (DWS, 2013[10]), agriculture is the largest water use with 61% of total water use, followed by municipal use at 27% (including industrial and commercial uses serviced by municipal systems), and power generation, mining and bulk industrial use, livestock and conservation and afforestation jointly making up the remaining 12%. According to the Department of Water and Sanitation Strategic Plan for the years 2020/21 to 2024/25 (DWS, 2019[9]), the level of assurance at which agricultural water is supplied is lower than that of the other sectors (90%). Water for power generation is seen as strategically important and is provided with the highest assurance of supply (99.5%) (which translates to 1: 200-year risk of failure).

In 2019, 88% of households had access to at least a basic water supply:[1] 76% had access to water in the house or yard and 12% had access to a public standpipe within 200 m walking distance from home. When minimum standards for reliability of water supply services[2] are taken into account, the percentage of households served drops to 74%. In 2019, 79% of households benefitted from at least basic sanitation services (DWS, 2019[4]). Although the percentage of people lacking access to basic water and sanitation services has declined steadily since 1994, the absolute number of unserved people has remained relatively constant due to population growth (DWS, 2019[4]).

Note: 1. According to DWS National Norms and Standards for Domestic Water and Sanitation Services (DWS, 2017[11]), a basic water supply is defined as a minimum volume of 6 000 litres (or 25 litres per person per day) of potable water made available to a household per month by a formal connection point at the boundary of a stand/yard, or in a site of a public institution (school, clinic, hospital, etc.) as prescribed by the Minister responsible for water supply.
2. According to DWS National Norms and Standards for Domestic Water and Sanitation Services, the minimum reliability standard is defined for a basic water supply as availability for at least 350 days per year, and not interrupted for longer than 48 consecutive hours.
Source: DWS (2013[10]), *National Water and Sanitation Master Plan*, https://www.gov.za/sites/default/files/gcis_document/201911/national-water-and-sanitation-master-plandf.pdf; DWS (2019[9]), *Strategic Plan (Vote 41) for the Fiscal Years 2020/21 and to 2024/25*, https://static.pmg.org.za/Department_of_Water_and_Sanitation_Strategic_Plan_2020_21_to_2024_25.pdf; IMF (2020[8]), *World Economic Outlook Database*, International Monetary Fund; DWS (2019[4]), *National Water and Sanitation Master Plan*, http://www.dwa.gov.za/National%20Water%20and%20Sanitation%20Master%20Plan/DocumentsReports.aspx; FAO (2016[5]), "Country profile – South Africa" , http://www.fao.org/3/i9821en/I9821EN.pdf; World Bank (2019), *The World Bank in South Africa, Overview*, World Bank, https://www.worldbank.org/en/country/southafrica/overview; World Bank (2019), *Population Growth (Annual %) - South Africa*, World Bank Database, https://data.worldbank.org/indicator/SP.POP.GROW?locations=Z; World Bank (2019), *Population, Total – South Africa*, World Bank Database, https://data.worldbank.org/indicator/SP.POP.TOTL?locations=ZA.

In the province of the Western Cape, situated on the southwestern coast of the country, a high population density, which is steadily increasing through migration, converges in an area with low available water resources, resulting in an accentuation of water scarcity issues that are experienced across the country which reached its peak during the Cape Town water crisis between 2015 and 2019. Water demand is predicted to outstrip current supply in the Greater Cape Town Region by 2021. Current forecasts suggest that an additional 300-350 million litres (0.3-0.35 million m^3) of water a day will be needed by 2028 to ensure supply meets demand (The Nature Conservancy, 2018[12]).

Cape Town relies heavily on surface water. The Western Cape is supplied by two water management areas (WMAs): Berg-Olifants and Breede-Gouritz (Figure 1.1). The Breede-Gouritz catchment supplies 59% of the Cape Town supply while the Berg-Olifants WMA supplies 41%. These catchments are also used extensively for irrigation (Western Cape Government, 2018[13]) in the surrounding areas. Indeed, the city of Cape Town receives 95% of its water from a system of 6 rain-fed dams that also supply agriculture and other urban areas (Berg, Lower Steenbras, Theewaterskloof, Upper Steenbras, Voëlvlei, Wemmershoek). On average, during a non-drought year, the city of Cape Town uses around 64% of the Western Cape Water Supply System's (WCWSS) available drinking water, agriculture uses 29% and smaller towns use around 7% (City of Cape Town, 2018[14]). In the absence of a bulk water utility, three of the WCWSS dams (Upper and Lower Steenbras, Wemmershoek) have been built and are owned by the city of Cape Town. However, it is the national DWS which fulfils regulatory control and allocates all water from the "big six" dams that Cape Town relies on.

Figure 1.1. Water management areas (WMAs), South Africa

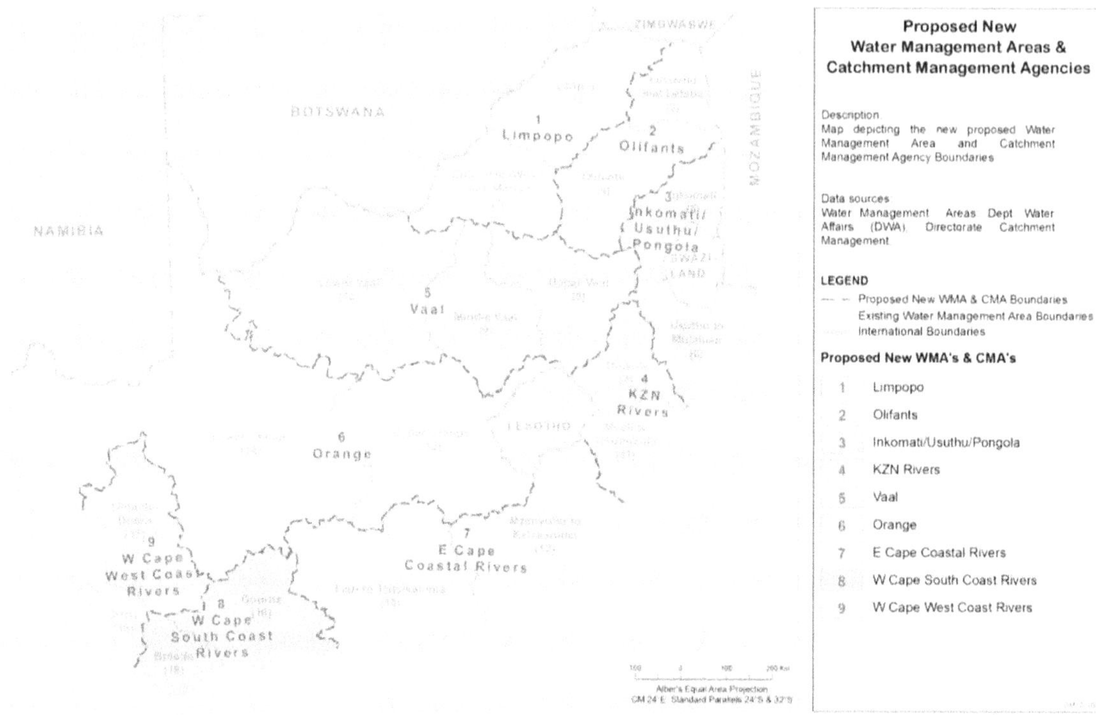

Source: DWS (n.d.[15]), *Water Management Area (WMA) Map*, http://www.dwa.gov.za/IO/wmamap.aspx.

The city of Cape Town provides water and sanitation services to more than 4.2 million people via water and sewer connections that supply nearly 600 000 domestic properties (City of Cape Town, 2018[14]) and basic services comprising public water points and shared toilet facilities to about 230 000 households living in informal settlements (City of Cape Town, 2020[16]). However, the city is growing rapidly and this figure increases every year due to population growth and migration. Each year, on average, the Water and Sanitation Department of Cape Town provides connections to 8 500 new customers (City of Cape Town, 2018[14]). In terms of access to water and sanitation, in 2016, 88% of Cape Town's population reported access to water inside the dwelling or yard, and 11.8% reported access outside their yard. A total of 91% of the population reported access to a flush toilet connected to the sewerage system or septic tank and 1.5% reported access to chemical toilets (City of Cape Town, 2017[17]).

The city of Cape Town started experiencing drought in 2015 and water reservoirs further reached critically low levels in 2017/18. The drought was driven by physical factors such as a lack of winter rainfall and increasing temperatures attributable to the effects of climate change. It was exacerbated by anthropic factors such as rising urban population and and competition among local water users, all placing enormous stress on limited resources (Climate Institute, 2018[18]). The 16 April 2018 was supposed to be the day that Cape Town switched off its taps, known as Day Zero, defined as the point at which the dam levels fell to 13.5%, therefore requiring taps in the city of Cape Town to be shut off and severe water rationing to be implemented, requiring citizens to fetch a daily 25 litres per person allocation at public points of distribution (PODs). Although Day Zero did not happen, the Cape Town water crisis exposed a serious vulnerability to water scarcity issues for the city, the surrounding urban agglomerations and the country at large.

Water and the environment

The Western Cape Province is abundantly rich in biodiversity, which is crucial to conserve in order to protect the water cycle. Although the Cape Floristic Region is the smallest of six recognised floral kingdoms in the world, it is a biodiversity hotspot. It is an area of high endemism and diversity, meaning that it has the highest concentration of plant species in the world (CapeNature, 2020[19]) and was inscribed on the World Heritage List in 2004. The vegetation of this floral kingdom is pyrophytic and requires fire in its lifecycle. Droughts dry the vegetation and make it prone to burning and this poses a risk to the wildland-urban interface especially since the Table Mountain National Park is completely within the city's urban boundaries. The Western Cape is also prone to extremely strong winds which not only enhance the evaporation rates but also dry out vegetation and quickly fan any fires into uncontrollable blazes. Nevertheless, the maintenance of these complex and varied natural systems is crucial to ensure sufficient clean water in the province. One of the most salient of these opportunities to augment water supply in the city of Cape Town is through investment in the clearing of alien species in catchment areas. These plants can have a severe effect on water resources, reducing water runoff by as much as 30% in heavily infested areas (CapeNature, 2020[20]) as invasive trees and shrubs use a significantly larger amount of water than indigenous plants. According to The Nature Conservancy, an investment of ZAR 372 million (USD 25.5 million) to clean invasive plants would increase streamflow by over 55 million m^3 a year within 6 years compared to a business-as-usual scenario – equivalent to one-sixth of the city of Cape Town's current supply needs – increasing to 100 million m^3 a year in avoided water losses within 30 years (The Nature Conservancy, 2018[12]).

The natural environment has been negatively affected by urban development, particularly by population growth in Cape Town, and impacted by various threats associated with urbanisation. Those threats have adversely affected water and air quality through pollution and the disruption of ecological functions, disturbing the delicate balance in biological diversity in the Western Cape Province. Human development has also increased the demand for water and sanitation services. Ongoing organic and inorganic pollution and littering of Cape Town's stormwater and freshwater systems pose a threat to both biodiversity and human health. In 2016, 10 out of 14 river systems and 9 out of 13 wetlands exhibited eutrophic or hypertrophic[1] characteristics. Furthermore, according to 2016 water quality data, only 2 of the 14 water bodies achieved 100% targeted guideline adherence to the intermediate contact guideline and less than half of all rivers achieved 80% adherence to the national freshwater quality targets (City of Cape Town, 2018[21]). Contamination of the city of Cape Town's freshwater systems is primarily due to contaminated urban stormwater and raw sewage from informal settlements, leaking sewers and pump stations. The continuously increasing rate of urbanisation, the rapid expansion of informal areas and an increase in backyard dwellings further strain Cape Town's capacity to service and build new infrastructure.

Several strategies have been launched by the city and the Western Cape Government to address these serious environmental issues in an effort to contribute to the water scarcity problem. Cape Town promotes the concept of water-sensitive urban design (WSUD) to move towards a "water-sensitive city" (Box 1.2). This approach includes the management of stormwater using established urban watershed and sustainable urban drainage system (SUDS) management tools. Cape Town's new Water Strategy issued in 2019 aims specifically to turn Cape Town into a water-sensitive city through the exploitation of diverse water resources, diversified infrastructure, making optimal use of stormwater and urban waterways for the purposes of flood control, aquifer recharge, water reuse and recreation, all based on sound ecological principles. One of the aims of the city of Cape Town's 2017 Environmental Strategy is to work towards significant improvements in water quality of the city of Cape Town's watercourses, including rivers and wetlands, with the aim to use these assets as recreational and community spaces that support Cape Town's biodiversity and social well-being, and allow for sustainable urban stormwater management. Other projects are ongoing to improve water quality. These include, for instance, an increase in maintenance for clearing litter and dumped material from stormwater systems, improving aquatic weed and algae management measures, improving informal settlement servicing and managing databases to include downstream water quality criteria, and eliminating sewer-to-storm-water cross-connections. Furthermore, the city of Cape Town has partnered with a number of public, private and/or civil society entities to promote the improvement of freshwater quality and to manage water pollution. Cape Town has also implemented the national Adopt-a-River Programme to encourage communities to adopt and clean dirty rivers. Furthermore, the Western Cape Government launched the Western Cape Ecological Infrastructure Investment Framework (EIIF) in 2019 to create strategies to tackle invasive species in the province and improve water security.

Box 1.2. An application of the "water-sensitive" city in Cape Town, South Africa

Context of the water-sensitive city

There are several theories integrating water management and urban or development planning, such as the Water Sensitive Urban Design (WSUD), Integrated Water Resource Management (IWRM), Integrated Urban Water Management (IUWM) and One Water. Variations of these concepts also include the Blue-Green City concept that originated in the United Kingdom as well as the Sponge City concept hailing from the People's Republic of China. In water management, integrated water management approaches recognise that water acts in accordance with geographical and hydrological factors, rather than administrative boundaries. Therefore, stakeholders in water catchment basin areas must work across territorial and administrative boundaries, which can occasionally lead to even further fragmentation. Land-use planning and land governance, on the other hand, are some of the main competencies of cities and municipalities, in which their powers as an authority stand out. Cities can rarely make water management decisions on their own but they do have the prerogative to respond to water risks effectively through their urban planning and development processes and tools.

Originating in Australia, the water-sensitive city (WSC) or WSUD theory foresees six development stages of urban water management to protect the degradation of urban water resources and manage and recycle stormwater so that cities become sustainable, liveable and resilient (Wong and Brown, 2009[22]; Ashley et al., n.d.[23]). The transition towards a WSC model holds promise for metropolitan water policy. Beyond merely recognising the need for environmental sustainability, a "water-sensitive cities" model requires reform of the existing contract between citizens and governments over water policy, infrastructure, technologies and urban form, and would reinforce water-sensitive behaviour. This can be carried out through a flexible institutional regime that would co-manage water resources through multiple government levels, communities and economic sectors. Such a transition would entail intergenerational equity and resilience to climate change (OECD, 2011[24]).

WSUD and planning in Cape Town

Since the water crisis, the city of Cape Town developed an extensive policy outlook that actively facilitates the transition towards a WSC. Its integrated development plan (IDP) and spatial development framework (SDF) – two documents encompassing the city's medium-term strategic vision for development – provide the foundation for water-sensitive designs.

Cape Town reinforces this general support of water sensitivity principles – included in the IDP and SDF – by developing policy that addresses the transition to a WSC directly. Its Stormwater Impacts Policy was developed to minimise the negative effects of stormwater runoff within the city by introducing WSUD principles to urban planning and stormwater management. The policy introduces best practice criteria for achieving sustainable urban drainage objectives in various development scenarios and requires all stormwater management systems to be planned and designed in accordance with these criteria. In addition to its stormwater management policy, the city of Cape Town has also recently developed a Water Strategy contributing to facilitating the transition of Cape Town to a WSC by 2040 "with diverse water resources, diversified infrastructure and one that makes optimal use of stormwater and urban waterways for the purposes of flood control, aquifer recharge, water reuse and recreation, and that is based on sound ecological principles". It aims to achieve this through incentive and regulatory mechanisms and new investment initiatives.

Source: Helen Suzman Foundation (2019[25]), *Developing Water-Sensitive Cities III: A Case Study of Two South African Metros*, https://hsf.org.za/publications/hsf-briefs/developing-water-sensitive-cities-iii-a-case-study-of-two-south-african-metros; Wong, T. and R. Brown (2009[22]), "The water-sensitive City: Principles for practice", http://dx.doi.org/10.2166/wst.2009.436; Ashley, R. et al. (n.d.[23]), "Water-sensitive urban design: opportunities for the UK", http://dx.doi.org/10.1680/muen.12.00046; OECD (2011[24]), *Water Governance in OECD Countries: A Multi-level Approach*, https://dx.doi.org/10.1787/9789264119284-en.

Water and the economy

The city of Cape Town is the economic hub of the Western Cape Province and a key economic hub of the national economy. It is home to 70% of the Western Cape GDP and 63% of the provincial population. Cape Town contributes to 9.7% of the national GDP (City of Cape Town, 2019[26]). The key industries include the financial and business services industry, manufacturing and wholesale and trade. Important exports include oils petroleum and citrus fruit, grapes and apples. The agricultural products are mostly sourced from outside the metropolitan area of the city of Cape Town. However, these can be processed within the city before being exported.

Though agriculture represents a smaller part of national GDP, the Western Cape region, due to its climate, provides a very productive environment for crop growth. In fact, the region produces between 55% and 60% of South Africa's agricultural exports. It also contributes approximately 20% towards South Africa's total agricultural production (Water Research Commission, 2014[27]). In the Western Cape, 43% of available water is used for irrigation and it sustains a ZAR 530 billion (USD 36.3 billion) economy in the province alone. This sector employs around 180 000 workers, while the agri-processing sector adds another 126 000 jobs to the economy. Together, these sectors employ 15% of the provincial labour force (WWF, 2018[28]).

Increased domestic demand due essentially to the inflow of migration causes tensions between different water users (domestic, industrial, agricultural ones). However, there is an interdependent relationship between the city of Cape Town and the surrounding agricultural area. For example, on the one hand, the surrounding rural areas depend on visitors to the city of Cape Town for their own touristic sector. On the other hand, increased pollution from industrial use and deteriorating sewerage systems in the city are resulting in lower-quality water that represents a cost to all users.

Water scarcity issues put greater pressure on the rural-urban interdependent relationship. The 2015-18 drought had a significant impact on agriculture, livelihoods and communities, with an estimated economic loss of ZAR 5.9 billion (USD 0.4 billion) for agriculture in the Western Cape alone, 30 000 job losses and 13%-20% exports drop (WWF, 2018[28]). Tourism accounts for 10% of South Africa's economic output and provides 1.5 million jobs – around 10% of total employment in the country (Parks et al., 2019[29]). Negative press on the crisis resulted in a clear decrease in the number of visitors in 2017 compared to previous years due to the Day Zero campaign (Box 1.3). Similarly, a preliminary impact assessment of the COVID-19 crisis on the South African tourism industry has shown that during the first 6 weeks of the pandemic, 99% of tourism firms claim to be negatively affected and only 23% feel neutral or optimistic about the future (Department of Tourism, South Africa, 2020[30]).

Box 1.3. Tourism in Cape Town

Tourism is an important economic sector to Cape Town, and South Africa at large. The Western Cape attracted around 1.7 million international tourists and generated ZAR 16.3 billion (about USD 985 million) in foreign spending in 2018 (Wesgro, 2019[31]). Cape Town is one of the most visited towns in South Africa and is a tourism hub for the African continent.

The drought had an impact on tourist arrivals in the Western Cape, particularly at its peak between 2017 and 2018, and further translated into a decline in arrivals in South Africa. This consequently affected potential revenue for the city of Cape Town, the province and the country. In April 2017-18, the tourism industry recorded a 12.6% decline in overseas arrivals, with a further decline of 3.7% and 1.3% observed in May and June respectively.

The effects of the drought on the local tourism industry have further been compounded by the effects of the COVID-19 pandemic which triggered an unprecedented crisis in the tourism economy, given the immediate and immense shock to the sector. Revised OECD estimates on the COVID-19 impact point to 80% decline in international tourism in 2020 (OECD, 2020[32]). While country response measures continue to focus on public health issues, governments have also moved quickly to introduce extraordinary initiatives to mitigate the economic impact of COVI-19 crisis on businesses and workers. The tourism sector is greatly benefitting from these general economic support measures, which are relevant and accessible to workers and tourism businesses of all sizes. In South Africa, the Tourism Relief Fund, available from 7 April, provides once-off capped grant assistance to micro-, small- and medium-sized enterprises in the tourism value chain to ensure their sustainability during and post the implementation of government measures to curb the spread of COVID-19 in South Africa. Capped at ZAR 50 000 per entity, grant funding can be used to subsidise expenses towards fixed costs, operational costs, supplies and other pressure cost items. Categories eligible to apply for the Tourism Relief Fund include accommodation establishments, hospitality and related services, travel and related services.

Source: Dube, K., G. Nhamo and D. Chikodzi (2020[33]), "Climate change-induced droughts and tourism: Impacts and responses of Western Cape province, South Africa", *Journal of Outdoor Recreation and Tourism*; Wesgro (2019[31]), *Western Cape Destination Performance Report: Annual 2018*, https://wesgro.co.za/uploads/files/Research/DPR-2018.pdf; OECD (2020[34]), *Tourism Policy Responses to the coronavirus (COVID-19)*, https://www.oecd.org/coronavirus/policy-responses/tourism-policy-responses-to-the-coronavirus-covid-19-6466aa20/.

Ensuring more sustainable and water-wise agriculture and efficient municipal use is a key priority of the Western Cape region to maintain economic growth and regional development. During the drought, both the city of Cape Town and agricultural users made important efforts to decrease their water use significantly. For example, between 2017 and 2018, the agriculture sector in the Western Cape cut its water use by 60% on average. Water restrictions varied from 50% in the Breede Valley to 60% in the Berg River and Riviersonderend region and 87% in the Lower Olifants River Valley, with consequences on output value (WWF, 2018[28]). Cape Town residents also experienced severe water restrictions and lowered their water consumption by 55%.

Water and social inclusion

Though South Africa is recognised for its progressive 1998 water legislation to formally erase racial and class discrimination in the access to water, the country still struggles with inequality with regards to water justice. Dynamics of spatial and economic segregation of people of colour before 1994 resulted in the displacement of hundreds of thousands of "coloured" and "black" Capetonians to inferior housing in low-lying areas prone to flooding and with limited access to water, sanitation and other services (Enqvist and Ziervogel, 2019[35]). Though the national and local policy has strived to promote water justice for all citizens, municipalities have struggled with implementation, especially in rapidly growing informal settlements, where a significant part of immigrants are located.

The province is currently experiencing a significant inflow of migration from other areas of the country. The Western Cape has the second-highest rate of positive net migration after the province of Gauteng. Between 2001 and 2016, domestic net migration added an estimated 450 546 people to the province's population, with migrants from other provinces accounting for 27% of population growth over that period (Western Cape Government, 2017[36]). This inflow of migration has led to serious housing issues in the city of Cape Town with subsequent implications on the quality of water and sanitation provision to residents.

To promote more equal service delivery, the South African government passed the Free Basic Water Policy in 2001, mandating that municipalities provide a daily 25 litres per person, or a monthly 6 m^3 for a household of 8, at no cost to end-users and accessible no more than 200 m from their homes (Beck et al., 2016[37]). Following subsequent revisions, this policy now only applies to indigent households.[2] The city of Cape Town currently supplies free water to approximately half a million people living in informal settlements. On average, actual net water use by households in informal settlements is less than the basic-need amount: water is heavy to carry and a household of 4 would need to carry 28 buckets of water every day to use 50 litres per person. Total gross usage in informal settlements, including all types of use and losses, is about 50 litres per person per day (7 buckets), constituting only 5% of total usage in Cape Town (City of Cape Town, 2019[38]).

The gap in social inclusion when it comes to access to water and sanitation services may be exacerbated with the COVID-19 crisis. It is still early to tell how Cape Town will recover from the economic and social strife caused by the pandemic and its consequences on longer-term social and economic equality among all members of its population. However, some signs indicate that the pandemic is making it even harder for vulnerable citizens to have access to water and sanitation (UN-Habitat, 2020[39]).

The impacts of global megatrends on water risks

The onset and consequences of the Cape Town water crisis were exacerbated by megatrends such as climate change, the implications of economic growth on water demand and the continuation of demographic and urbanisation patterns. The figure on drought categories from the draft National Disaster Risk Reduction and Management Plan (DWS, forthcoming[40]) illustrates these multifaceted causes and exacerbating factors, including climate change impacts, increasing water demand or insufficient water infrastructure (Figure 1.2). Though Day Zero was avoided by the joined efforts of all stakeholders, extreme events will continue jeopardising water scarcity in the country and Cape Town. In fact, it is estimated that, at the current rate, South Africa will experience a 17% water deficit by 2030 if no action is taken to respond to existing trends (DWS, 2013[10]).

Climate change

The Western Cape was projected as one of the South African provinces most at risk of climate-induced warming and rainfall change. Evidence suggests that a significant cause of the drought could be attributed to climate change and that more events of this type can be expected in the future (Schiermeier, 2018[41]). This makes the city of Cape Town's resource management more challenging, especially since it has been estimated that human-induced climate change tripled the likelihood of the 2015-17 drought based on historical rainfall and dam inflow data (Otto et al., 2018[42]). These results point out important water-related climate risks that the city needs to be prepared for. For instance, since 2007, South Africa's Department of Water Affairs (currently the Department for Water and Sanitation, DWS) has underscored the need for diversification of water supply sources. Indeed, almost all of the city's water still comes from 6 dams (95%) dependent on rainfall, a risky situation in a semi-arid region with climate change forecasts predicting that Cape Town will get hotter and drier over the next 50 years (Schiermeier, 2018[41]). Climate change and globalisation have also triggered and exacerbated the spread of water-thirsty alien plant species in crucial catchment areas for Cape Town. This resulted in a decrease in water supply estimated to 30 million m^3 per year.

Figure 1.2. Drought categories according to their causes and impacts

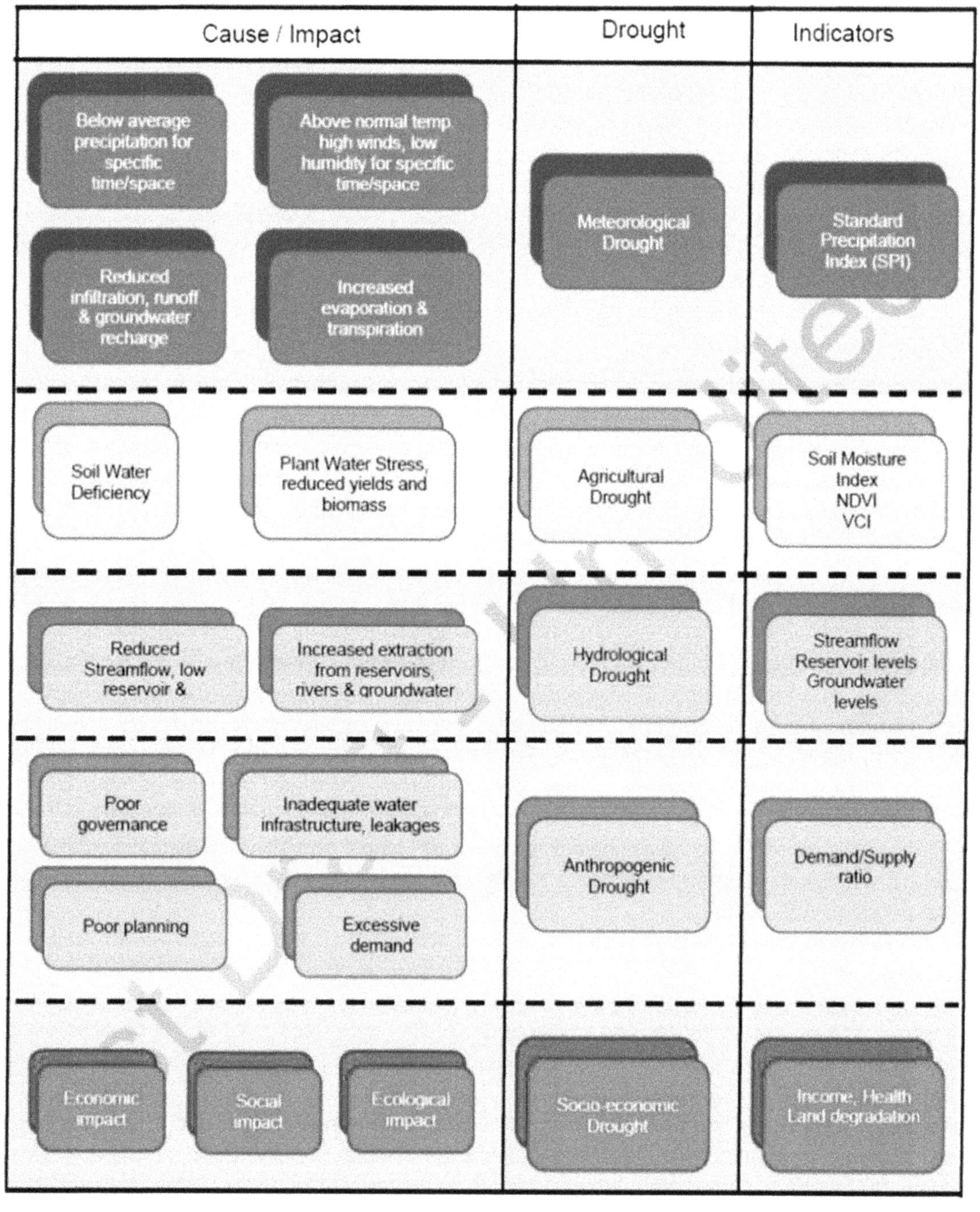

Source: DWS, (forthcoming[40]), Draft National Disaster Risk Reduction and Management Plan

In the context of increasing competition for water in the region and the potential surface water dam yields reduction due to climate change, Cape Town plans to become a water-sensitive city, where natural resources and engineered water services are planned and managed in an integrated and holistic way. Part of this approach to ensure resilience against climate change include water augmentation schemes (i.e. several options to increase water supply). For example, the DWS is currently implementing the Berg River to Voëlvlei Dam Augmentation Scheme as the next water resource scheme to increase the WCWSS capacity. A number of additional schemes are being implemented or investigated by the city including groundwater use, water reclamation for potable use, IUWM or seawater desalination. Furthermore, greater recognition for the value-added of investing in green infrastructure has taken form since the remission of the drought. The Nature Conservancy launched the Greater Cape Town Water Fund to increase collective support by a range of stakeholders to clear alien invasive vegetation from the catchments for the purpose of augmenting water yield in the bulk water system.

The Cape Town Resilience Strategy developed in 2019 is a direct response to the water crisis after the recognition that the implementation of severe water restrictions may not be enough to ensure supply the next time a drought of the same or greater magnitude arises (Box 1.4). The resilience strategy aims to integrate further climate adaption into all types of municipal planning and to integrate spare capacity to be better prepared for times of disruption. It also explicitly recognises the importance of partnerships through improved stakeholder engagement for water governance, holistic water resilience and collective ownership of water-related topics in the city. Indeed, the drought had a strong impact on municipal adaptation to climate change with, for instance: household installation of rainwater tanks, boreholes and well points, driving down consumption in homes through conservation and use of greywater; the creation of spring water collection points in communities; a greater understanding of climate risk; advanced pressure management in the city distribution system; and new water supply systems rapidly installed by the city. These measures as well as the change in water bylaws and building requirements within the metropolitan area of Cape Town adopted in 2019, placed more responsibility on property owners to provide for onsite water storage, water reuse and water efficiency.

Box 1.4. Cape Town Water Resilience Strategy

The Cape Town Resilience Strategy was adopted in the aftermath of the worst drought that the city-region has confronted in recorded history. The development of this strategy went through a number of phases and milestones including considerable stakeholder engagement: 11 000 Capetonians were interviewed in face-to-face interviews during January and February 2018, and approximately 200 thematic experts from community-based organisations, non-governmental organisations (NGOs), business, academia and other spheres of government shared their insights and advice during various stages of the strategy development process. The processes and tools used in the development of the strategy are similar to those used in other cities in the 100 Resilient Cities Network.

Five pillars form the core of Resilient Cape Town:

- **Pillar One - Compassionate, holistically-healthy city**

  Apartheid, high crime rates, substance abuse and poverty: the legacies of these challenges have culminated in a base level of trauma faced by Capetonians in all parts of society. This has resulted in a high incidence of mental health disorders – which often exacerbates the quadruple burden of disease. This pillar focuses on a more holistic approach to building a healthier city, including improving access to mental health services and affordable, nutritious food, strengthening social cohesion and ensuring that children have the best possible start to life, with the intention of disrupting the intergenerational transfer of trauma.

- **Pillar Two – Connected climate-adaptive city**

  Cape Town's unique geography makes our city very vulnerable to the impacts of climate change. These impacts, which can manifest as a variety of shock events, are known to be multiplied by existing societal stresses such as poverty, food insecurity and a lack of social cohesion. In this vein, the residents of informal settlements and backyards are often the most vulnerable to climate-related shock events. This pillar focuses on overcoming the spatial legacies of our divided past through partnership at all scales – community, city and regional – allowing us to enact climate-adaptive measures that simultaneously build urban resilience, with co-benefits that include improved mobility, place-making and social cohesion.
- **Pillar Three – Capable, job-creating city**

  The performance of the Cape Town economy and its ability to create jobs is heavily intertwined with national and global trends. The impacts of climate change can result in resource constraints, while a variety of shock events – from a cyberattack to infrastructure failure – can affect supply chains and productivity. Rapid technological change has the potential to exclude more work-seekers from the economy, while globalisation and increased connectivity makes the environment for attracting new investment more competitive. This pillar focuses on building resilience for the purpose of sustaining and growing new opportunities in the context of change. A resilient city, working to overcome its risks and turning them into new market advantages, is an attractive city for growth and new investment.
- **Pillar Four – Collectively shock-ready city**

  The nature of a rapidly changing urban environment impacted by climate change, urbanisation, rapid technological change and globalisation means that the nature of shocks that can impact Cape Town are varied beyond those that we are commonly prepared for and they can be more complex in terms of scale and impact considering the continuous stresses that are pervasive in our city. This pillar focuses on preparing capabilities for some new, known shocks that could impact us in the future but, more broadly, works to build the capacity of individuals, households and communities to respond to shocks, no matter what kind of shocks may occur, with particular focus on vulnerable households and communities.
- **Pillar Five - Collaborative, forward-looking city**

  The city government operates in a complex legislative environment with limited resources. It has an extensive service offering to Capetonians and a number of transformational goals set out in the integrated development plan (IDP) but is cognisant of the fact that shocks and stresses can negatively affect its ability to deliver these services and goals. This pillar focuses on how the city government will work with other spheres of government and organisations to improve the functioning of certain key city systems. It also focuses on how the city government will work with partners such as data and technology providers, modellers and researchers, to be reflective aftershock events and to mainstream resilience into planning and decision-making.

Source: City of Cape Town (2019[43]), *Cape Town Resilience Strategy*, https://resource.capetown.gov.za/documentcentre/Documents/City%20strategies%2C%20plans.

Economic growth

The South African economy is largely based on services, manufacturing and mining (FAO, 2016[5]) in which water plays a critical role. Prior to the COVID-19 crisis, South Africa's economy was growing moderately: real GDP grew at an estimated 0.7% in 2019, down from 0.8% in 2018, and was projected to rise to 1.1% in 2020 and 1.8% in 2021 amid domestic and global downside risks (AFDB, 2019[44]). The COVID-19 pandemic and the ensuing lockdown have led to a sharp economic contraction and rising unemployment, particularly affecting youth (OECD, 2020[34]). Post lockdown, mid-September estimates of 2020's second quarter-point to the economy contracting by 51% quarter on quarter. All sectors, except – notably – agriculture, printed a negative output (Stats South Africa, 2020[45]). The early and strict lockdown from mid-March to the end of June explains the severity of the contraction but monthly indicators point to a rebound of activity since July which is confirmed by a rebound of 66.1% for the third quarter (quarter on quarter).

Despite economic progress since the transition to democracy in the mid-1990s, South Africa retains one of the highest inequality rates in the world and significant poverty prevails. South Africa had a Gini coefficient of 0.63 in 2015 (World Bank, 2019[46]). Inequality has been persistent and is perpetuated by a legacy of exclusion and the nature of economic growth, which is not pro-poor and does not generate sufficient jobs. Inequality in wealth is even higher: the richest 10% of the population held around 71% of net wealth in 2015, while the bottom 60% held 7% of the net wealth (World Bank, 2019[46]). Furthermore, intergenerational mobility is low, meaning inequalities are passed down from generation to generation with little change in inequality over time.

As in most African countries, the economic landscape of South Africa is dependent on the effects of climate change and this also has significant implications for water. Higher temperatures and a reduction in rainfall expected as a result of climate change will reduce already depleted water resources, contributing to an increasing number of droughts in the country. South Africa's development is highly dependent on climate-sensitive sectors such as agriculture and forestry. Increases in temperature and reductions in rainfall threaten the productivity of these sectors. Tourism is another key driver of South Africa's economic growth. Ranked third in the world in terms of biological diversity, desertification caused by a hotter drier climate could potentially reduce biodiversity, threatening the tourism industry. Temperature rise and changes in rainfall patterns also increase the potential for malarial disease, with significant impacts on health and the economy (UNDP, 2020[47]).

Cape Town is a critical economic hub in South Africa and presents its own unique characteristics. Cape Town's economy has progressively shifted towards a predominantly service-driven one with growth in tertiary sector industries outpacing growth in both primary and secondary sector industries in the last decade. The local economy has recently grown faster than the national economy primarily because it is not heavily dependent on the mineral sector, which has experienced a recent downturn. Cape Town's unemployment rate at the end of 2018 was 21.2% on the narrow definition and 23.1% on the broad definition (City of Cape Town, 2019[43]). While Cape Town's narrow unemployment rate is significantly lower than the country as a whole and the broad unemployment rate is the lowest out of all metropolitan municipalities, half a million Capetonians are unemployed. High unemployment is a significant stress in Cape Town and is a contributing factor to high levels of poverty and inequality. Increasing employment is thus a crucial component of building resilience to shocks and improving quality of life.

In times of crisis, finding a balance between protecting the general interest and ensuring economic activity for the continuance of livelihoods is a challenge. During the water crisis, the authorities implemented measures to reduce water consumption while supporting economic activities. Despite the emergency, all around Cape Town wine production continued in order to prevent an ensuing economic crisis (ISPI, 2018[48]), which caused notable tension between water user categories due to differentiated restriction measures. This "water versus wine" polemic clearly illustrates the tensions created by the water balance between both "essential" and "non-essential industries" especially in times of crisis. Nonetheless, winemakers still experienced a notable decline in their activity, owing to water use restrictions.

Demographic changes

In the past decade, Cape Town experienced a population growth rate of 2.5%, exacerbated by significant and fast migration into the city. Cape Town is the second-most populous city in South Africa, behind Johannesburg, and the 10th most populous city in Africa. From 2011 to 2016, Cape Town had the

4th-highest annual population growth of all the metropolitan municipalities in South Africa, increasing from 1.5% between 2011 and 2012 to 1.6% between 2015 and 2016. This rapid urbanisation is largely the result of inward migration of South Africans, particularly from the Eastern Cape, Gauteng and other parts of the Western Cape (Stats South Africa, 2018[49]). A significant number of new migrants to Cape Town find a residence in one of the city's many informal settlements (City of Cape Town, 2019[43]).

Although the city now continues to grow at a slower pace, this demographic upward trend has many water-related impacts. For example, urban sprawl contributes to increasing the ground sealing thus exacerbating flood risks and reducing groundwater recharge. The loss of agricultural land and areas with high biodiversity conservation potential induce water conservation, runoff and quality issues. In the city's growth areas, the water and sewer infrastructure is stressed. The pressing housing challenge has given rise to a growing number of backyard dwellers which increases the water demand and sewer load on existing infrastructure. For instance, contamination of the city's freshwater systems is primarily due to contaminated urban stormwater and raw sewage from informal settlements, leaking sewers and pump stations.

Cape Town's success will be contingent on its capacity to manage the implications of these demographic changes. The city has managed a relatively stable water demand over the last 20 years, despite a rapidly increasing population, thanks to the implementation of water demand management measures and various city initiatives. There is also an increased consumer awareness of water-saving, with improved maintenance of household plumbing by fixing leaks and installing more water-wise toilets, taps and showerheads. The city has increased its efforts in reusing water for industry and for watering golf courses and sports grounds. However, significant inequities stemming from apartheid still plague the city, highlighting the unique importance of human capital development in order to mitigate the consequences of poverty. In this sense, the city's resilience strategy considers the role of water in reducing urban inequalities and promoting health and safety for all its residences. For example, one strategy-based objective recognises the current poor state of Cape Town's rivers and waterways as a breeding ground of inequality and focuses on rejuvenating rivers and spaces around them to create healthy, safe and productive urban waterways which produce multiple resilience dividends, including flood mitigation, new work and recreation opportunities, improved water quality and crime reduction.

Urbanisation trends

As a result of long-standing inequities and the rate of population growth in the city, Cape Town is facing a serious housing crisis which affects the quality of basic services provision. The city of Cape Town has an estimated population of just over 4 million people, with most recent official population Census data showing that 20.5% of households live in informal housing (13.5% in informal settlements and 7% in informal backyard dwellings) (City of Cape Town, 2012[50]). According to Stats South Africa's General Household Survey of 2018, the Western Cape, after Gauteng, has the second-highest proportion of households living in informal dwellings (Stats South Africa, 2018[51]). Most of the informal settlements in Cape Town are situated on city-owned land; however, some are located on private land, which creates unique and complex legal challenges for the provision of basic services to these specific informal settlements and for the implementation of informal settlements regeneration projects.

The growing challenge of informal housing due to immigration has resulted in increasing demands on water and sanitation services and increased inequalities in access to basic services. There are approximately 230 000 informal households (City of Cape Town, 2020[16]) in 204 informal settlements throughout the city, which are serviced by approximately 10 000 communal taps and 50 000 toilets (City of Cape Town, 2018[14]). In terms of water use, residents in formal housing use 66% of the city's water, while informal settlements account for only around 4%-5% of total water consumption (City of Cape Town, 2018[21]; 2018[14]). Informal settlements are characterised by a lack of formal tenure, insufficient public space and facilities, inadequate access to municipal services and poor access ways. Some informal settlements are built on dangerous sites such as unplanned landfills, wetlands or retention and detention ponds, which intensify the likelihood of disasters such as flooding. From a social point of view, these areas often overlap with high social vulnerability such as poverty, unemployment and high crime rates (City of Cape Town, 2019[43]).

Cost recovery and sustainable funding of water is another challenge and the dynamics of class and race reflect themselves in water funding strategies. About 1.5 million people, making up more than a third of the total population in the city, cannot afford to pay for water and therefore are eligible for a free allocation each month. The policy intention is for water tariffs to fully recover the cost of the water service except for the allocation of free water, which is paid from a national operation grant known as the Equitable Share. However, in practice, cash revenues are insufficient to cover all of the costs, especially timely rehabilitation and replacement of existing infrastructure (Ziervogel, 2019[52]). This situation for low-income households significantly contrasts with the trends of urban development in Cape Town for middle and upper classes with low-rise buildings, swimming pools and lawns, which also hold implications for water use and demand in the city.

The Cape Town Resilience Strategy specifically recognises the need to innovate for improved conditions, service delivery and well-being in informal settlements as a way to achieve a connected and climate-adapted city. This goal specifically envisages two actions: exploring alternative, innovative and financially feasible mechanisms of service delivery in informal settlements which are acceptable to local residents, and co-designing informal settlement upgrading projects with local residents. Clear alignment between city officials and NGOs and informal settlements is a key necessity for these actions to be implemented effectively as well as accurate up-to-date data and information.

Cape Town's drought crisis: Key lessons

The water crisis took the form of drought, rare in its intensity and duration. The El Niño-triggered drought in the Western Cape developed over a period of three years from June 2015 through to June 2018. Rainfall over this period represented 50% to 70% of the long-term average (Wolski, 2018[53]). In 2017, many rainfall records were the lowest since the 1880s (Wolski, 2018[53]). This low rainfall resulted in increasingly lower and lower dam levels. In fact, the overall level of storage in the 6 largest dams, accounting for over 99% of total system storage, dropped from 100% in 2014 to 71%, 60% and 38% in the subsequent years (as measured at the start of each hydrological year, 1 November, also marking the start of the dry season) (Figure 1.3) (Ziervogel, 2019[52]).

Institutional, technical and communication responses during the water crisis

Institutional responses during the peak months of the drought between 2017 and 2018 included risk assessments, communications and stakeholder engagement efforts, and regulatory changes. The City Council appointed a Water Resilience Task Team (WRTT) in May 2017, headed by the Chief Resilience Officer, within the Directorate of the Mayor, which designed a Water Resilience Plan outlining water supply augmentation targets. On the technical side, groundwater and desalination were identified by city officials as potential techniques for supply augmentation. In August 2017, the Water Resilience Advisory Committee (WRAC), was established in the city to convene monthly external advisors, share knowledge and plan actions with a number of stakeholders outside of the municipal administration. This committee included around 15 members from academia, business, NGOs, non-profit organisations (NPOs), provincial and national government, among others.

Figure 1.3. Dam levels, urban and agricultural use and rainfall in the Western Cape from 2014 to 2018

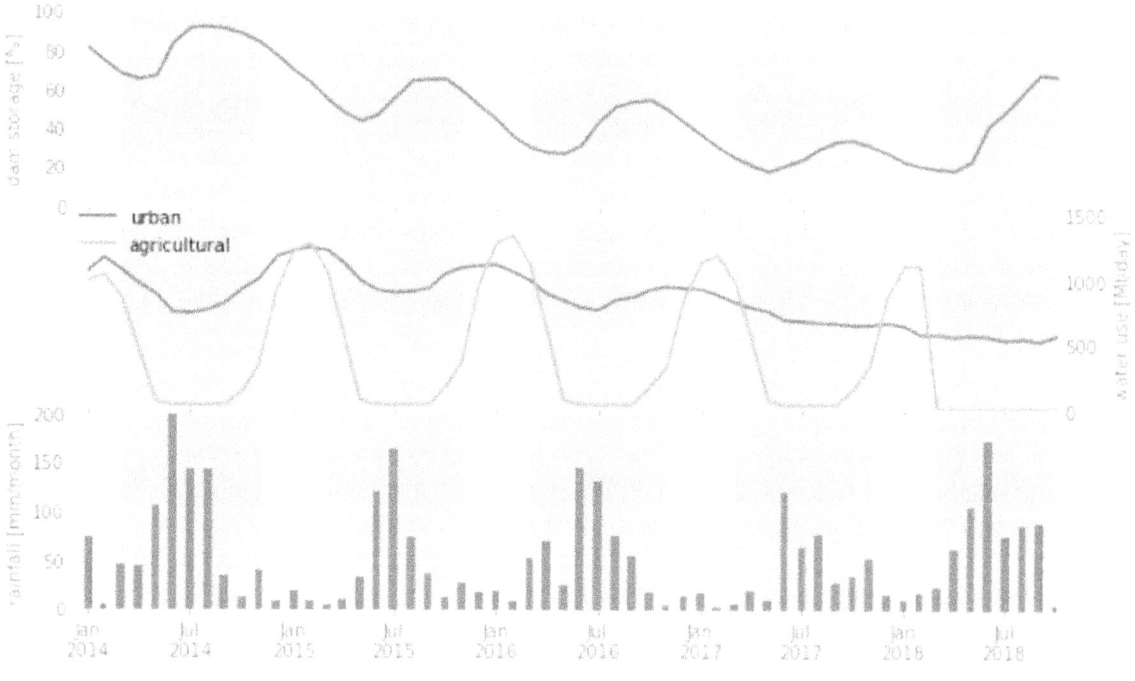

Source: Wolski in Ziervogel, G. (2019[52]), *Understanding the Cape Town Drought: Lessons Learned*, https://www.africancentreforcities.net/wp-content/uploads/2019/02/Ziervogel-2019-Lessons-from-Cape-Town-Drought_A.pdf.

On the technical side, responses focused on demand management. In this sense, the city scaled up the installation of household flow regulator devices to target households using large amounts of water (i.e. houses with large gardens, etc.) and effluent reuse schemes were stepped up to increase the amount of potable water that could be used. In order to strengthen the effect of these technical measures, the city engaged in a strong communication campaign and stakeholder engagement strategy to make everyone aware of the crisis and increase water conservation efforts (Box 1.5).

Box 1.5. Cape Town's Drought Crisis Communication

During the tipping point of the water crisis between 2017 and 2018, the city ran an exhaustive, sustained communication campaign through channels ranging from print, radio, billboards and social media to displays in shopping centres, with the aim of making stakeholders keenly aware of the consequences of the crisis and maximise the effectiveness of institutional and technical measures which included stringent water use restrictions, steep tariff increases (especially for those who used the most water) and technical interventions such as pressure management.

In July 2017, daily use was reduced to 87 litres per person per day by the city of Cape Town, which imposed further restrictions while raising tariffs. In November 2017, the long-standing weekly dam level report available on the city's website was expanded into a "water dashboard" that gave useful information and projections about consumption, supply and water-related matters. In order to stop the spread of misinformation, toolkits were also developed to ensure that private sector partners and communities and organisations with limited resources could access communication material in an open-source manner.

Stakeholders were informed and engaged through numerous briefings to provide them with mailers, rates bill inserts, educational materials or templates that could be customised for their own use. The city ran a Water Star rating certification system to recognise companies and organisations for best practices in water management. Partnerships with companies and non-profit organisations assisted to extend the reach of water-saving messaging.

With the inflow of tourists expected during the year-end holiday season, the city launched the Save Like a Local campaign that urged visitors to embrace water-saving habits. This campaign was rolled out in all tourist hot spots. Brochures and leaflets were made available to hotels and hospitality outlets.

As the water crisis worsened at the start of 2018, the first Water Outlook, a comprehensive report on the steps the city was taking in its drought management and augmentation efforts, was published. This was complemented with a live Water Map where householders could access an online map and easily see how they and other residents were performing against the targets.

Source: City of Cape Town (2020[54]), *Cape Town's Drought Crisis Communication,* https://www.arcww.co.za/wp-content/uploads/2016/09/24589-COCT-Drought-Crisis-case-study.pdf.

At the start of the height of the crisis in late 2017, the municipal Department of Safety and Security released a Critical Water Shortages Disaster Plan that laid out three phases for demand management based on the gravity of the depletion of water resources:

- Phase 1: Water rationing through pressure management and supply limitation.
- Phase 2: Disaster restrictions aimed at intensive water rationing, prioritising human life and critical services.
- Phase 3: Full-scale disaster implementation where non-surface drinking water supplies, sourced from groundwater abstraction from various aquifers and spring water, would be available for drinking purposes only and where critical services would be significantly reduced.

Although the Critical Water Shortages Disaster Plan was never implemented and Phase 1 was never surpassed, it was an ambitious exercise that ensured a city plan for water shortage, if it ever came to fruition.

In January and February 2018, at the peak of the crisis, fear spread across city residents after municipal authorities aggressively restricted water use to 50 litres per person per day by limiting supply and enforcing tariffs and initiated more active communications campaigns. Residents and businesses reduced water use and daily use in the city was driven down to just below 500 000 m^3 several times, which was about 50% of the pre-drought usage. No other city has ever achieved this level of reduction without resorting to intermittent supply (Ziervogel, 2019[52]). At this point, the concept of Day Zero, coined by a provincial government official, entered the public consciousness. The term was originally meant as when the dams would run dry but the city started defining it as the time when the water supply to homes would be cut off and residents would have to collect water from public collection points. However, the idea of "zero" was a powerful one and encouraged residents to use even less water. Day Zero was initially forecast by city officials for April 2018 but through a combination of stringent water consumption restrictions, temporary infrastructure interventions and late-season rainfall, it was then pushed back to 2019 and then later cancelled. The restrictions were accompanied by strict tariffs. The cost of water for non-domestic use, which accounts for about 30% of city usage, more than doubled (to over ZAR 40 or USD 3), making it very expensive to use more water than restrictions allowed. Commercial and industrial water use declined by about 20% (Ziervogel, 2019[52]). The city maintained its social tariff, providing 10.5 m^3 per month at no charge to the approximately 270 000 residential properties with a property value below ZAR 400 000 (which is about 30% of the total formal housing) and free water through public standpipes to a further 180 000 households living in informal settlements. Other domestic users faced a very steep inclining block tariff with very large increases if they used more than restrictions allowed. The winter rainfalls during 2018 filled the dams to above 75% by the end of the winter, marking the beginning of the recovery with dams reaching 100% in 2020.

Lessons from the water crisis

Several factors brought the city of Cape Town to the brink of a water crisis in early 2018. First, planning models had not been updated using the latest hydrology data available and the potential effects of climate change on dam inflows had likely been underestimated (the hydrology in the planning models was last updated based on 2004 rainfall/runoff information). While the baseline study on reconciling demand and supply, completed in 2007, was updated each year, changes in water availability as a result of changes in vegetation and other factors were overlooked. The plans used at the city, provincial and national levels initially indicated that the city was water-secure until 2022. But it turned out that the city was more vulnerable than these plans indicated. While the severity of the drought, a 1-in-590-year event, could not have been foreseen, resilience planning, including extensive use of climate change scenarios, might have helped to be better prepared (Water Research Commission, 2018[55]).

Second, the city's reliance on traditional surface water sources made it more vulnerable in the context of much-reduced rainfall. The city had run a successful groundwater abstraction and recharge system for a number of years and had also begun investigating other alternatives including more extensive groundwater abstraction, reuse and desalination before the drought. Nevertheless, when the drought hit, the city had limited ability to abstract water from these alternative sources and thus mitigate the impact of the drought.

Third, some weaknesses in governance and water management became evident during the drought. While the drought brought many organisations together and united residents and businesses towards conserving water to the best extent possible given the circumstances, it also exposed gaps in co-ordination, leadership and capacity with delayed water restriction decisions and enforcement, for instance. Though restriction measures and temporary infrastructure implemented by the city eventually averted the crisis, these gaps will remain in the long run. As a response, in 2019, the city of Cape Town developed its Water Strategy which aims to take a more holistic approach to water management and focuses on what is needed to build resilience (Kaiser and Macleod, 2018[56]) through five commitments: safe access to water and sanitation; wise use of water; sufficient, reliable water from diverse sources; shared benefits from regional water resources; and a water-sensitive city. Part of this strategy includes improved stakeholder engagement through collaboration, thus recognising that multiple actors need to be engaged to manage water across levels of government and between organisations. The COVID-19 disruption may challenge and delay the achievement of these goals but is also an important testing ground for some lessons learned during the water crisis (Box 1.6).

Box 1.6. How Cape Town Water Crisis paved the way for COVID-19 crisis management

Covid-19 impacts on South Africa and Cape Town

Like most other countries around the globe, South Africa has been hit hard by the COVID-19 pandemic, with over 1 346 000 confirmed cases of COVID-19 and over 37 400 deaths (to date) (WHO, 2021[57]). Though the impact of the pandemic has been relatively mitigated on the African continent in relation to other regions, South Africa has the continent's highest caseload to date and continues to bear the highest burden of the pandemic, with 69% of total deaths (as of January 2021) and 57% of all reported and confirmed cases in the African region (WHO, 2021[58]). In addition to human casualties, the COVID-19 pandemic and the ensuing lockdown have triggered a sharp drop in economic activity.

South Africa reacted quickly to the outbreak by establishing a nationwide lockdown on March 26. Economic activity was reduced in mining and industry and stopped in the tourism, entertainment and passenger transport sectors. The OECD (2020[34]) estimates that in a double-hit scenario, a new outbreak affecting South Africa and its trading partner countries will curtail exports, deepening the recession to -8.2% in 2020 and limiting the recovery in 2021, with GDP growth at 0.6%.

The Western Cape has been one of the hardest-hit provinces in the country, with over 9 400 deaths and over 257 000 cases (Western Cape Government, 2021[59]). The Cape Town metropolitan area accounted for around 70% of total cases in the province. In terms of water management and service provision, the pandemic has emphasised the already existing inequalities in access to water and sanitation services in townships, informal settlements and among the homeless in Cape Town. The national Department of Human Settlements, Water and Sanitation procured 41 000 water tanks for national distribution to ensure water supply during the lockdown so that people in these living conditions can still have enough drinking water and maintain adequate and healthy hygiene routines. However, there are very significant concerns about the spread of COVID-19 in informal settlements through communal toilets and taps, as well as security concerns around the use of water tanks (Hara, Ncube and Sibanda, 2020[60]).

COVID-19 poses many challenges to the water sector encompassing economic and social issues. A sustainable and financial funding model for water and sanitation is needed, but under so many stressed conditions and with tariffs set below cost-recovery level, it will be challenging to finance all of the necessary water investments to achieve resilience while addressing basic human and social needs. The National Water and Sanitation Plan, which sets outs the country's approach to address, among other issues, inequalities in access to water and sanitation for the poor in cities, will be tested through the pandemic, especially with regards to the co-ordination between funding capacity and funding needs, in light of the added pressure that the pandemic entails in terms of resources.

From crisis management to the "new normal"

Lessons learned during the critical stages of Cape Town's 2017-18 water crisis have helped the city cope with the hardships imposed by the pandemic in 2019-20.

In fact, terminology now used globally, such as the "new normal" which makes a reference to the realisation that the crisis brought on by the pandemic will bring about permanent change, was already used by stakeholders in the Western Cape to reference the effects of the drought and the predicted impacts of climate change. Like the drought, the pandemic has precipitated changes that had profound economic impacts, with direct losses in earnings at many levels experienced by individuals, as well as countries' GDP and growth rates. In addition, social changes in the way people live and work have been brought about. Furthermore, the environmental aspect of both crises is undeniable, with the longer-term impacts of climate change becoming more and more visible.

Some important lessons learned during the drought shaped the city's response to COVID-19. For example, both crises led the Western Cape and Cape Town governments to value the importance of effective communication with citizens and stakeholders for co-ordinated action and trust-building. This need for collaborative and open interactions between stakeholders has also become apparent during the COVID-19 crisis, where, despite the difficult conditions, municipal stakeholders have worked together through transversal committees to minimise the impact of COVID-19 on its residents in a more cohesive way, a method that was put into practice with the water crisis.

COVID-19 may provide the impulse necessary towards a green recovery, building off the 2019 Cape Town Resilience Strategy implemented as a response to the water crisis. For example, the impulse to prioritise investment in ecosystem services such as the clearing of alien invasive species as a more cost-effective way to augment water supply may become stronger now, in times of funding limitations brought about by the pandemic. However, the full impact of COVID-19 is yet to be seen and the future remains uncertain as long as the pandemic remains rampant.

Source: Author's elaboration based on Hara, M., B. Ncube and D. Sibanda (2020[60]), "Water and Sanitation in the Face of Covid-19 in Cape Town's townships and informal settlements"; OECD (2020[34]), *OECD Economic Surveys: South Africa 2020*, https://doi.org/10.1787/530e7ce0-en; Western Cape Government (2020[61]), *Covid-19 Dashboard*, https://coronavirus.westerncape.gov.za/covid-19-dashboard; WHO (2021[57]), *South Africa: WHO Coronavirus Disease (COVID-19) Dashboard*, https://covid19.who.int/region/afro/country/za; WHO (2021[58]), "COVID-19 situation update for the WHO Africa region" , https://apps.who.int/iris/bitstream/handle/10665/336181/SITREP_COVID-19_WHOAFRO_20201021-eng.pdf;
Western Cape Government (2021[59]), Covid-19 Dashboard | Covid-19 Response, Western Cape Government official website. https://coronavirus.westerncape.gov.za/covid-19-dashboard

References

AFDB (2019), *South Africa Economic Outlook*, African Development Bank, https://www.afdb.org/en/countries/southern-africa/south-africa/south-africa-economic-outlook. [44]

Ashley, R. et al. (n.d.), "Water-sensitive urban design: opportunities for the UK", *Municipal Engineer*, Vol. 166/2, pp. 65-76, http://dx.doi.org/10.1680/muen.12.00046. [23]

Beck, T. et al. (2016), "Institutional and policy mapping of the water sector in South Africa", Program on Water Governance and University of British Columbia, Vancouver, http://edges.sites.olt.ubc.ca/files/2016/12/Institutional-Map-of-SA-Water-Sector-Final.pdf. [37]

CapeNature (2020), *Alien Vegetation Management*, https://www.capenature.co.za/care-for-nature/conservation-in-action/integrated-catchment-management/alien-vegetation-management/. [20]

CapeNature (2020), *Cape Floristic Region*, https://www.capenature.co.za/care-for-nature/biodiversity/cape-floristic-region/. [19]

City of Cape Town (2020), *Cape Town's Drought Crisis Communication*, https://www.arcww.co.za/wp-content/uploads/2016/09/24589-COCT-Drought-Crisis-case-study.pdf. [54]

City of Cape Town (2020), "Human settlements strategy: Draft version for public comment", http://resource.capetown.gov.za/documentcentre/Documents/City%20strategies%2C%20plans%20and%20frameworks/Draft_Human_Settlements_Strategy.pdf. [16]

City of Cape Town (2019), *Cape Town Resilience Strategy*, https://resource.capetown.gov.za/documentcentre/Documents/City%20strategies%2C%20plans%20and%20frameworks/Resilience_Strategy.pdf. [43]

City of Cape Town (2019), *Economic Performance Indicators for Cape Town*, https://resource.capetown.gov.za/documentcentre/Documents/City%20research%20reports%20and%20review/EPIC%202019%20Q1%20FINAL.pdf. [26]

City of Cape Town (2019), "Our shared water future: Cape Town's Water Strategy", https://resource.capetown.gov.za/documentcentre/Documents/City%20strategies,%20plans%20and%20frameworks/Cape%20Town%20Water%20Strategy.pdf. [38]

City of Cape Town (2018), *City of Cape Town State of the Environment Report 2018*, http://resource.capetown.gov.za/documentcentre/Documents/City%20research%20reports%20and%20review/State%20of%20the%20Environment%202018%20Report.pdf. [21]

City of Cape Town (2018), *Water Services and the Cape Town Urban Water Cycle*, https://resource.capetown.gov.za/documentcentre/Documents/Graphics%20and%20educational%20material/Water%20Services%20and%20Urban%20Water%20Cycle.pdf. [14]

City of Cape Town (2017), "2016 Community Survey. Cape Town trends 1996 to 2016", http://resource.capetown.gov.za/documentcentre/Documents/Maps%20and%20statistics/2016%20Community%20Survey%20Cape%20Town%20Trends.pdf. [17]

City of Cape Town (2012), *2011 Census – Cape Town, Trends and Change*, http://resource.capetown.gov.za/documentcentre/Documents/Maps%20and%20statistics/2011_Census_Cape_Town_Profile_Change. [50]

Climate Institute (2018), *Delaying Day Zero: Fighting Back Against Water Insecurity*, http://climate.org/wp-content/uploads/2018/04/Day-Zero-Water-Article.pdf. [18]

Department of Tourism, South Africa (2020), *Tourism Industry Survey of South Africa: COVID-19, Preparedness for Reopening*, https://www.tourism.gov.za/CurrentProjects/Tourism_Relief_Fund_for_SMMEs/Documents/South%20Africa%20Tourism%20Survey%202%20on%20COVID-9%20(June%202020)%20Results.pdf. [30]

Dube, K., G. Nhamo and D. Chikodzi (2020), "Climate change-induced droughts and tourism: Impacts and responses of Western Cape province, South Africa", *Journal of Outdoor Recreation and Tourism*. [33]

DWS (2019), *National Water and Sanitation Master Plan*, Department of Water and Sanitation, http://www.dwa.gov.za/National%20Water%20and%20Sanitation%20Master%20Plan/DocumentsReports.aspx. [4]

DWS (2019), *Strategic Plan (Vote 41) for the Fiscal Years 2020/21 and to 2024/25*, Department of Water and Sanitation, https://static.pmg.org.za/Department_of_Water_and_Sanitation_Strategic_Plan_2020_21_to_2024_25.pdf. [9]

DWS (2017), "National norms and standards for domestic water and sanitation services", *Government Gazette*, No. 982, Department of Water and Sanitation, https://cer.org.za/wp-content/uploads/1997/12/National-norms-and-standards-for-domenstic-water-and-sanitation-services.pdf. [11]

DWS (2013), *National Water and Sanitation Master Plan*, Department of Water and Sanitation, https://www.gov.za/sites/default/files/gcis_document/201911/national-water-and-sanitation-master-plandf.pdf. [10]

DWS (forthcoming), *National Disaster Risk Reduction and Management Plan*, National Department for Water and Sanitation. [40]

DWS (n.d.), *Water Management Area (WMA) Map*, Department of Water and Sanitation, http://www.dwa.gov.za/IO/wmamap.aspx. [15]

Enqvist, J. and G. Ziervogel (2019), "Water governance and justice in Cape Town: An overview", *WIREs Water*, Vol. 6/4, https://onlinelibrary.wiley.com/doi/full/10.1002/wat2.1354. [35]

FAO (2016), "Country profile – South Africa", *FAO AQUASTAT Reports*, Food and Agriculture Organization, United Nations, http://www.fao.org/3/i9821en/I9821EN.pdf. [5]

Food and Agriculture Organization of the United Nations (2017), *Aquastat*, http://www.fao.org/aquastat/statistics/query/index.html;jsessionid=C37B4C7FABC0A0DB6430C76AFB8C1547. [1]

Hara, M., B. Ncube and D. Sibanda (2020), "Water and Sanitation in the Face of Covid-19 in Cape Town's townships and informal settlements". [60]

Helen Suzman Foundation (2019), *Developing Water-Sensitive Cities III: A Case Study of Two South African Metros*, https://hsf.org.za/publications/hsf-briefs/developing-water-sensitive-cities-iii-a-case-study-of-two-south-african-metros. [25]

IMF (2020), *World Economic Outlook Database*, International Monetary Fund. [8]

ISPI (2018), "Cape Town's water crisis: Governance hindrances in the age of climate change", Istituto per gli Studi di Politica Internazionale, https://www.ispionline.it/sites/default/files/pubblicazioni/commentary_montanini_23.03.2018.pdf. [48]

Kaiser, G. and N. Macleod (2018), "Cape Town - Where we've been and where we want to go", *Civil Engineering*, Vol. 9/October, pp. 8-12. [56]

Marron Institute of Urban Management (2019), *Urban Land Expansion*, https://marroninstitute.nyu.edu/programs/urban-expansion. [3]

Minister of Human Settlements, Water and Sanitation (2019), "Statement by L.N. Sisulu, South African Minister of Human Settlements, Water and Sanitation, Budapest Water Summit 2019", http://www.dhs.gov.za/sites/default/files/speeches/budapest. [2]

OECD (2020), *OECD Economic Surveys: South Africa 2020*, OECD Publishing, Paris, https://doi.org/10.1787/530e7ce0-en. [34]

OECD (2020), "Tourism Policy Responses to the coronavirus (COVID-19)", *OECD Policy Responses to Coronavirus (COVID-19)*, OECD, Paris, https://www.oecd.org/coronavirus/policy-responses/tourism-policy-responses-to-the-coronavirus-covid-19-6466aa20/. [32]

OECD (2011), *Water Governance in OECD Countries: A Multi-level Approach*, OECD Studies on Water, OECD Publishing, Paris, https://dx.doi.org/10.1787/9789264119284-en. [24]

Otto, F. et al. (2018), “Anthropogenic influence on the drivers of the Western Cape drought 2015-2017”, *Environmental Research Letters*, Vol. 13, pp. 1-10, https://doi.org/10.1088/1748-9326/aae9f9. [42]

Parks, R. et al. (2019), “Experiences and lessons in managing water from Cape Town”, *Grantham Institute Briefing Paper*, No. 29, Imperial College London, https://www.imperial.ac.uk/media/imperial-college/grantham-institute/public/publications/briefing-papers/Experiences-and-lessons-in-managing-water.pdf. [29]

Schiermeier, Q. (2018), “Droughts, heatwaves and floods: How to tell when climate change is to blame”, *Nature*, https://www.scientificamerican.com/article/droughts-heat-waves-and-floods-how-to-tell-when-climate-change-is-to-blame/. [41]

Stats South Africa (2020), “Steep slump in GDP as COVID-19 takes its toll on the economy”, Statistics South Africa, http://www.statssa.gov.za/?p=13601. [45]

Stats South Africa (2018), “General Household Survey”, Statistics South Africa, http://www.statssa.gov.za/publications/P0318/P03182018.pdf. [51]

Stats South Africa (2018), “Mid-year population estimates 2018”, Statistics South Africa, http://www.statssa.gov.za/publications/P0302/P03022018.pdf. [49]

The Nature Conservancy (2018), *The Greater Cape Town Water Fund, Assessing the return on Investment for Ecological Infrasytructure Restoration, Business Case*, The Nature Conservancy, https://www.nature.org/content/dam/tnc/nature/en/documents/GCTWF-summary-11.14.18.pdf. [12]

UNDP (2020), *Climate Change Adaptation: South Africa*, United Nations Development Programme, https://www.adaptation-undp.org/explore/africa/south-africa#:~:text=South%20Africa's%20development%20is%20highly,of%20South%20Africa's%20economic%20growth. [47]

UN-Habitat (ed.) (2020), *COVID-19 in African Cities: Impacts, Responses and Policies*, https://unhabitat.org/covid-19-in-africa-cities-impacts-responses-and-policies. [39]

Water Research Commission (2018), “Day Zero on the back of drought in southern Africa – Lessons for the future”, *Fluid Thoughts*, http://www.wrc.org.za/wp-content/uploads/mdocs/WWMarch18_Upfront_web.pdf. [55]

Water Research Commission (2014), *Water in the Western Cape Economy*, http://www.wrc.org.za/wp-content/uploads/mdocs/2075-1-13.pdf. [27]

Wesgro (2019), *Western Cape Destination Performance Report: Annual 2018*, https://wesgro.co.za/uploads/files/Research/DPR-2018.pdf. [31]

Western Cape Government (2021), *Covid-19 Dashboard*, https://coronavirus.westerncape.gov.za/covid-19-dashboard. [59]

Western Cape Government (2020), *Covid-19 Dashboard*, Covid-19 Response, Western Cape Government, https://coronavirus.westerncape.gov.za/covid-19-dashboard. [61]

Western Cape Government (2018), *Western Cape Sustainable Water Management Plan 2017-2022*, https://www.westerncape.gov.za/eadp/files/atoms/files/WC%20Sustainable%20Water%20Management%20Plan%202018.pdf. [13]

Western Cape Government (2017), “Futurescape policy brief: Migration trends in the Western Cape”, https://pardee.du.edu/sites/default/files/MigrationBrief_AJM_FINAL.pdf. [36]

WHO (2021), “COVID-19 situation update for the WHO Africa region”, *External Situation Report*, No. 34, World Health Organization, https://apps.who.int/iris/bitstream/handle/10665/336181/SITREP_COVID-19_WHOAFRO_20201021-eng.pdf. [58]

WHO (2021), *South Africa: WHO Coronavirus Disease (COVID-19) Dashboard*, World Health Organization, https://covid19.who.int/region/afro/country/za. [57]

Wolski, P. (2018), “What Cape Town learned from its drought”, *Bulletin of the Atomic Scientists*, https://thebulletin.org/2018/04/what-cape-town-learned-from-its-drought/. [53]

Wong, T. and R. Brown (2009), “The water-sensitive City: Principles for practice”, *Water Science and Technology*, Vol. 60/3, pp. 673-682, http://dx.doi.org/10.2166/wst.2009.436. [22]

World Bank (2019), *Population Growth (Annual %) - South Africa*, World Bank Database, https://data.worldbank.org/indicator/SP.POP.GROW?locations=ZA. [7]

World Bank (2019), *Population, Total – South Africa*, World Bank Database, https://data.worldbank.org/indicator/SP.POP.TOTL?locations=ZA. [6]

World Bank (2019), *The World Bank in South Africa, Overview*, World Bank, https://www.worldbank.org/en/country/southafrica/overview#:~:text=South%20Africa%20remains%20a%20dual,increased%20from%200.61%20in%201996. [46]

WWF (2018), “Agricultural water file: Farming for a drier future”, World Wildlife Fund, https://www.wwf.org.za/water/?25441/Agricultural-water-file-Farming-for-a-drier-future. [28]

Ziervogel, G. (2019), *Understanding the Cape Town Drought: Lessons Learned*, https://www.africancentreforcities.net/wp-content/uploads/2019/02/Ziervogel-2019-Lessons-from-Cape-Town-Drought_A.pdf. [52]

Notes

[1] Usually low or very low levels of species diversity; usually very highly productive systems; nuisance growth of aquatic plants and blooms of blue-green algae, often including species which are toxic to humans, wildlife and livestock.

[2] Municipalities determine their own criteria for identifying and registering indigents. In 2017, 147 municipalities (out of 257) classified an indigent household as a family earning a combined income of less than R3 200 per month (http://www.statssa.gov.za/).

2 Mapping water governance in Cape Town, South Africa

This chapter firstly proposes an institutional mapping of the three-tiered governance system in place in South Africa and describes who does what at national and subnational levels. It thus underlines the fragmentation and complexity of water policy and management in South Africa. It then focuses on the water allocation principles in force in the country, as well as the water supply system in place in Cape Town which involves a variety of stakeholders across sectors and levels of government. As such, the Western Cape Water Supply System also appears fragmented both vertically and horizontally, thus requiring important co-ordination efforts. Finally, it presents the financing framework for water resources and services management in Cape Town and South Africa which relies on a funding scheme composed of seven elements.

A three-tiered water governance system

As in many countries, water governance in South Africa is a shared responsibility across levels of government. Key roles and responsibilities for policymaking, policy implementation, operational management, information, monitoring, regulation and financing are allocated across a broad range of stakeholders, thus reflecting the fragmentation and complexity of water policy and management. As a consequence, Cape Town, like all municipalities in South Africa, needs to co-ordinate with upper levels of government, and vice versa, when designing and implementing water policies. Mapping who does what is the first step to clearly represent the allocation of roles and responsibilities of actors at different levels of government and across water management functions for water resources management (Figure 2.1) and water services provision (Figure 2.2).

Who does what at the national level?

The **National Department of Water and Sanitation** (DWS) is the lead national entity for water policy. The DWS's main responsibilities include the development and revision of national policies, the oversight of all legislation that impacts the water sector (including setting national norms and standards), co-ordination with other national departments on policy, legislation and other water-related issues, national communication strategies and the development of national water strategies. The DWS currently fulfils some regulatory functions for the water sector. This encompasses water use authorisation, compulsory national standards for water services, infrastructure regulation, oversight of public entities reporting to the minister, regulation of competition, and some aspects of economic regulation (including setting raw water tariffs and overseeing the setting of bulk water tariffs by water boards and retail tariffs by water service authorities). A further role entails monitoring sector performance, including conformity to national norms and standards. At present, the DWS manages most of the national water resources infrastructure through its Water Trading Entity and National Water Resources Infrastructure Branch.

The **Water Trading Entity** (WTE) is in charge of developing, operating and maintaining specific water resources infrastructure and managing resources in specific areas.

The **National Water Resources Infrastructure Branch** that comes under the DWS is responsible for the development of new water resources infrastructure and the rehabilitation, maintenance and operation of existing infrastructure.

The **Trans-Caledon Tunnel Authority** (TCTA) is a state-owned entity (SOE) specialising in project financing, implementation and liability management. It finances and manages the implementation of economically viable projects, as directed by the National Minister. It also provides integrated treasury management and a financial advisory service to the DWS, water boards, municipalities and other entities that are linked to bulk raw water infrastructure. TCTA projects are financed off-budget and the investment costs are repaid through user charges.

Established in 1998, the aim of the **Water Tribunal** is to hear appeals against directives and decisions made by responsible authorities or water management agencies about matters such as the issuing of licences to use water. It is an independent body and can hold hearings anywhere in the country.

The **National Treasury** administers grants for water infrastructure and provides funds to water service authorities for the provision of Free Basic[1] services through the equitable share of nationally-derived revenue.

The **National Department for Cooperative Governance and Traditional Affairs** ensures that all municipalities perform their basic responsibilities and functions consistently. This includes the delivery of municipal services to the right quality and standard, the promotion of good governance, transparency and accountability, the fulfilment of sound management of finances and accounting, and administrative capacity building.

Figure 2.1. Institutional mapping for water resources management in Cape Town, South Africa

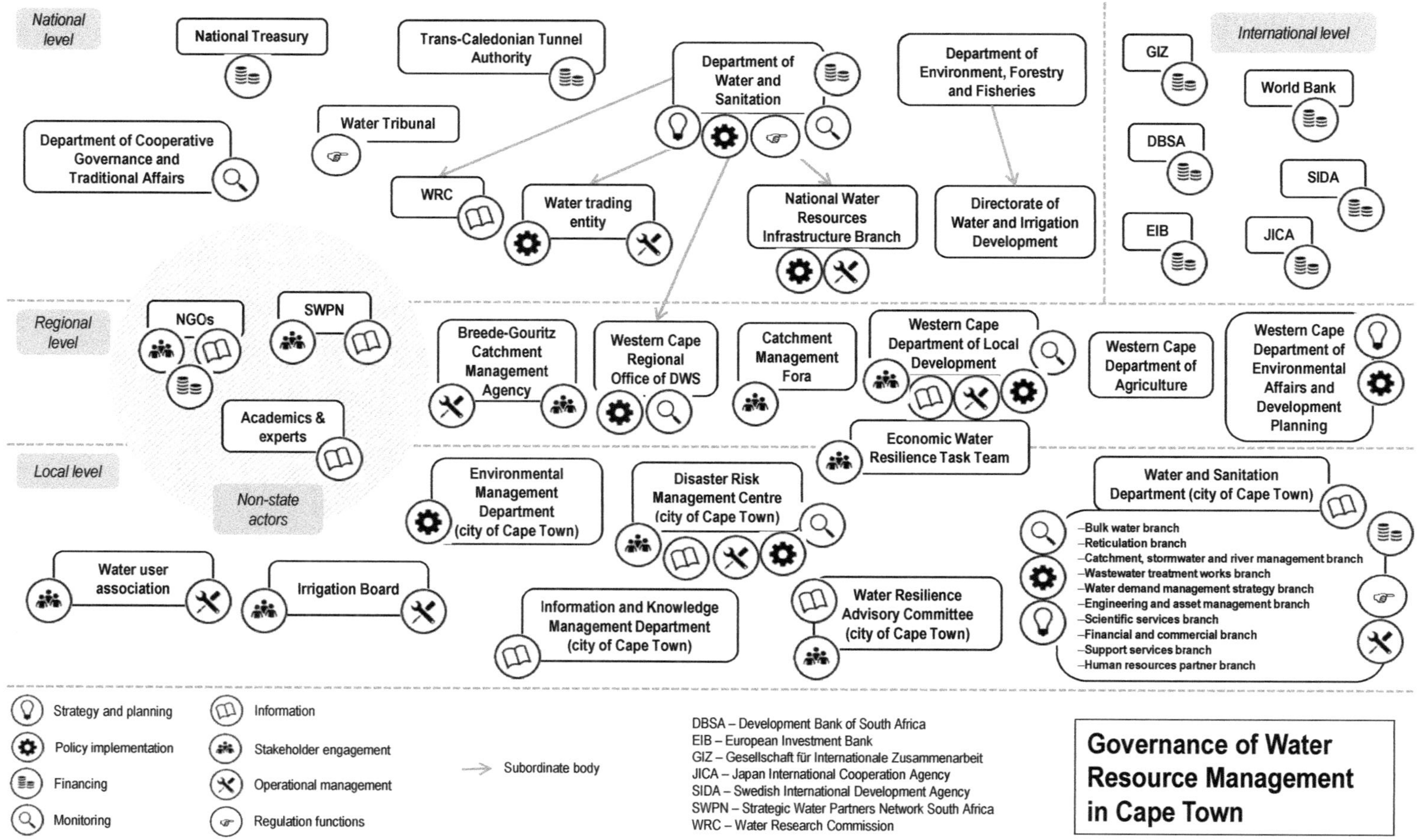

Source: Author's elaboration based on OECD (2011[1]), *Water Governance in OECD Countries: A Multi-level Approach*, https://dx.doi.org/10.1787/9789264119284-en.

Figure 2.2. Institutional mapping for water and sanitation services in Cape Town, South Africa

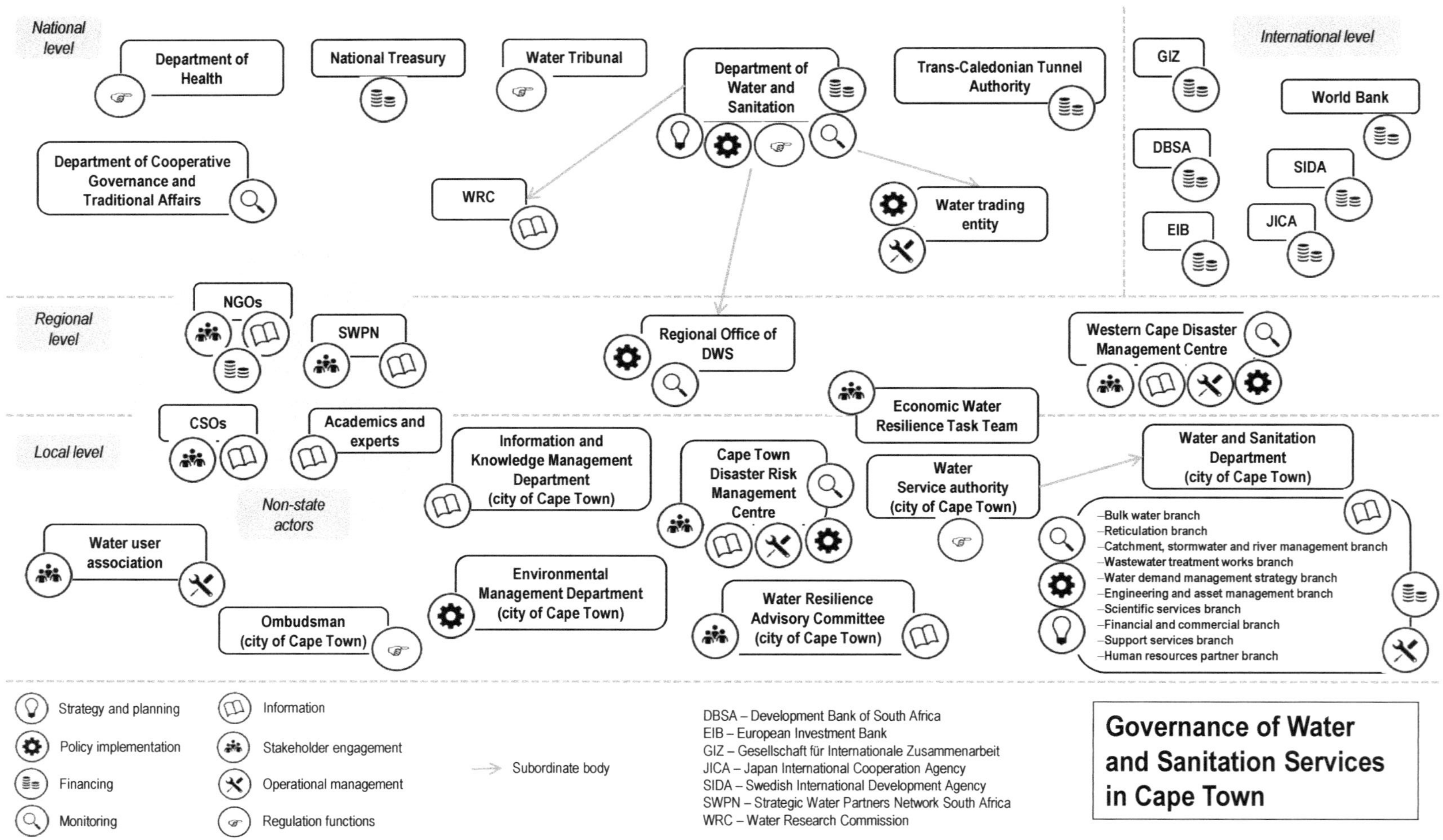

Source: Author's elaboration based on OECD (2011[1]), *Water Governance in OECD Countries: A Multi-level Approach*, https://dx.doi.org/10.1787/9789264119284-en.

The **National Department of Health** is responsible for setting the norms and rules regarding domestic water supply quality standards.

The **National Department of Agriculture, Land Reform and Rural Development**, through its **Directorate for Water Use and Irrigation Development** in its Agriculture Production, Health and Food Safety Management Branch, aims to ensure the efficient development and revitalisation of irrigation schemes and water use.

The **Water Research Commission** (WRC) plays a key role in water research by establishing needs and priorities, stimulating and funding research, promoting the transfer of information and technology, and enhancing knowledge and capacity building in the water sector. Its fields of focus encompass water resources management, water-linked ecosystems, water use and waste management, and water use in agriculture.

A series of national water legislation provides an overarching framework for water management across South Africa. These elements are completed by national, regional and local water-related policies (Box 2.1).

Box 2.1. National overarching water framework and dedicated water policies in South Africa

At the national level, six key pieces of legislation set overarching principles for water management in South Africa:

- The Constitution of South Africa, adopted in 1996, states the right for everyone to have access to sufficient water and specifies the allocation of water responsibilities across the different levels of government.
- The National Water Act (NWA) 1998 (Act 36), which replaced the previous Water Act 1956 that was based on riparian rights and was racially discriminating for water allocation, redefines water rights and establishes a new framework to regulate water resources through licensing, while water was previously considered attached to the land. Finally, it also promotes integrated water management and declares afforestation as a "stream flow reduction activity" due to its impact on the flow of rainwater into streams, and downstream hydrological balance.
- The Water Services Act 1997 (Act 108) prescribes the duty of municipalities to provide water supply and sanitation according to national standards and norms. It also defines the roles of the DWS as a regulator and the role of water boards as bulk providers. Both acts are being reviewed and it is expected that they may be merged into one single act to improve integration of resources management.
- The Municipal Systems Act (2000) and the Municipal Structures Act (1998) also have relevance to the role of municipalities for water and sanitation service provision.
- The National Environmental Management Act 1998 (Act 107) and its amendments of 2003, 2004, 2008 on waste and of 2009 on integrated management complete the legislation in relation with water.

In addition to these pieces of legislation, a number of water-related policies have been passed at the national level:

- The White Paper on Water Supply and Sanitation (1994) addresses inequity in water services and water supply development.
- The Strategic Framework for Water Services (2003) which sets out a comprehensive approach with respect to the provision of water services in South Africa, ranging from small community

water supply and sanitation schemes in remote rural areas to large regional schemes supplying water and wastewater services to people and industries in our largest urban areas.

- The White Paper on a National Water Policy for South Africa (1997) defines water as a public trust and states three fundamental principles for managing water resources: equity, environmental sustainability and efficiency.
- The Water Allocation Reform Strategy (2008) that seeks to address past water allocation inequity.
- The National Water Resource Strategy (2004) that was reviewed in 2012 with the Second National Water Resources Strategy (NWRS 2) to operationalise the establishment of catchment management agencies (CMAs), in particular from a financial perspective with a framework for water allocation and taxes. It ensures that water resources are protected and conserved for the long term while contributing to reaching social and economic goals for the country. The NWRS 2 includes a National Desalination Strategy and a National Strategy for Water Reuse.
- The National Groundwater Strategy (2010) intends to make the best use of this resource while protecting it.
- The Water and Sanitation Master Plan (2017) has been developed by the national DWS to ensure a more co-ordinated approach to water and sanitation management, planning, implementation, monitoring and evaluation. The master plan points out the priority actions required until 2030 and beyond to ensure the water security and equitable access to water and sanitation services for all in South Africa.

Source: Author's elaboration based on the White Paper on Water Supply and Sanitation (1994); the Constitution of South Africa (1996); the Water Services Act (1997); the White Paper on a National Water Policy for South Africa (1997); the National Environmental Management Act (1998); the National Water Act (1998); the Municipal Systems Act (2000); the Strategic Framework for Water Services (2003); the Water Allocation Reform Strategy (2008); the National Groundwater Strategy (2010); the Second National Water Resources Strategy (2012); the Water and Sanitation Master Plan (2017).

Who does what at the regional level?

The DWS has 9 **DWS regional offices** implementing the water policy, as well as controlling and monitoring services. The Western Cape DWS Regional Office has jurisdiction over water resources in the Western Cape Province.

Water user associations (WUAs) are defined under the National Water Act (1998) as "associations of individual water users who wish to undertake water-related activities for their mutual benefit with voluntary membership intended to support the management of local water resources in the common interest". When the National Water Act came into force, **Irrigation Boards** were to be restructured into WUAs. However, there are still 220 Irrigation Boards in existence. There are currently 90 WUAs, comprising both new WUAs and transformed Irrigation Boards.

The **Breede-Gouritz Catchment Management Agency** (CMA) is responsible for the management of water resources at the catchment level in collaboration with local stakeholders. Although much of the water for the city of Cape Town is sourced from the Berg-Olifants catchment (which does not have an installed CMA), the biggest dam of the Western Cape Water Supply System (Theewaterskloof Dam) is located in the Breede-Gouritz CMA.

Catchment management fora are entities gathering local stakeholders to ensure engagement and participation with regard to water-related topics.

The **Provincial Department of Agriculture** provides a wide range of development, research and support services to the agricultural community in the Western Cape. It serves on the Steering Committee of the

Western Cape Water Supply System and makes the link with the network of farm dams across the greater Cape Town Functional Area.

The **Provincial Department of Local Government** hosts the Provincial Disaster Management Centre which oversees all declared provincial disasters and forms Joint Operating Committees which bring together all Provincial level entities and national stakeholders to align disaster response.

The **Provincial Department of Environmental Affairs and Development Planning** has a contaminated land and water pollution oversight mandate, as well as an estuary and coastal mandate, under the National Environmental Management Act. It is also the oversight Department for **CapeNature**, a Western Cape public entity which manages all provincial conservation areas as well as much of the public land.

At the regional level, the following water-related policies have been adopted: the Western Cape Sustainable Water Management Plan dated 2014 and revised in 2019; the Western Cape Climate Change Response Strategy (2014); and the Western Cape Biodiversity Economy Strategy (2016).

Who does what at the local level?

Following the constitution provisions, the responsibility for "potable water supply systems and domestic wastewater and sewage disposal systems" is assigned to local governments. The city of Cape Town acts as the **Water Service Authority** (WSA) responsible for the provision of water services in its area of jurisdiction. In South Africa, there are currently 144 WSAs.

The **Water and Sanitation Department** of the city of Cape Town acts as the water service provider for the city of Cape Town, and Drakenstein and Stellenbosch municipalities. As such, it is in charge of providing water (including bulk water) and sanitation services, as well as managing water catchment areas and water storage. The department comprises the following branches: bulk water; reticulation; catchment, stormwater and river management; wastewater treatment works; water demand management strategy; engineering and asset management; Informal Settlements Water and Sanitation Services; scientific services; financial and commercial; support services; and human resources partner.

The **Environmental Management Department** of the city of Cape Town co-ordinates and facilitates the implementation of the city's environmental strategy. Working with a range of other departments, it manages and protects the environment and ensures Cape Town's long-term environmental sustainability.

The **Information and Knowledge Management Department** of the city of Cape Town closely works with city departments to improve the management and accessibility of corporate information assets and to provide specialised information services to city departments with regard to information and knowledge management; records management; geomatics; and geographic information system (GIS) mapping and data management.

The **Disaster Risk Management Centre** of the city of Cape Town identifies, prevents or reduces the occurrence of disasters and softens their impacts. It facilitates the co-ordination, integration and efficiency of multiple emergency and essential services. It is in charge of the preparation and execution of the city's Municipal Disaster Risk Management Plan. In the event of a disaster or a large-scale emergency, the Disaster Coordinating Team assembles in the Disaster Operations Centre and acts as a central information point to communicate swiftly with the public during emergencies.

The **Water Resilience Advisory Committee** (WRAC) was established in August 2017 by the city. It meets monthly since its creation and comprises 15 members from academic institutions, businesses, NGOs or provincial and national governments. Building on an important community of practice in Cape Town, the WRAC gathers a variety of stakeholders outside the municipal administration in order to encourage information and knowledge sharing.

The **Ombudsman of the City of Cape Town** is responsible for investigating and facilitating the resolution of public complaints against the administration.

The city of Cape Town and Western Cape Government (WCG) formulated an approach together with key partner organisations to support the city's economy in the face of water scarcity and restricted consumption. This translated into the **Economic Water Resilience Task Team** which is primarily a group of interested and involved organisations who wanted to contribute to the drought response in addition to supporting their various constituencies or stakeholders. The task team includes the following stakeholders:

- WCG's Department of Economic Development and Tourism (DEDAT) and Department of Environmental Affairs and Development Planning (DEADP).
- The Enterprise and Investment and Water and Sanitation Directorates of the city of Cape Town.
- GreenCape, a technical not-for-profit organisation which supports the growth of green businesses.
- Wesgro, the tourism, trade and investment promotion agency for Cape Town and the Western Cape.
- The National Business Initiative, a voluntary coalition of South African and multinational companies.
- The Western Cape Economic Development Partnership (EDP), a non-profit organisation focused on providing partnering solutions to improve economic performance.

At city level, the Cape Town Water and Sanitation Department comprises eleven branches. Three of these branches correspond to the stages of water and wastewater services provision (bulk water, reticulation, wastewater treatment works). One branch focuses on catchment, stormwater and river management thus reflecting the city of Cape Town's objective to become a water-sensitive city through an integrated urban water management approach. These branches are complemented by branches dedicated to infrastructure (engineering and asset management), water demand (water demand, regulation and planning) and water quality monitoring and compliance (scientific services). In addition, three branches provide specific support for finance, capital contracts management, and, information, communication and stakeholder management (auxiliary services). Finally, the Human Resources Business Partner Branch provides an administrative role to the Water and Sanitation Department which includes training and human relations support. As of April 2019, the Informal Settlement and Basic Services branch returned to the Water and Sanitation Department. A new Customer Services Branch was also developed since 2019, to focus on customer relationship and improve metering and billing effectiveness (Table 2.1).

Table 2.1. Branches composing the Water and Sanitation Department of Cape Town

Bulk Water Branch	Management of water catchment areas, storage dams, city groundwater sources, water treatment works and bulk water supply lines.
Reticulation Branch	Drinking water distribution to consumers and conveyance of wastewater to the treatment works through a network of pipelines, pump stations and reservoirs. They also convey treated effluent (recycled) water to users of large water volumes and collection points for construction and industrial contractors.
Catchment Storm Water and River Management Branch	Strategic planning for the city's stormwater system, including management of river systems and their drainage catchments to manage flood risk, improve water quality and optimise harvesting of stormwater as a valuable water resource.
Wastewater Treatment Works Branch	Operation of wastewater treatment works.
Water Demand, Regulation and Planning Branch	Planning service responsible for policy development and enforcement of by-laws; co-ordination of water demand management programmes, quality management, awareness programmes, information management and business reporting.
Engineering and Asset Management Branch	Electrical and mechanical maintenance of water and sanitation equipment and facilities. They also provide risk management, fleet management and health and safety services for the Water and Sanitation Department.
Scientific Services Branch	Water quality compliance through strict water quality checks as prescribed by the national DWS.
Finance Branch	Revenue management (including meter reading and billing), budgeting and accounting.

Capital Contracts Management Branch	Management of capital contracts with regard to the water and sanitation infrastructure of the city
Auxiliary Services Branch	Information, record and facilities management and communication and stakeholder management.
Informal Settlement and Basic Services for Water and Sanitation	Management and implementation of informal settlements water and sanitation policy.
Customer Services	Management of customers relationships and improvement metering and billing effectiveness.

Source: City of Cape Town, (2019[2]), *Departmental Buniess Plan 2019/2020*, Department of Water and Sanitation.

At the local level, the city adopted the following water-related policies:

- City of Cape Town Stormwater By-law (2005)
- City of Cape Town Management of Urban Stormwater Impacts Policy (2009)
- City of Cape Town Floodplain and River Corridor Management Policy (2009)
- City of Cape Town Inland and Coastal Water Quality Improvement Strategy and Implementation Plan (2012)
- City of Cape Town Environmental Strategy (2017)
- City of Cape Town Preliminary Resilience Assessment (2018)
- City of Cape Town Water Strategy (2019)
- City of Cape Town Resilience Strategy (2019)
- City of Cape Town Integrated Development Plan (2017-22).

Water and sanitation services regulation

In order to complement the institutional mapping of water roles and responsibilities in Cape Town, a more specific analysis of regulatory functions allocation for Cape Town water and sanitation service has been conducted based on the OECD analytical framework on the governance of regulators (OECD, 2015[3]). Regulatory functions in water and sanitation services encompass economic, environmental and social aspects. They can be shared among several institutions. However, they need to be clearly defined and allocated to avoid overlaps and incoherence. Table 2.2 provides a list of regulatory functions for water and sanitation services and the level and institution to which they are allocated in the case of Cape Town.

Table 2.2. Allocation of regulatory functions for water and sanitation, Cape Town, South Africa

Regulatory function	Level in charge of exercising the function	Type of institution in charge of exercising the function
Tariff regulation	National/Local	DWS/City of Cape Town
Quality standards for drinking water	National	Department of Health
Quality standards for wastewater treatment	National	DWS
Defining public service obligations	National	DWS
Defining technical/industry and service standards	National	DWS
Setting incentives for efficient use of water resources	Local	City of Cape Town
Setting incentives for efficient investment	*Not allocated*	*Not allocated*
Information and data gathering	Local	City of Cape Town
Monitoring of service delivery performance	National/Local	National Treasury/DWS/City of Cape Town
Customer engagement	Local	City of Cape Town
Consumer protection and dispute resolution	Local	City of Cape Town

Regulatory function	Level in charge of exercising the function	Type of institution in charge of exercising the function
Licensing of water abstraction, wastewater treatment plants and wastewater discharge conditions	National	DWS
Supervision of contracts with utilities/private actors	Local	City of Cape Town
Analysing water utilities' investment/business plans	National/Local	National Treasury/DWS/City of Cape Town

Source: Based on OECD (2015[3]), *The Governance of Water Regulators*, https://doi.org/10.1787/9789264231092-en.

As is the case in many countries, key regulatory functions for water supply and sanitation are spread across levels of government and institutions, thus reflecting the mutual dependency and needed co-ordination of responsible authorities. At the horizontal level, several line departments are involved in the regulation of water services, including the DWS, the Department of Health and the National Treasury. At the vertical level, water supply and sanitation (WSS) are characterised by multi-level regulatory governance from national to the local level. In practice, OECD (2011[1]) shows that the multiplicity of actors across ministries and public institutions, between levels of government and at the subnational level, intrinsically raises multi-level governance challenges. With so many participants, a clear definition of roles and responsibilities, as well as the establishment of co-ordination mechanisms, are therefore crucial to manage water services effectively and efficiently.

Another characteristic of water and sanitation services in South Africa is that some stages of service provision are being regulated, delivered and managed by the same institution, i.e. the DWS and its decentralised offices. Although there are successful examples of self-regulation, the absence of any separation between regulation and operation may generate conflicts of interest. For instance, for electoral purposes, the operator may be forced to adopt an unsustainable economic policy causing service sustainability/quality/efficiency to decline, or, on the contrary, may divert part of the monopoly rent for its own benefit or that of the public authority. In the context of South Africa, where capture has been identified in the literature as a major issue (Dassah, 2018[4]) (Roux, 2019[5]) (Solomon, 2016[6]), the establishment of an independent regulator may be preferred to a self-regulation model. In this model, the regulatory framework for WSS services is organised around the establishment of a dedicated agency that supervises and regulates the water sector independently from the operators, the government and the consumers. This model allows separation of powers between the regulator and the line ministers. This separation concentrates the regulatory functions and powers into a single body and limits potential conflicts between policy formulation and enforcement.

Water allocation and supply system

Overarching principles for water allocation

Replacing the previous Water Act 1956 that was based on riparian rights and was racially discriminating for water allocation, the 1997 Water Policy, the 1998 National Water Act and the 2008 Water Allocation Reform Strategy established the basic principles for water allocation in South Africa. These principles follow a clear allocation hierarchy. First, provision is made in the act for "the Reserve, which consists of two parts – the basic human needs reserve and the ecological reserve. The basic human needs reserve provides for the essential needs of individuals served by the water resource in question and includes water for drinking, for food preparation and for personal hygiene. The ecological reserve relates to the water required to protect the aquatic ecosystems of the water resource. The reserve refers to both the quantity and quality of the water in the resource". After the reserve water allocation is met, international obligation, strategic uses and future uses are the next level of water allocation priority. Then come all other uses (Figure 2.3).

Figure 2.3. Water allocation hierarchy in South Africa

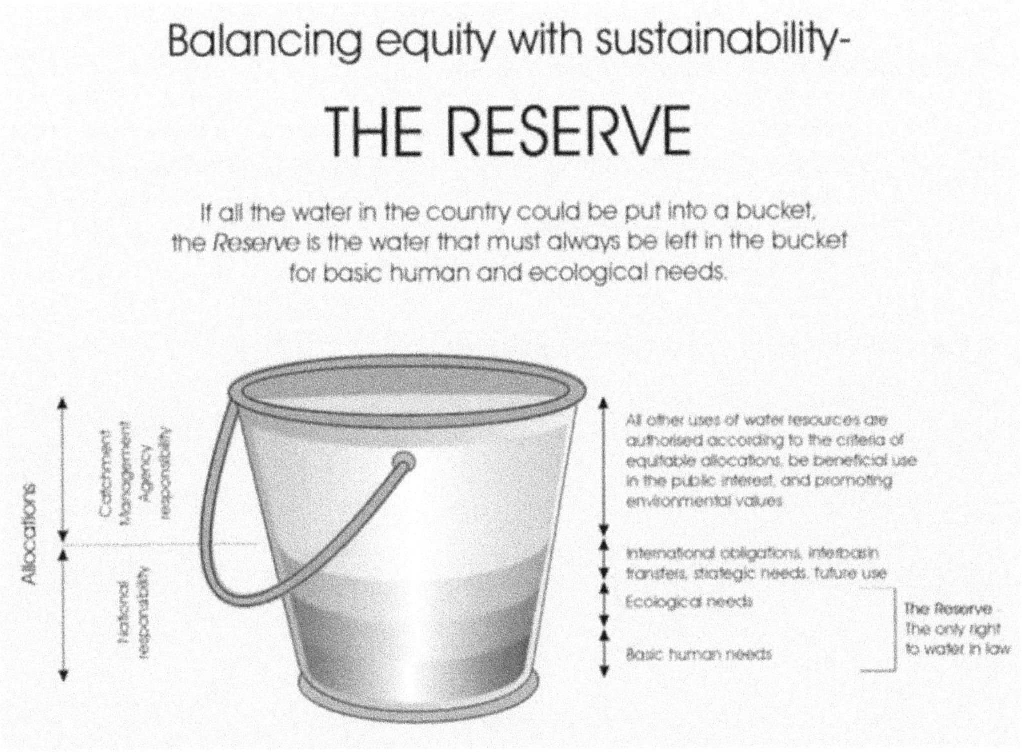

Source: DWS, Manyaka Greyling Meiring, (2003[7]), *Balancing equity with sustainability, The Reserve*

These water allocation principles are implemented using the following mechanisms:

- A water resources planning methodology, including determination of the Basic Human Needs Reserve and an Ecological Reserve, led and managed by the DWS.
- A national water pricing strategy which dates back to 2007 and is currently under discussion to be revised.
- Scheme-based financing agreements used to develop new urban water schemes, secured on the basis of an off-take agreement with users. This approach was applied, for example, for the financing of the Berg River Dam, the last major scheme to supply Cape Town.
- Authorisation licenses of water use by the DWS. The new (post-1997) authorisation process sits alongside a system that recognises existing lawful use pending a transfer of these uses into licensed use, and a mechanism to issue general authorisations. The process of converting existing lawful use into licensed use is still incomplete, and licence application processes have been subject to long delays.
- Compulsory licensing. It is a mechanism allowing DWS to review all the water use in an area that is or is soon likely to be under water stress, or where it is necessary to review prevailing water use to achieve equity of access to water. This is done by converting existing lawful water use into licences.
- Catchment-based water allocation plans. This process is still largely undeveloped as the roll-out of CMAs has been stalled.

In accordance with these mechanisms, for each catchment area, the DWS allocates water according to licenses for municipal needs, irrigation and other activities such as hydropower, industrial and commercial uses. It also makes decisions on how use is restricted during periods of drought in accordance with agreed processes and rules.

A multi-level Western Cape Water Supply System

Unlike other cities in South Africa, the city of Cape Town enjoys a unique situation as it is a major actor of the Western Cape Water Supply System (WCWSS) which is an integrated and collectively managed water system of dams, pump stations, pipelines and tunnels (Figure 2.4). The city of Cape Town uses around 58% of the WCWSS available yield, agriculture 26%, smaller towns around 6% and approximately 10% is lost to evaporation and other losses from the bulk water system.

Figure 2.4. Map of the Western Cape Water Supply System

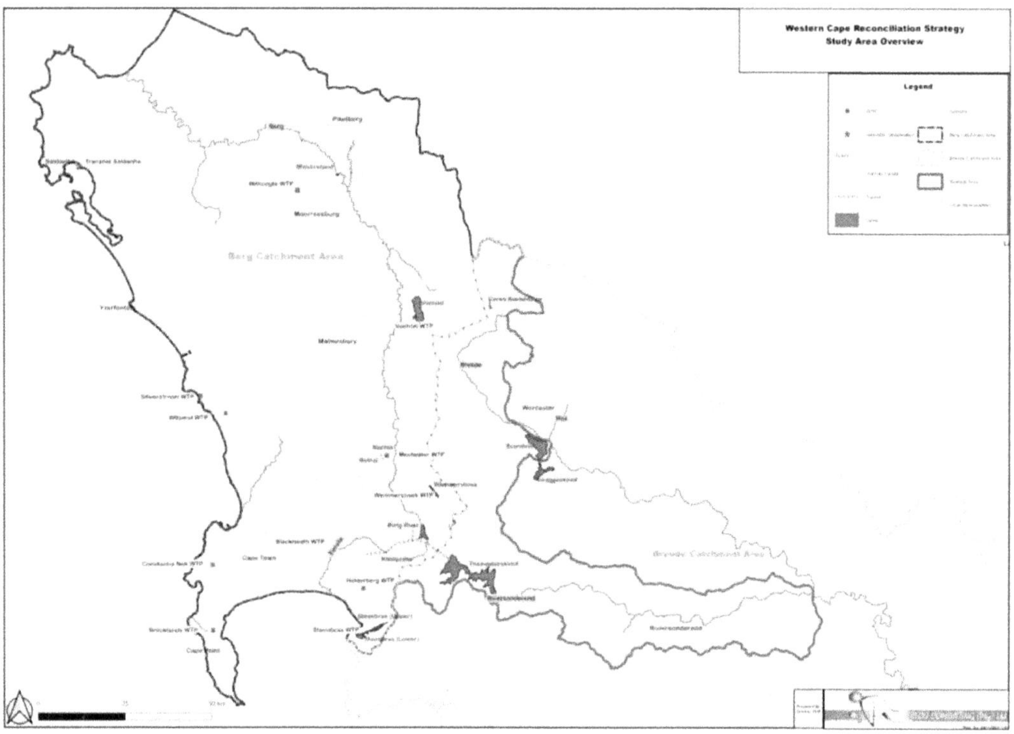

Source: DWS (forthcoming[8]), *Western Cape Water Supply System Reconciliation Strategy, Status Report 2019*

The WCWSS involves a variety of stakeholders across sectors and levels of government. As such, it appears fragmented both vertically and horizontally, thus requiring important co-ordination efforts (Figure 2.5).

Figure 2.5. Allocation of responsibilities related to water resources and services within the WCWSS

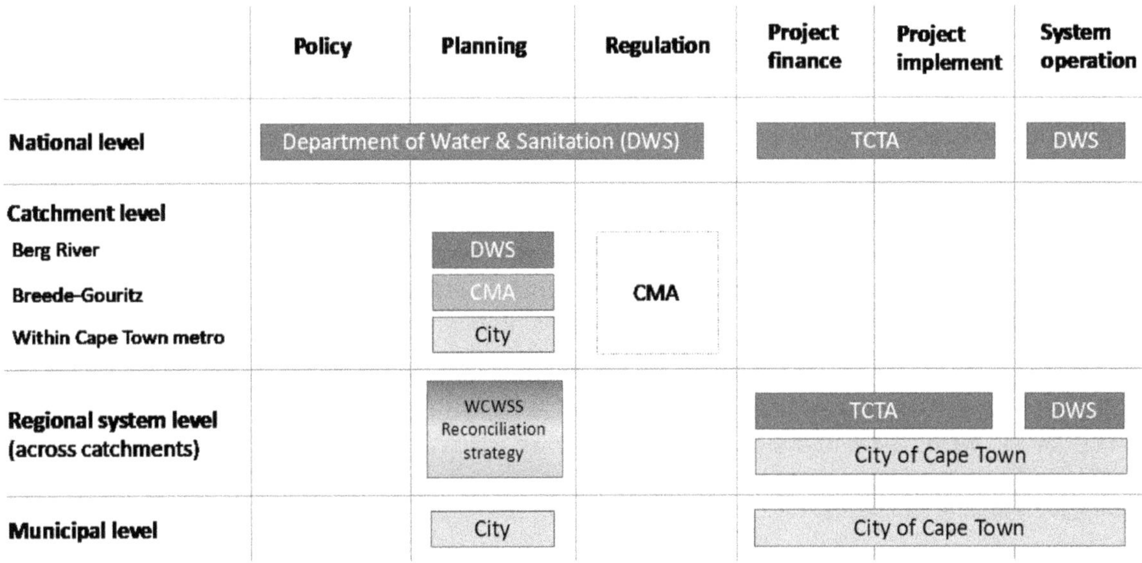

Note: for water resource planning, the function sits primarily with DWS; for water services planning, it sits primarily with the city of Cape Town.
Source: City of Cape Town, (2020[9]), *Western Cape Water Supply System*

Within this system, the national DWS fulfils the water policymaking and regulation functions for both water resources and services. It also manages and operates the major dams of the WCWSS (Table 2.3). The TCTA finances and implements off-budget bulk raw water infrastructure projects in South Africa, such as the Berg River Dam in the Western Cape.

Table 2.3. Dams of the Western Cape Water Supply System

Dam name	Location	Water source	Ownership	Completion year	Storage capacity (million m^3/year)
Theewaterskloof	Villiersdorp	Riviersonderend River	DWS	1978	480.25
Voëlvlei	Gouda	Klein Berg, Leeu and Twenty-Four Rivers	DWS	1971	164.12
Berg River	Franschhoek	Berg River	DWS	2009	130.00
Wemmershoek	Franschhoek	Wemmers River	City of Cape Town	1957	58.64
Steenbras Lower	Gordon's Bay	Steenbras River	City of Cape Town	1921	33.52
Steenbras Upper	Gordon's Bay	Steenbras River	City of Cape Town	1977	31.77

Source: DWS, (forthcoming[8]) *Western Cape Water Supply System Reconciliation Strategy, Status Report 2019*

At the catchment level, the National Water Act mandates the decentralisation of water resource management through CMAs. CMAs play a range of functions related to water resource management and also undertake water allocation and regulatory functions. Originally, 19 CMAs were envisaged throughout the country but this number was rationalised to 9 by the minister in March 2012 and confirmed as stated in the NWRS 2 published in 2013. Of these, only two have been established to date and are operational (Breede-Gouritz CMAInkomati-Usuthu CMA).

Two main water management areas cover the Western Cape area, the Berg-Olifant and the Breede-Gouritz. However, only the Breede-Gouritz CMA has been established and the Western Cape regional office of the DWS retains water resource management functions for the Berg-Olifants catchment in the absence of an operational CMA to date. Catchment management is predominantly undertaken by the conservation authorities that manage state-owned land, much of which is previous state forest. CapeNature, the Western Cape Conservation public entity, manages provincial conservation areas as well as much of the public land around Berg River, Steenbras and Wemmershoek Dams as well as many other state-owned landholdings.

At the regional level, the DWS and the city of Cape Town manage and operate the WCWSS, while the TCTA undertakes the financing and implementation of water resources infrastructure as directed by the Minister of Human Settlements, Water and Sanitation as off-budget activities.

At the municipal level, the city of Cape Town is responsible for water resources planning and funding. In the absence of a bulk water utility, three of the WCWSS dams (Steenbras, Lower and Upper, Wemmershoek) were built and are owned by Cape Town which operates them. This situation allows the city of Cape Town to retain a say in the upstream-downstream water resource management, which makes it a unique case in South Africa.

Water resources and services financing

Overarching principles for water resources and services financing

The National Water Act 1998, the Water Services Act 1997 and the National Pricing Strategy for Raw Water Charges 2007 set a sound and coherent system of finance for water resources and services management. The National Pricing Strategy establishes social equity, ecological sustainability, financial sustainability and economic efficiency as the key objectives to achieve while stating that water charges are set with the purpose of funding water resource development and management (Box 2.2).

Box 2.2. The National Pricing Strategy for Raw Water Use Charges, South Africa

This strategy refers to pricing for the use of water from South Africa's water resources and not to the pricing of water services, which is dealt with separately under the Water Services Act, 1997. In other words, the approach deals with first-tier water, i.e. the use of raw (untreated) water from the water resource and/or supplied from a government waterworks. It does not deal directly with second- and third-tier water, i.e. water supplied in bulk (often by water boards) and distributed to households (usually via a water services authority), except for water supplied from government water schemes. The strategy deals with all first-tier water as reflected in the use of ground and surface water resources and covers the setting of prices by the Department for Water Affairs and Forestry (DWAF) as well as by water management institutions as defined in the National Water Act (NWA).

The pricing strategy contains the objectives, methodology and implementation strategy for setting water use charges for purposes of:

- Funding water resource management by the DWAF and water management institutions, through water use charges, Section 56 (2) (a).
- Funding water resource development and use of waterworks by the DWAF and water management institutions, Section 56 (2) (b).

- Achieving the equitable and efficient allocation of water, through a charge hereafter referred to as the "economic charge", Section 56 (2) (c).
- Providing for a differential rate for waste discharges, Section 56 (5).

The following objectives are shaping the pricing strategy:

1. **Social equity**

   The Pricing Strategy for Water Use Charges coupled to the granting of financial assistance will contribute to social equity and redress of the imbalances of the past, both with respect to equitable access to water supply services and direct access to raw water.

2. **Ecological sustainability**

   In terms of Chapter 3 of the NWA, the water needs for the effective functioning of aquatic ecosystems must be protected. The water required for the ecological reserve must be safeguarded and the cost of managing the reserve must be paid for by all registered and billable users in terms of Section 56(2) (a) (iv) of the NWA. To promote the preservation of resource quality, the polluter pays principle for waste discharge is adopted in this pricing strategy.

3. **Financial sustainability**

   In order to ensure financial sustainability adequate revenue must be generated to fund the annual cost related to:

   - The management of the country's water resources.
   - The operations, maintenance, refurbishment and betterment of existing government water schemes and waterworks owned by water management institutions.
   - The development of new user-funded schemes.

   The financial framework makes accommodation for the financial autonomy of water user associations (WUAs) and catchment management agencies (CMAs). As stated in the previous pricing strategy, the full financial cost of water resource management and supplying water should be recovered from water users, including the cost of capital. While it is important to keep water prices as low as possible, the DWAF has to ensure that water is priced at levels consistent with efficient and effective delivery of services.

4. **Economic efficiency**

   In the context of water scarcity, ensuring an efficient allocation of scarce water resources requires that the price of water is set to reflect its scarcity value, first to ensure that water is conserved and, second, that some water used for low-value purposes is redirected to alternative high-value purposes. This can be done administratively or by using market-related mechanisms. It is also critical to ensure that the water resource management systems implemented are cost-effective and do not become an unnecessary financial burden on the water users.

Source: Author's elaboration based DWS (2007[10]), *Pricing Strategy for Raw Water Use Charges*, Department of Water and Sanitation.

This funding scheme includes seven elements: a water resource management charge, a raw water tariff, a bulk water tariff, a retail water tariff, a sanitation charge, a bulk wastewater tariff and a water discharge charge (Figure 2.6).

The **water resource management charge** and the **waste discharge charge** are set and collected by the CMA and by the DWS when no CMA has been established, as per the National Water Act. In all cases, these charges are regulated by the DWS following the provisions of the National Pricing Strategy for Raw Water Use Charges (Box 2.3).

The **water resource management charge** aims to recover the costs associated with water resources management including evaluating and issuing licences, monitoring water resource quality against national standards, detecting and prosecuting unlawful water use, promoting water conservation and demand management, and removing and managing alien vegetation. This charge applies to all water users but is capped for the forestry and irrigation sectors thus constituting an implicit subsidy to those sectors. For emerging farmers, this charge is explicitly subsidised. At present, this charge is not very significant. The implementation of the water discharge charge is based on the polluter pays principle as it charges for the discharge of water containing waste into a water resource or onto land.

Figure 2.6. Water resources and services funding scheme in South Africa

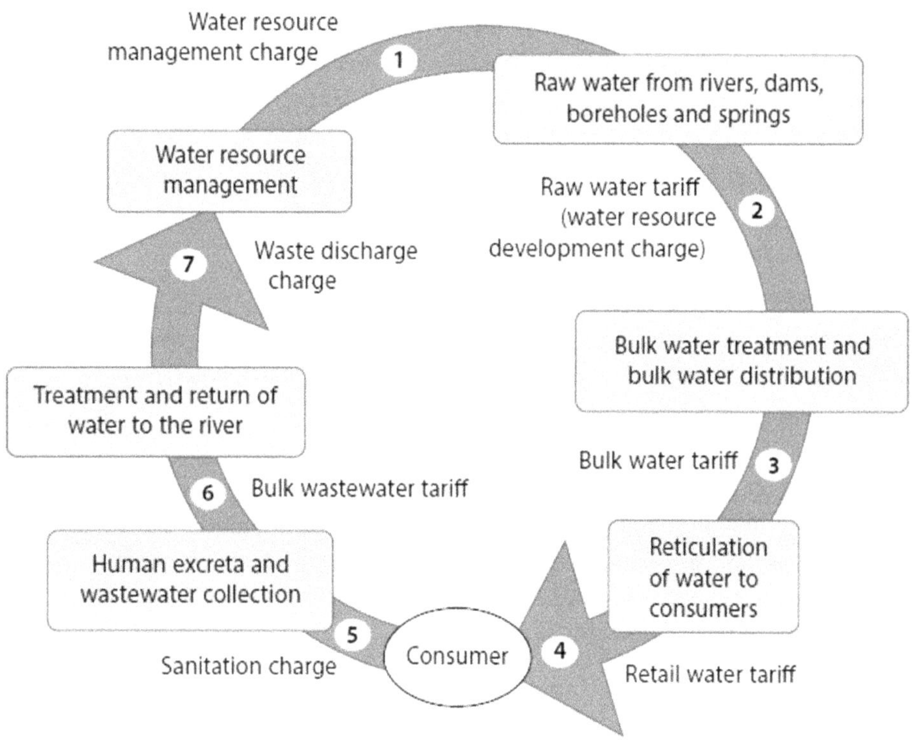

Source: Department of Water Affairs and Forestry (2003[11]), *Strategic Framework for Water Services*.

The **raw water tariff** (or **water resource development charge**) is set by the DWS following the national water resource management pricing strategy. This tariff includes water management and infrastructure charges related to the development and use of waterworks, covering planning, capital costs, operation and maintenance, depreciation and future infrastructure build on government water schemes. The tariff policy requires a 4% real return on the depreciated current asset value. In 2019, it amounted to R3.59/m^3 on average at the national level for domestic and industrial use (DWS). This charge applies to all water users, except stream flow reduction activities. Subsidies can be granted to emerging farmers.

The **bulk water and wastewater tariffs** are set by water boards or Water Service Authorities as per the Water Services Act. They are collected by Water Service Authorities. They are regulated by the DWS following the *Norms and Standards in Respect of Tariffs for Water Services* (2001[12]). They should also be formally approved by the DWS although no clear approval criteria and method have been elaborated. In 2017, the bulk water tariffs averaged ZAR 7.44/m^3, varying from ZAR 4.18/m^3 to ZAR 15.86/m^3 throughout the country (DWS).

The **retail water and sanitation tariff** paid by customers is set and collected by the WSA. It is established following the rules provided in the Water Services Act stating that tariffs should notably cover:

- All reasonable costs directly and indirectly[1] associated with the operation, maintenance, refurbishment and development of water services, water services customer care and all costs associated therewith.
- Payments required to redeem water services related loans over a reasonable period.
- A net surplus of a minimum of 6% per annum on revenue.

Box 2.3. Setting water resource management charge and waste discharge charge according to the Pricing Strategy for Water Use Charges

According to the *Pricing Strategy for Water Use Charges* (DWS, 2007[10]), their setting method is based on the actual cost recovery of the activities required "to protect, allocate, conserve, manage and control the water resources and manage water quality".

> *"These costs could include but are not limited to the following activities:*
>
> - *Planning and implementing catchment management strategies.*
> - *Monitoring and assessing water resource availability and use.*
> - *Water use allocations.*
> - *Water quantity management, including flood and drought management, water distribution, control over-abstraction, storage and streamflow reduction activities.*
> - *Water resource protection, resource quality management and water pollution control.*
> - *Water conservation and demand management.*
> - *Institutional development and enabling the public to participate in water resources management decision-making."*

DWS and CMAs are the authorities in charge of budgeting annually for the estimated costs of these activities and thus determining the level of water resource management charges and waste discharge charges. The activities that may be partially or completely funded from the water resource management charge and the waste discharge charge are explicitly listed in the Pricing Strategy for Water Use Charges (Table 2.4).

Table 2.4. Activities funded from the water resource management charge and the waste discharge charge

Functions/Activities	Taking water (abstraction activities)	Waste discharge activities
1. Catchment management strategy and Water resources planning	Resource studies, investigations and integrated strategy development	
	Allocation plans	Water quality management plan
2. Resource directed measures	Implement programmes to monitor Resource Quality Objectives (RQOs) Implement source-directed controls to achieve resource quality objectives Report against the achievement of the Class and RQOs Report on the water balance per catchment (i.e. water available for allocation after consideration of ecological requirements)	
3. Water use authorisation	Registration of water use	
	Abstraction and stream flow reduction activities authorisation	Waste discharge activities authorisation
4. Control and enforcement of water use	Control monitoring and enforcement of water use	
	Abstraction and stream flow reduction activities Dam safety control (private dams)	Water discharge control

5. Disaster management	Planning and management of disaster (administration)	Pollution incident planning and response (management)
6. Water resources management programmes	Integrated water resources programmes	
	Implementing of water management strategies (e.g. water conservation and water demand management)	Implementing of water management strategies (e.g. cleaner technology, dense settlements, waste discharge strategies)
7. Water-related institutional development (stakeholder management empowerment)	Stakeholder participation, empowerment, institutional development and co-ordination of activities o Establishment and regulation of water management institutions o Stakeholder consultations o Capacity and empowerment of stakeholders	
8. Waterweed control	Aquatic weeds control	
9. Maintenance and restoration of ecosystems to improve water resources	Planning and implementation of ecosystem maintenance and rehabilitation programmes, required for water resource protection, e.g. sediment control, nutrient trapping, riparian rehabilitation Control of invasive alien plants with acknowledged negative impacts on water resources, e.g. riparian zones, mountain catchment areas, wetlands and in areas where there could be an impact of aquifers	
10.Geo-hydrology and hydrology	Groundwater and surface water monitoring Compiling of maps and yield information Extending and maintaining the hydrological database and compilation of information	
11. Administration and overheads	Administrative, institutional and overheads for regional office or CMA	

Source: Author's elaboration based on DWS (2007[10]), *Pricing Strategy for Raw Water Use Charges*, Department of Water and Sanitation.

Table 2.5 details the institutions responsible for setting, regulating, collecting and cashing in each type of charge included in the overall water price.

Table 2.5. Responsible institutions for setting, regulating, collecting and cashing in water charges

Type of charge	Set by	Regulated by	Collected by	Cashed in by
Water resource management charge	CMA or DWS (when no CMA established)	DWS	CMA or WTE	CMA or DWS
Water resource development charge	DWS	DWS	WTE	DWS
Bulk water tariff	Water Boards or WSA (when no Water Board established)	DWS or WSA (when no Water Board established)	WSA	Water Boards or WSA
Retail water tariff	WSA	WSA	WSA	WSA
Sanitation charge	WSA	WSA	WSA	WSA
Bulk wastewater tariff	Water Boards or WSA (when no Water Board established)	DWS or WSA (when no Water Board established)	WSA	Water Boards or WSA
Waste discharge charge	CMA or DWS (when no CMA established)	DWS	CMA or WTE	CMA or DWS

Source: Based on DWS (2007[10]), *Pricing Strategy for Raw Water Use Charges*, Department of Water and Sanitation.

Water and sanitation service provision is financed through tariffs paid by the different categories of users, and subsidies stemming from national and local budgets. Subsidies are used to finance both capital and operational expenditures (Figure 2.7). Although the Water Service Act (1998) stipulates that water economic flux should be ring-fenced, in Cape Town, for instance, WSS revenues are only separately accounted for since 2018.

Figure 2.7. Water services financial framework, South Africa

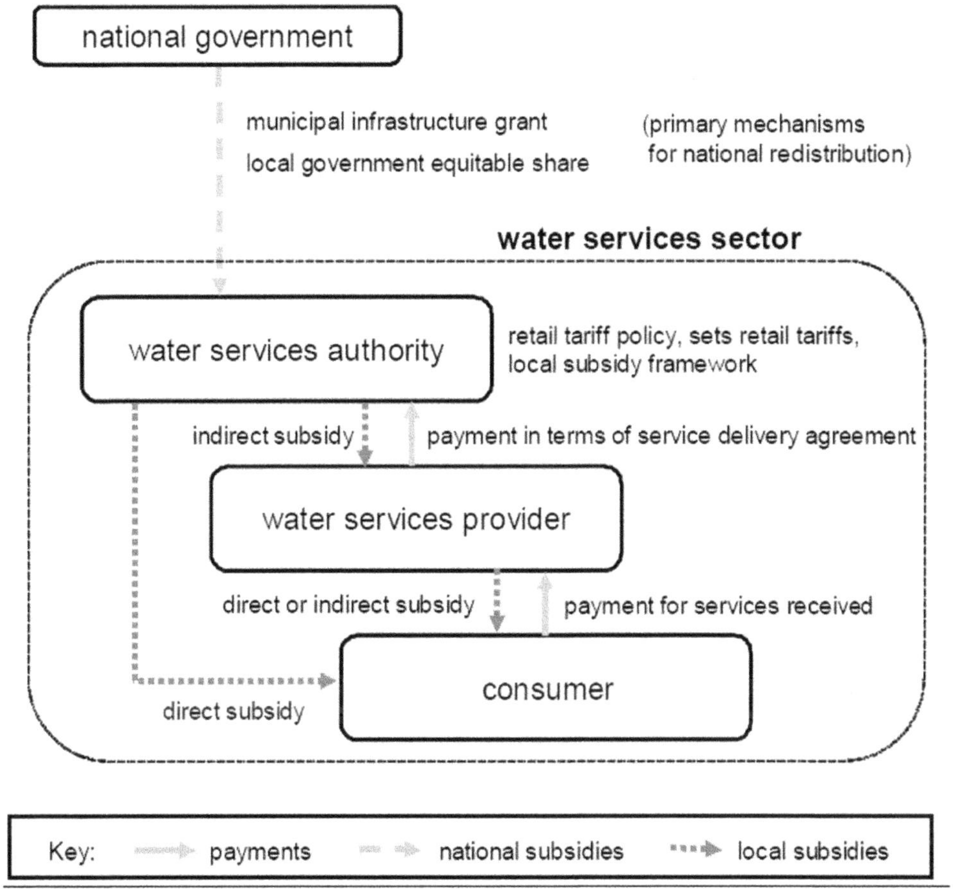

Source: Eberhard, R. (2002[13]), "Administered prices: Water".

Cape Town Water Service Provider

According to the Water Services Act 1997, the city of Cape Town is the WSA responsible for service provision at the municipal level. Thus, Cape Town Water Service Provider services more than 4.2 million people via water and sewer connections that supply more than 600 000 domestic properties and 230 000 households living in informal settlements. However, as the city of Cape Town is growing rapidly, the number of connections increases every year due to population growth (5% per year during the past decade according to Africapolis) and migration. Each year, on average, the Water and Sanitation Department provides connections to 8 500 new customers. Table 2.6 describes Cape Town water service customer base.

Table 2.6. Customer base of Cape Town water service

Type of water customer	Number
Domestic	600 000
Housing complexes and blocks of flats	6 500
Informal households (in 204 informal settlements throughout the city, serviced by approximately 10 000 communal taps 50 000 toilets)	230 000
Commercial	13 000
Industrial	4 500
Municipalities (Drakenstein) and winelands (Stellenbosch)	2

Source: City of Cape Town (2018[14]), *Water Outlook 2018 Report*, https://resource.capetown.gov.za/documentcentre/Documents/City%20research%20reports%20and%20review/Water%20Outlook%202018%20-%20Summary.pdf. City of Cape Town (2019[15]), "Cape Town Water Strategy", http://resource.capetown.gov.za/documentcentre/Documents/City%20strategies%2c%20plans%20and%20frameworks/Cape%20Town%20Water%20Strategy.pdf.

All water consumption from formal properties in Cape Town is metered and consumers are billed according to their consumption for the variable part of the invoice. The current residential WSS tariff is composed of a fixed charge (established in 2018) which varies according to the size of the connection and a variable part that follows four increasing blocks, and that can be modulated according to four restriction levels depending on the dam level (Table 2.7 and Figure 2.8). However, it should be noted that during the water crisis, the number of restrictions level were greater as restrictions went up to level 6B which is no longer in force today. One-off connection charges are also applied when new connections are installed and set at the full costs of connection installation.

Table 2.7. Water restriction levels, Cape Town

Restrictions measures permanently in place	Restriction level				
	No restriction (water-wise)	Level 1	Level 2	Level 3	Emergency responses
Watering: hosepipes/sprinklers	Allowed	1 hour (Tuesdays and Saturdays)	1 hour (Saturdays)	Not allowed	Not allowed
Watering: drippers/drip line/soaker hose or bucket/watering can	Allowed	Allowed	Allowed	1 hour (Tuesdays and Saturdays)[2]	Not allowed
Sports fields/parks (sprinklers)	Allowed	1 hour (Tuesdays and Fridays)	1 hour (Tuesdays)[3]	1 hour (Tuesdays)[3]	By exemption only
Swimming pools	Allowed subject to conditions[4]	Allowed subject to conditions[4]	-Topping up allowed subject to conditions[4] -No filling/refilling	-Topping up allowed subject to conditions[4] -No filling/refilling	-No topping up -No filling
Car washing (privately)	Allowed	Bucket or high pressure/ low volume cleaner	Bucket only	Not allowed	Not allowed
Informal car washes	Allowed	Bucket or high pressure/ low volume cleaner	Bucket only	Bucket only	Not allowed
Commercial car washes	Allowed[5]	Allowed[5]	Allowed[5]	Allowed[5]	Not allowed
Water features	Allowed	Allowed	Not allowed	Not allowed	Not allowed

Restrictions measures permanently in place	Restriction level				
	No restriction (water-wise)	Level 1	Level 2	Level 3	Emergency responses
Other	-	-	-	-	Additional emergency restrictions may be determined
Targeted water pressure[6] (bar)	> 2.4	> 2.4	> 2.4	> 1.2	> 0.5

Note:
1. Restriction measures only apply to the use of municipal drinking water and not alternative water such as rainwater, greywater or groundwater. Groundwater use must comply with the National Department of Water and Sanitation regulations.
2. Drippers or soaker hose irrigation allowed for areas not exceeding 100 m² per property.
3. High priority parks, public open spaces and sports fields and subject to any additional conditions determined by the Director of Cape Town Water and Sanitation Department.
4. Topping up or filling of swimming pools with municipal drinking water is allowed subject to: i) the pool is covered with a non-permeable solid pool cover when not in use; and ii) the recovery of backwash water and the use of rainwater for pool topping up where practically possible.
5. Commercial car washes may use municipal drinking water subject to industry best practice water conservation norms and the recycling of at least 50% of the water used.
6. Targeted water network zone pressure as measured at the zone critical point at ground level. Zone pressure is expected to be lowest at the critical point, thus most of the zone should experience pressure higher than at the critical point.
Source: City of Cape Town (n.d.[16]), *Homepage*, https://www.capetown.gov.za/ (accessed on 02 February 2021).

Figure 2.8. Water restriction levels according to dam levels, Cape Town

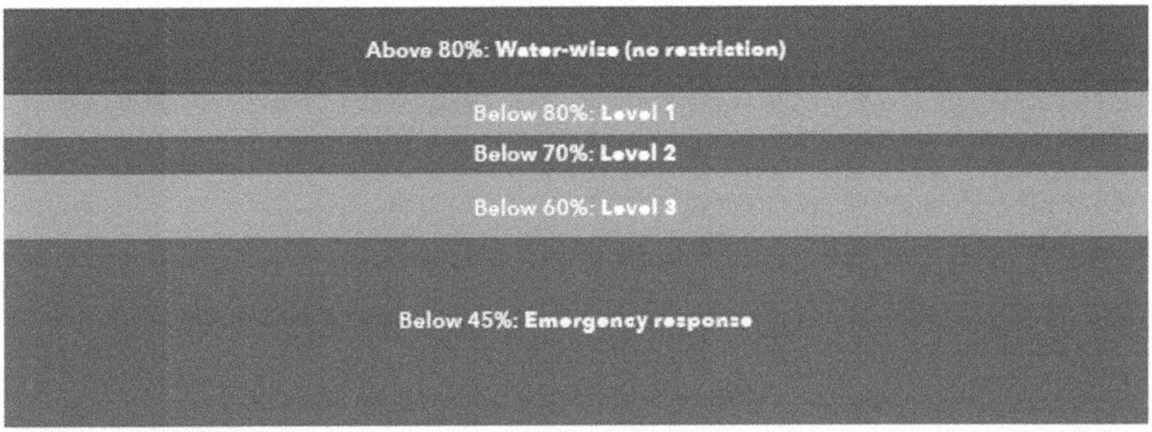

Source: City of Cape Town (2019[15]), *Cape Town Water Strategy*, http://resource.capetown.gov.za/documentcentre/Documents/City%20strategies%2c%20plans%20and%20frameworks/Cape%20Town%20Water%20Strategy.pdf.

The Water and Sanitation Department of the city of Cape Town has set up 36 key performance indicators (KPI) to assess and monitor the service quality. They are part of a broader corporate monitoring and appraisal system at the city level. For each of these 36 KPIs a target value is defined each year and KPI monitoring is shared monthly with the Water and Waste Portfolio Committee, the Executive Mayor and the Mayoral Committee and the City Council. However, the outcomes of the Water and Sanitation Department monitoring are not publicly available.

References

City of Cape Town (2020), *Western Cape Water Supply System.* [9]

City of Cape Town (2019), *Cape Town Water Strategy*, Department of Water and Sanitation, http://resource.capetown.gov.za/documentcentre/Documents/City%20strategies%2c%20plans%20and%20frameworks/Cape%20Town%20Water%20Strategy.pdf. [15]

City of Cape Town (2019), *Departmental Business Plan 2019/2020, Department of Water and Sanitation.* [2]

City of Cape Town (2018), *Water Outlook 2018 Report*, Department of Water and Sanitation, https://resource.capetown.gov.za/documentcentre/Documents/City%20research%20reports%20and%20review/Water%20Outlook%202018%20-%20Summary.pdf. [14]

City of Cape Town (n.d.), *Homepage*, https://www.capetown.gov.za/ (accessed on 2 February 2021). [16]

Dassah (2018), "Theoretical analysis of state capture and its manifestation as a governance problem in South Africa", *The Journal for Transdisciplinary Research in Southern Africa*, Vol. 14(1), p. 4. [4]

Department of Water Affairs and Forestry (2003), *Strategic Framework for Water Services.* [11]

DWS (2007), *Pricing Strategy for Raw Water Use Charges*, Department of Water and Sanitation. [10]

DWS (2001), *Norms and Standards in Respect of Tariffs for Water Services*, Department of Water and Sanitation. [12]

DWS (forthcoming), *Western Cape Water Supply System, Reconciliation Strategy, Status Report 2019.* [8]

Eberhard, R. (2002), "Administered prices: Water". [13]

Meiring, M. (2003), *Balancing equity with sustainability, The Reserve.* [7]

OECD (2015), *The Governance of Water Regulators*, OECD Studies on Water, OECD Publishing, Paris, https://doi.org/10.1787/9789264231092-en. [3]

OECD (2011), *Water Governance in OECD Countries: A Multi-level Approach*, OECD Studies on Water, OECD Publishing, Paris, https://dx.doi.org/10.1787/9789264119284-en. [1]

Roux, G. (2019), "Dam state capture: its cascading effect on the Department of Water and Sanitation". [5]

Solomon, M. (2016), "Understanding the Phenomenon of "State Capture" in South Africa", *Southern African Peace and Security Studies*, Vol. 5/1. [6]

Notes

[1] The Free Basic policy passed by the South African government in 2001 that promotes more equal service delivery, mandates that municipalities provide 25 litres per day per person, or 6 m^3 per month for a household of 8, at no cost to end users and accessible within 200 m from their homes.

[1] These costs include notably staff costs, debts repayment, depreciation costs, bulk water and electricity tariffs, contracted services.

3 Key water governance challenges in Cape Town, South Africa

This chapter analyses the key governance challenges for water resources management and water and sanitation services in Cape Town and South Africa. The chapter uses the OECD Principles on Water Governance to assess key issues related to policy and institutional fragmentation, scale mismatch, policy coherence, capacity, data and information, funding, regulation, integrity, transparency, stakeholder engagement, trade-off management and evaluation. It stresses in particular the multi-level and multi-stakeholder co-ordination issues. It highlights the capacity gaps across levels of government as well as challenges regarding the production and use of data to effectively manage water balance and restrictions. It stresses how trust was undermined among stakeholders. Finally, it explains how below-cost recovery charges generate funding gaps at the national and local levels.

Key messages

Using the 12 OECD Principles on Water Governance (2015[1]) as an analytical grid, the following key governance challenges for water resources management and water and sanitation services have been identified for Cape Town and South Africa. They encompass issues related to policy and institutional fragmentation, scale mismatch, policy coherence, capacity, data and information, funding, regulation, integrity, transparency, stakeholder engagement, trade-off management and evaluation. Remedial actions already taken to address these challenges have also been highlighted (Table 3.1).

Table 3.1. Key water governance challenges in Cape Town and South Africa

OECD Principle on Water Governance	Associated governance challenge identified	Remedial action already taken
1. Clearly allocate and distinguish roles and responsibilities for water policymaking, policy implementation, operational management and regulation, and foster co-ordination across these responsible authorities	Although roles and responsibilities are defined in a set of acts, multi-level co-ordination issues have occurred for water resource and conservation policy implementation, especially in a context of poorly funded mandates.	To address this co-ordination challenge in a context of poorly funded mandates, Western Cape Water Supply System (WCWSS) stakeholders have set up a dedicated water fund for invasive alien plant (IAP) clearing campaigns.
2. Manage water at the appropriate scale(s) within integrated basin governance systems to reflect local conditions and foster co-ordination between the different scales	Co-ordination of policies and stakeholders at the catchment level has proven difficult as catchment management agency (CMA) instalment process has stalled.	
3. Encourage policy coherence through effective cross-sectoral co-ordination, especially between policies for water and the environment, health, energy, agriculture, industry, spatial planning and land use	Challenges occurred with water restriction co-ordination, implementation and enforcement across levels of government and sectors.	
4. Adapt the level of capacity of responsible authorities to the complexity of water challenges to be met and to the set of competencies required to carry out their duties	Capacity gaps identified across levels of government encompass important turnover and vacancies, ageing staff and difficulty to attract the adequate number of skilled staff.	- The National Department of Water and Sanitation (DWS) recognised the need to build and strengthen capacity in the National Water and Sanitation Master Plan (DWS, 2019[2]), where an action plan details and costs a series of eight measures to implement by 2030. - Cape Town plans a revision of its organisational structure, as well as its working processes and the competencies required inhouse as stated in its Water Strategy 2019
5. Produce, update and share timely, consistent, comparable and policy-relevant water and water-related data and information, and use it to guide, assess and improve water policy	The planning models used to determine water balance were interpreted according to unjustified assumptions including, for instance, an effective eradication programme for invasive alien plants, up-to-date hydrology systems or effective operation of water systems.	Cape Town partners and collaborates with universities and research centres to develop applied research to better support evidence-based decision-making.
6. Ensure that governance arrangements help mobilise water finance and allocate financial resources in an efficient, transparent and timely manner	Below-cost recovery charges generate important funding gaps at the national and local levels.	Cape Town is considering a mix of solutions to fill the funding gap, including tariff increase, economic and technical efficiency gains, pooled financing strategy as well as grants.
7. Ensure that sound water management regulatory frameworks are effectively implemented and enforced in pursuit of the public interest	Despite the existence of a Pricing Water Strategy, charges and tariffs are set too low.	In its 2019 Water Strategy, Cape Town recognises that the water tariff has to better reflect costs of service provision.
8. Promote the adoption and implementation of innovative water governance practices across responsible authorities, levels of government and relevant stakeholders		Towards the end of the crisis, Cape Town started to use data and information-driven tools to communicate, including an Open Data Portal, or a Collaborative Resilience Action Plan platform.

OECD Principle on Water Governance	Associated governance challenge identified	Remedial action already taken
9. Mainstream integrity and transparency practices across water policies, water institutions and water governance frameworks for greater accountability and trust in decision-making	Public procurement was characterised by irregular expenditure and harmful delays.	In its 2019 Water Strategy, Cape Town ambitions to optimise procurement processes "with particular attention to value for money and the time taken to contract".
10. Promote stakeholder engagement for informed and outcome-oriented contributions to water policy design and implementation	At the beginning of the water crisis, stakeholder engagement was limited and communication was done on a "command and control" mode before evolving towards a more collaborative approach.	During the crisis, Cape Town set up the Water Resilience Advisory Committee. The city also set up a strategy for building water resilience through partnering and collaboration with a wide variety of national, regional and local stakeholders from all sectors.
11. Encourage water governance frameworks that help manage trade-offs across water users, rural and urban areas, and generations	During the crisis, water allocation from the Western Cape Water Supply System exceeded its yield, thus triggering the need to revisit water balances and requirements.	
12. Promote regular monitoring and evaluation of water policy and governance where appropriate, share the results with the public and make adjustments when needed	The yearly updates of the Reconciliation Strategy Status and of the Blue and Green Drop reports were not consistently and timeously performed.	

The present chapter uses the OECD Principles on Water Governance (OECD, 2015[1]) to assess the performance of water policy in Cape Town and analyse key water governance challenges that emerged during the crisis although some of them existed before.

Adopted by all OECD countries in 2015, the OECD Principles on Water Governance aim to enhance water governance systems that help manage "too much", "too little" and "too polluted" water and foster universal access to drinking water and sanitation, in a sustainable, integrated and inclusive way, at an acceptable cost and in a reasonable time frame. The principles acknowledge that good governance is a means to an end to master complexity and managing trade-offs in a policy domain that is highly sensitive to fragmentation, silos, scale mismatch, negative externalities, monopolies and large capital-intensive investment. The principles consider that governance is good if it can help to solve key water challenges, using a combination of bottom-up and top-down processes while fostering constructive state-society relations. It is bad if it generates undue transaction costs and does not respond to place-based needs (Box 3.1).

Box 3.1. The OECD Principles on Water Governance

The OECD Principles on Water Governance intend to contribute to tangible and outcome-oriented public policies, based on three mutually reinforcing and complementary dimensions of water governance (Figure 3.1).

1. Effectiveness relates to the contribution of governance to define clear sustainable water policy goals and targets at all levels of government, to implement those policy goals and to meet expected targets.
2. Efficiency relates to the contribution of governance to maximise the benefits of sustainable water management and welfare at the least cost to society.
3. Trust and engagement relate to the contribution of governance to building public confidence and ensuring the inclusiveness of stakeholders through democratic legitimacy and fairness for society at large.

Figure 3.1. Dimensions of water governance

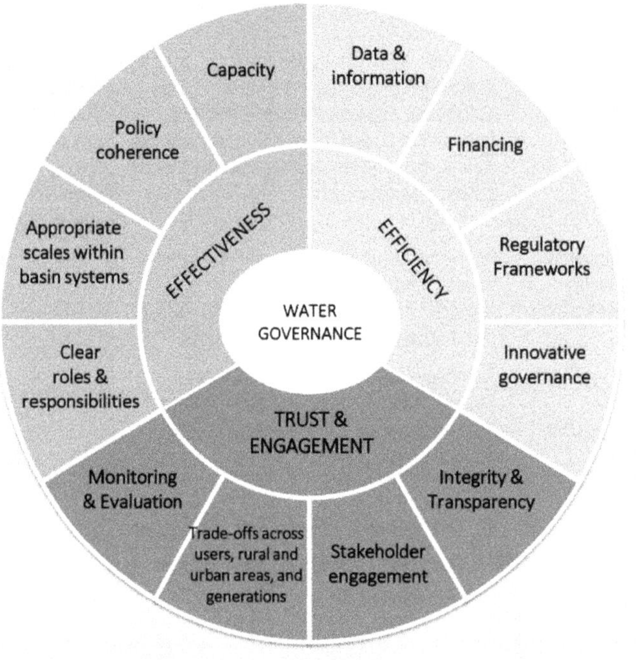

Source: OECD (2015[1]), *OECD Principles on Water Governance*, https://www.oecd.org/gov/regional-policy/OECD-Principles-on-Water-Governancebrochure.pdf.

Enhancing the effectiveness of water governance

- Principle 1. Clearly allocate and distinguish roles and responsibilities for water policymaking, policy implementation, operational management and regulation and foster co-ordination across these responsible authorities.
- Principle 2. Manage water at the appropriate scale(s) within integrated basin governance systems to reflect local conditions and foster co-ordination between the different scales.
- Principle 3. Encourage policy coherence through effective cross-sectoral co-ordination, especially between policies for water and the environment, health, energy, agriculture, industry, spatial planning and land use.
- Principle 4. Adapt the level of capacity of responsible authorities to the complexity of water challenges to be met and to the set of competencies required to carry out their duties.

Enhancing the efficiency of water governance

- Principle 5. Produce, update and share timely, consistent, comparable and policy-relevant water and water-related data and information, and use it to guide, assess and improve water policy.
- Principle 6. Ensure that governance arrangements help mobilise water finance and allocate financial resources in an efficient, transparent and timely manner.
- Principle 7. Ensure that sound water management regulatory frameworks are effectively implemented and enforced in pursuit of the public interest.
- Principle 8. Promote the adoption and implementation of innovative water governance practices across responsible authorities, levels of government and relevant stakeholders.

Enhancing trust and engagement in water governance

- Principle 9. Mainstream integrity and transparency practices across water policies, water institutions and water governance frameworks for greater accountability and trust in decision-making.
- Principle 10. Promote stakeholder engagement for informed and outcome-oriented contributions to water policy design and implementation.
- Principle 11. Encourage water governance frameworks that help manage trade-offs across water users, rural and urban areas, and generations.
- Principle 12. Promote regular monitoring and evaluation of water policy and governance where appropriate, share the results with the public and make adjustments when needed.

Source: OECD (2015[1]), *OECD Principles on Water Governance*, https://www.oecd.org/gov/regional-policy/OECD-Principles-on-Water-Governancebrochure.pdf.

Challenging co-ordination across stakeholders and levels of government

The Western Cape Water Supply System (WCWSS) multi-level institutional setting requires strong and effective vertical and horizontal co-ordination between levels of governments and across sectors to manage and efficiently use water resources. Although overarching principles and roles allocation are duly stated in the legislation and co-ordination mechanisms are in place (see Chapter 2), Cape Town's 2017-18 water crisis highlighted challenges to implement and achieve effective co-ordination within the WCWSS and at the catchment level.

Co-ordination challenges within the Western Cape Water Supply System

The WCWSS is managed by multi-stakeholder instances. The Strategy Steering Committee, formed after the completion of the Reconciliation Strategy[1] in 2007, gathers representatives from all provincial government departments, from the agriculture sector, the Breede-Gouritz Catchment Management Agency (CMA), the city of Cape Town, relevant districts and local municipalities, and the DWS regional and national offices. In addition to this committee, a WCWSS Strategic Operating Forum is held yearly to discuss the operational state of the WCWSS dams and to determine the need to impose water restrictions.

Despite the existence of such multi-stakeholder instances, co-ordination has, at times, proven challenging, especially during the 2017-18 water crisis. The Strategy Steering Committee typically meets twice a year but did not meet during 2016 and 2017 (Ziervogel, 2019[3]) in the absence of an appointed service provider to support the DWS and the committee. The role of the service provider was to update the status of system demand and supply, and the various intervention measures underway, and to put forward recommendations to the committee for consideration and decisions. However, as no service provider was appointed, these tasks were not timeously fulfilled. In addition, a yearly status update of the Reconciliation Strategy for the Western Cape should be published but no update was produced for 2017. A draft was however prepared for 2018 but not finalised. A 2019 status update is currently waiting for final approval before release.

Co-ordination for the implementation of the invasive alien plant (IAP) species clearing programme, to prevent the further reduction of the WCWSS water yield, also proved challenging. Although the responsibility for environmental conservation issues lies within the national Department for Environment, Forestry and Fisheries (DEFF) and the provincial Department for Environmental Affairs and Development Planning (DEADP), several institutions need to co-ordinate to fund and implement these programmes.

Funding comes from national, provincial and catchment levels when a CMA is installed and a great variety of national and subnational stakeholders are involved in environmental and water conservation (DWS, DEFF, DEADP, farmers, municipalities, non-governmental organisations [NGOs], etc.). As such, IAP clearing programmes tend to exacerbate multi-level co-ordination issues especially when mandates are poorly funded. These funding and co-ordination issues currently hamper environmental restoration and ecological infrastructure investment to protect water sources and ensure water security at the catchment level. To address this co-ordination challenge, WCWSS stakeholders set up a dedicated water fund for IAP clearing campaigns that sits outside of the CMA (Box 3.2). This allows funding to flow to IAP control from a range of sectors but it also creates challenges with co-ordination due to some overlaps between concurrent responsibilities for environmental management.

Box 3.2. The Greater Cape Town Water Fund

While until recently the focus has been on "grey", or engineered, infrastructure solutions to combat water scarcity, there is another cost-effective option with the potential to augment water supply. Long-term water security in the Greater Cape Town Region, as elsewhere, begins at the source with the ecological infrastructure (native vegetation, wetlands, etc.) that regulates source water quality and supply. Over two-thirds of the sub-catchments supplying the WCWSS are affected by alien plant invasions, reducing the amount of water that reaches the rivers and dams that feed the region by 55 billion litres (55 Mm^3) per year. In a place where every drop of water counts, these losses are significant. These plants, trees such as pine and eucalyptus, quickly replace native species if unmanaged and threaten the diversity of native plant life in the Cape Floral Region, where 70% of plants are found nowhere else on the planet, and alter the habitat for the region's fauna. IAP species alter soil ecology, increase the frequency and severity of wildfires and significantly impact river flow and aquifer recharge. Despite ongoing efforts to remove invasive trees by programmes such as Working for Water, the problem is increasing. In response, a coalition of partners – The Nature Conservancy, the National Department of Water and Sanitation (DWS), the National Department of Environmental Affairs (Environmental Programmes), the provincial DEADP, the city of Cape Town, SANBI, CapeNature, Coca-Cola Peninsula Beverages, Nedbank, Remgro Ltd and the World Wildlife Fund (WWF) – came together under the auspices of the Greater Cape Town Water Fund Steering Committee. The committee commissioned studies to evaluate the impact of nature-based solutions on water supply, beginning with targeted removals of alien plant invasions, and determine whether investing at scale in catchment restoration is cost-competitive with other supply-side solutions.

The business case analysis models a 30-year period, discounting both costs and water gains at 6% for surface water sub-catchments. Results show that investing ZAR 372 million here (USD 25.5 million; present value) will generate expected annual water gains of 100 billion litres (100 Mm^3) within 30 years compared to the business-as-usual scenario. Importantly, IAP removal would already yield up to an additional 50 billion litres (50 Mm^3) within 5 years. Approximately 350 job opportunities will be created in the first five years of implementation, as removing alien plant invasions is very labour intensive. Catchment restoration is significantly more cost-effective than other water augmentation solutions, supplying water at one-tenth the unit cost of alternative options. It produces greater water yields than all other supply options except desalination, which is far more costly. The results of catchment restoration programmes will be evident rapidly, with improved supply showing as soon as the first winter rains. Furthermore, catchment restoration produces water yield gains into perpetuity if areas cleared of IAP are maintained.

The Greater Cape Town Water Fund is bringing together private and public sectors stakeholders alongside local communities around the common goal of restoring the surface water and aquifer catchments which supply our water. The water fund aims to support and align with existing government initiatives and act as a catalyst for systemic change in catchment management by cost-effective use of on the ground resources, strengthened capacity and robust monitoring and evaluation. In addition, the water fund will stimulate funding and implementation of catchment restoration efforts and, in the process, create jobs and momentum to protect globally important biodiversity and build more resilient communities in the face of climate change.

Source: The Nature Conservancy, (2018[4]), The Greater Cape Town Water Fund, Assessing the return on Investment for Ecological Infrasytructure Restoration, Business Case, https://www.nature.org/content/dam/tnc/nature/en/documents/GCTWF-summary-11.14.18.pdf

Co-ordination challenges at the catchment level

While the National Water Act (NWA) 1998 mandates the decentralisation of water resources management through CMAs, thus aiming to enhance user involvement in the governance of water at the local and regional levels, progress in this sense has been slow. The incomplete process to establish the Berg-Olifant CMA, for example, has impeded the full implementation of Integrated Water Resource Management (IWRM) at the catchment level. As a result, WCWSS stakeholders have been unable to reap off the benefits from decentralised water management at catchment level through the implementation of CMAs as a co-ordination tool (Box 3.3).

Box 3.3. Awaited benefits from CMA establishment

1. CMAs are better positioned to deal with water allocation in light of droughts, current variability and the challenges of climate change.
2. CMAs support resource-poor farmers and are well-positioned to deal with the transformation of water institutions.
3. CMAs are up-to date on the licensing of water use and able to monitor compliance and act on compliance failures.
4. CMAs are able to focus on water quality and protection of water resources against pollution from dysfunctional wastewater works, mines, industry and agriculture.
5. CMAs are good at engaging the public for awareness and supporting the active participation of stakeholders in water resource management.
6. CMAs are able to plan strategically and respond to challenges through adaptive management.
7. Proto-CMAs are not able to operate to the same effect as CMAs.
8. CMAs will be positioned to deal with current failures in the water sector which are needing other actors to step in to fulfil functions neglected by the DWS in catchments.

Source: Munnik, V. (2020[5]), "The reluctant roll-out of Catchment Management Agencies: Assessing the key risks and consequences of delays in finalising institutional arrangements for decentralised water resource management", http://www.wrc.org.za/wp-content/uploads/mdocs/2943_final.pdf.

Even where CMAs have been established, the low level of funding and the incomplete delegation/assignment of functions by the DWS have limited their ability to undertake their functions effectively. CMAs are endowed with initial functions focusing mainly on co-ordination missions at the catchment level, as stated in the NWA:

> *"- to investigate and advise interested persons in the protection, use, development, conservation, management and control of the water resources in its water management area;*
> - *to develop a catchment management strategy;*
> - *to co-ordinate the related activities of water users and of the water management institutions within its water management area;*
> - *to promote the co-ordination of its implementation with the implementation of any applicable development plan established in terms of the Water Services Act, 1997 (Act No. 108 of 1997); and*
> - *to promote community participation in the projection, use, development, conservation, management and control of the water resources in its water management area."*

However, in addition to these initial functions, which limit CMAs' reach and effectiveness, complementary powers and functions may be delegated by the National DWS, as stated in Schedule 3 of the NWA. These complementary functions include for instance:

> *"- the power to manage and monitor permitted water use within its water management area;*
> - *the power to conserve and protect the water resources and resource quality within its water management area [...];*
> - *the power to do anything necessary to implement catchment management strategies within its water management area [...];*
> - *the power to make rules and regulate water use;*
> - *the power to temporarily control, limit or prohibit use of water during periods of water shortage."*

The priority action listed in the National Water and Sanitation Master Plan (DWS, 2019[2]) to "establish financially sustainable CMAs across the country, and transfer staff and budget and delegated functions, including licensing of water use and monitoring and evaluation of water resources" seems to point in the direction of delegating complementary functions to CMAs. However, this priority action was to be completed by 2020, which is still not the case. As a result, uncertainties remain with regard to the pace of the reform and its possible form and outcomes. These uncertainties and the slow pace of CMA instalment are hampering effective water resources management co-ordination at the catchment level.

Capacity gap across levels of government

Capacity gaps at the national level

At the national level, a long-lasting capacity gap has potentially undermined the ability of the DWS to fully take leadership and deliver water policy outputs and outcomes. It is argued that this capacity gap partly results from a possible phenomenon of political capture[2] (Dassah, 2018[6]; Martin and Solomon, 2016[7]) that has negatively affected the DWS and weakened its effectiveness (Galvin and Roux, 2019[8]). In their article, Galvin and Roux identify erosion of human resources as one of the various potential institutional impacts of capture (Table 3.2). In addition to the capacity gap, it is argued that capture also generated public procurement issues resulting in long delays to appoint service providers (see section on Undermined trust across levels of governments and among stakeholders) and financial mismanagement resulting in underinvestment and low asset maintenance (see section (see section on Undermined trust across levels of governments and among stakeholders).

Table 3.2. Institutional impacts of political capture

Erosion of human resources, including high staff turnover and vacancy rates
Erosion of financial management, including over-expenditure, accruals, increased debt, overdraft, irregular expenditure and poor revenue collection
Poor contract management
Erosion of procurement and supply chain management
Erosion of financial controls to identify unauthorised, irregular fruitless and wasteful expenditure

Increased risk of corruption
Reduced public participation
Reduced transparency and accountability
Increase in issuing inappropriate licences and authorisations
Reduced compliance monitoring and enforcement
Erosion of monitoring and reporting systems

Source: Galvin, M. and S. Roux (2019[8]), "Dam state capture: Its cascading effect on the Department of Water and Sanitation", *Transformation: Critical Perspectives on Southern Africa*, Vol. 100.

In 2015, the DWS was established out of the merger of the mandates of the Department of Water Affairs and the Sanitation function from the Department of Human Settlements. Following this merger, the Minister of Human Settlements, Water and Sanitation then commissioned a comprehensive organisational review of the DWS (Vienings, 2015[9]). The outcomes of this review highlighted important capacity gaps and issues, which have only been partially addressed since then.

Turnover and vacancies

The DWS has been suffering from high rates of turnover and vacancy for many years. In 2017, the National Treasury was reporting 900 vacant posts within the DWS. The latest figures reported by the DWS in its Annual Performance Plan 2019/20 to 2021/22 amount to 1 033 (13% of total positions), with 37% of vacant positions in the Chief Operational Office Branch and 31% in the Infrastructure Build Operation and Maintenance Branch.

In 2018, in a report on the functioning of the DWS (2018[10]), the Auditor-General made specific reference to the rate of turnover of directors-general and chief financial officers. From 2009 to 2017, the average duration of senior staff mandate was 11 months with the positions being filled in an acting capacity most of the time. Over this period, three of the four formally appointed directors-general resigned, which added to the instability of human resources management at the DWS. In her speech on DWS Budget 2020/21 (Minister of Human Settlements, Water and Sanitation, 2020[11]), the Water and Sanitation Minister acknowledges the need to "ensure that, especially at top management level, all incumbents are truly fit for purpose because that is the core of the delivery of the department's mandate".

Ageing staff and absence of replacement plan

The forthcoming retirement of 22% of experienced DWS workers is leaving significant gaps in skills and, in the absence of proper skills transfer, can put in jeopardy the institutional memory of water policy in South Africa (NIWIS).[3] Among the scientists and engineers with high-level skills working at the DWS, 86 would reach retirement age within the next 10 years and currently, no work plan exists to secure replacement and foster the preservation and continuity of the existing technical expertise. As a result, mentoring and training new staff in the water sector has become a major challenge due to the expected shortage of experienced personnel in the medium term. Moreover, as noted by the Auditor-General, a skills audit has not been conducted in the past 15 years at the DWS.

Adverse implications of the capacity gap on water policy

As noted in the Auditor-General report (2018[10]), the observed capacity issues within the DWS adversely affects its performance and its ability to deliver water policy outcomes.

For instance, the lack of staff and capacities is one of the reasons that is contributing to slow down the water use licenses (WUL) speed-up reform. Another reason is the many tools for the protection and use of water that can be overly complex and technical, and that generate significant delays (Centre for Environmental Rights, 2012[12]). The DWS, which is responsible for issuing WULs, was criticised by some stakeholders for taking too long, as the process can reach up to 300 days as per National Water Act regulations. Although the DWS is making changes to its regulatory regime to give effect to the 90-day WUL turnaround time (Minister of Human Settlements, Water and Sanitation, 2020[11]), delays remain long which prevents quick and adaptive reactions and responsiveness, especially during crises. Moreover, it has been noted by the Auditor-General that a number of WULs have been issued in protected areas with stringent conditions rather than being refused. As an illustration of this long-lasting situation, in a decision dated 21 July 2020, the Water Tribunal upheld an appeal to set aside two WULs granted by the DWS to ACWA Power for the development of a new coal-fired power station. The tribunal found that the WUL applications were procedurally flawed but also that the licensing authority had not adequately weighed up the impact of climate change on water security in the region (Final Appeal Decision of the Water Tribunal no WT02/18/MP dated 21 July 2020).

According to some stakeholders, the lack of staff and capacities has also adversely affected the maintenance and operation of DWS infrastructure. In 2016/17, it was suggested that the operation of the WCWSS dams owned by the DWS was not optimal due to non-operational pumps and silted canals among other factors (Ziervogel, 2019[3]).

The capacity to collect and process data and information and the capacity of regulatory authorities to interpret and respond appropriately and timeously based on these data and information is a major challenge. The failure to yearly publish the Blue Drop (water quality) and Green Drop (wastewater treatment) reports since 2013 is an illustration of this situation. The Blue Drop-Green Drop reports are comprehensive assessments, available to the public and water service authorities, on the functioning of water and wastewater treatment plants, and on the compliance with water quality standards. The absence of these reports and of the data and information they comprise has considerable implications for management, operation, risk mitigation, remedial action and refurbishment plans related to treatment plants – and hence water safety and quality (Figure 3.2).

Figure 3.2. Implications of the capacity gap on water policy

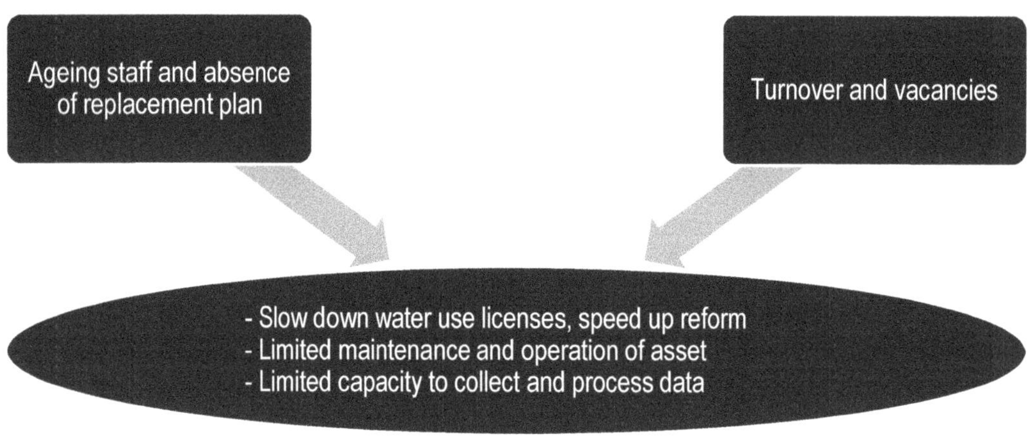

Taking stock of the abovementioned challenges, the DWS recognised the need to build and strengthen capacity in the National Water and Sanitation Master Plan (DWS, 2019[2]), where an action plan details and costs a series of eight measures to implement by 2030. Such measures include the production of a skills and institutional capacity development strategy for the sector aligned to the 2030 National Water and Sanitation Master Plan by indicating what skills (competencies and numbers) are needed by the different water sector institutions to achieve the sector goals and priorities. They also foresee the expansion and continued implementation of existing capacity building programmes such as the 2020 Vision of Water and Sanitation Schools Education Programme, the Community Water Education Programme incorporating climate change or the Water Councillor Leadership Programme. These measures also underline the key role that the Energy and Water Sector Education and Training Authority (EWSETA) will play as the institution responsible for co-ordinating and facilitating skills development and capacity building for the water sector.

In addition, the minister, in her speech on DWS Budget 2020/21 (Minister of Human Settlements, Water and Sanitation, 2020[11]), mentioned a programme to restructure the DWS. The new structure was signed off in 2020 and will be submitted to the Minister for the Public Service and Administration for his concurrence.

Capacity gap at the local level

While Cape Town is endowed with skilled staff and experts – although facing capacity issues below summarised – smaller municipalities in the Western Cape area struggle to attract adequate numbers of specialised technical staff to effectively operate and maintain water schemes. The situation is exacerbated by a below-cost-recovery tariff and a sub-optimal collection of revenue, which further prevents operational plans from being effectively implemented. Nationally, the ratio of civil engineering staff per 100 000 people is less than half of what is required to adequately plan, deliver, operate and maintain services, including water services (GreenCape, 2019[13]). These capacity constraints limit the ability of municipalities to efficiently implement or pilot water assets and technologies. The problem is further exacerbated by the lack of water revenues ring-fencing in most municipalities for reinvestment in water infrastructure, and a heavy reliance on these revenues to cross-subsidise other municipal functions. This leads to fundamental challenges in the local government financing model, especially for those municipalities that do not have strong revenue bases.

With more than 3 800 water and sanitation employees, the city of Cape Town Water and Sanitation Department is endowed with skilled staff and experts. For instance, the city of Cape Town Scientific Services Branch comprises a research facility and an accredited laboratory, under SANAS ISO 17025, that tests some 16 000 samples of drinking water each year, drawn from approximately 300 designated sampling points throughout the water system (boreholes, dams, treatment plants, reservoirs, distribution network). High levels of compliance with SANS 241 standards are attained and the water quality is rated as "excellent". In addition, the Scientific Services also test treated wastewater from wastewater treatment works and from rivers and perform air pollution testing. The city of Cape Town also has an inhouse mechanical workshop performing customised manufacturing for water and sanitation equipment, materials, spare parts and maintenance. The Cape Town Water and Sanitation Department has an asset register which uses IT inventory and monitoring solutions. These tools which were jointly developed by the city of Cape Town Engineering and Asset Management Branch and the Corporate IT Branch allow to developing an asset management system and department-wide processes with ISO 9001 quality certification. Moreover, the city is certified ISO 14001 and is currently working on getting ISO 45001 certification.

Nevertheless, Cape Town is also facing a high rate of vacancies with 15% of vacant positions, predominantly in the functional Branches of Reticulation, Bulk Water, Engineering and Asset Management and Wastewater Works (City of Cape Town, 2019[14]). Water and sanitation staff costs represent 17% of the total operating expenditure (City of Cape Town, 2019[14]) which is rather low compared to international practices and underlines the existence of several vacant positions to be filled. Furthermore, during the drought, high call volumes and a lack of capacity in the call centre, where some positions were not filled as a matter of urgency, left many calls unanswered (City of Cape Town, 2019[15]). For the past years, important staff retirement has generated some loss of information, experience and institutional memory within the city of Cape Town Water and Sanitation Department. A need for internal staff with experience and expertise in the development and maintenance of alternative sanitation technologies has been identified to fast track the efficiency of service delivery and to sustain technology lifecycle maintenance (City of Cape Town, 2019[14]). In addition, heavy and complex public procurement processes have generated delays in public purchase. In addition to this, budgetary constraints also hamper the creation and filling of potentially much-needed staff positions.

Taking stock of these issues, Cape Town plans a revision of its organisational structure, as well as its working processes and the competencies required inhouse as stated in its Water Strategy 2019 (section on translating the strategy into action and increasing capability) (City of Cape Town, 2019[16]). Emphasis will be placed on increasing fluidity and speed of execution within the organisation, particularly with respect to decision-making, appointments and procurement. The aim is to reduce vacancy rates and recruitment delays substantially but also to optimise procurement processes, with particular attention to value for money and the time taken to contract. Standard operating procedures will be reviewed and improved to retain institutional memory and ensure effective training. Talent management for succession planning and staff development will be emphasised.

Data and co-ordination challenges to effectively manage water balance and restrictions

Water resource planning data and models

"Since the 1980s, South Africa's major conurbations have used systems models to guide their water management. These models, run by the national government, are considered world-class. They map links between river basins, reservoirs and transmission channels and use historical hydrological data to predict probable stream flows. Those are then matched to projections of demand to assess how much storage is needed. The models support real-time operations of the water network as well as planning for development. Crucially, they allow planners to assess risks of supply failures to different categories of users and evaluate the effectiveness of responses such as restrictions" (Muller, 2018, p. 175[17]).

Over time, engineers in South Africa have developed a standardised methodology to model future water demand against available supply. Future rainfall is modelled stochastically based on historical rainfall records. The anticipated impacts of climate change are factored into the supply models. Options to balance demand and supply are investigated and evaluated using multi-criteria decision analysis. Timeframes for supply augmentation are typically long, between five and ten years from the commencement of a feasibility study to the supply of water from a new scheme.

The results of the models are yearly discussed by the Strategy Steering Committee comprising national government, city representatives and other stakeholders. Decisions on the augmentation of supplies to cities are typically joint decisions taken by both national and city government in light of the financial implications of projects for city water users who pay for the costs of the supply augmentation through their water tariffs.

However, in the case of the 2017-18 water crisis in Cape Town, the set of assumptions used in the models to determine water allocation and balance, and thus potentially commission an augmentation of the water yield in the WCWSS, turned out not to be justified. The assumptions included the following assertions: allocations are based on available yield; the system hydrology is up to date; there is effective enforcement of withdrawals; there is the timely and effective implementation of restrictions (as and when necessary); there is an effective programme in place to eradicate alien invasive vegetation, and the system is operated effectively in accordance with well-defined rules. Unfortunately, what happened in practice was substantially different from what had been assumed. As a result, the effective system yield was less than assumed and the water balance in 2015 was more potentially precarious than shown in the technical reports at the time (Box 3.4).

Box 3.4. Decision-making and data interpretation

As stated by the United Nations, "data is the lifeblood of decision-making and the raw material for accountability. Quality and timely data are vital for enabling governments, international organisations, civil society, private sector and the general public to make informed decisions and to ensure the accountability of representative bodies" (UN, n.d.[18]).

With today's available digital technologies, the OECD Principle 5 on Water Governance (2015[1]) related to data and information should be easy to implement: "produce, update and share timely, consistent, comparable and policy-relevant water and water-related data and information, and use it to guide, assess and improve water policy".

Nevertheless, many organisations are still struggling with data. Data and data-related analytics make it possible to understand complex water systems from a holistic perspective. An increasing number of institutions face a widening gap between emerging realities (like growing populations, climate change and rapid digitalisation) and their existing practices. Understanding water systems that get more and more complex in a rapidly changing environment is a huge challenge that water managers have to face. Water managers have to be better prepared for the unexpected (in particular extreme situations generated by climate change) and quality data is again the basic building block in the decision-making process, as existing knowledge and experience are not enough anymore. Continuous monitoring of water systems and processes is key.

In Cape Town during the drought crisis, water-related data and information were needed to describe what happened, to analyse and come up with a diagnosis (why did it happen and how was it avoided). Data can also help to be more predictive (what will happen) while analytics can help to be more prescriptive (what should we do).

Satellite images, multi-model simulations, networked sensor systems and improved forecasts of water-related variables (to name a few) already exist and are ready for exploitation. These tools can be used in rather easy-to-operate ways that consider economic and social factors and can support evidence-based decision-making. But it is important to realise that decisions are made on the interpretation of data. Even if data as such can be considered as objective, interpretation is always subjective.

In 2017, the city of Cape Town already developed a data strategy. Data and data analytics were available and used to solve the drought issue. This allowed the city to develop knowledge and insights, to plan and act accordingly. Timely sharing of data and information was needed to help the city water security.

As stated in the Cape Town Water Strategy (City of Cape Town, 2019[16]), "clear communication is critical in building a water resilient city, both within the municipality itself and externally with the public. Communication is as much about listening to and understanding the needs of others, as it is about conveying information or key messages to them". But most of the time, communication departments only focus on the conveyance of key messages. Listening to and understanding the needs of others, creating an inclusive and participative dialogue are not easy when some people experienced a lack of trust in the past. South Africa has experience with such dialogues; the 1991 Mont Fleur Scenario Exercise, facilitated by Adam Kahane,[1] being a famous example amongst others.

Note:
1. For more information, see https://reospartners.com/reos-management/adam-kahane/.

Source: Caroline Figuères, (OECD, 2021[19]), *Water Governance in Cape Town, South Africa*; UN (n.d.[18]), *Big Data for Sustainable Development*, https://www.un.org/en/sections/issues-depth/big-data-sustainable-development/index.html.

Sub-optimal management

The impact of sub-optimal management of the WCWSS was significant. The Department of Water and Sanitation of the city of Cape Town has estimated that if the system had been managed (regulated and operated) entirely according to the rules and an effective programme to eradicate alien invasive vegetation had been in place, as planned, the dams could potentially have been 18% fuller during the worst part of the drought, which would have allowed the more serious economic impacts of the drought to have been avoided (City of Cape Town, 2018[20]).

Anticipating the impact of climate change

Although climate change was factored into the demand and supply scenarios, it could be argued that insufficient account had been taken of the climate change risks and variability. The modelling assumed a gradual impact over time and no possible step changes. More recent studies have suggested that climate change may have increased the risk of low rainfall years by a factor of three (Otto et al., 2018[21]). These factors are now being considered in future planning.

Ground-breaking research initiated by the city now incorporates the potential for an increase in multi-year droughts. Previous modelling only considered changes in mean annual precipitation and associated runoff.

Challenges with water restriction co-ordination across levels of government and sectors

In accordance with the basic principles for water allocation established in the 1997 Water Policy and the 1998 National Water Act, the DWS allocates water to each catchment area according to licenses for municipal needs, irrigation and other activities such as hydropower, industrial and commercial uses. It also makes decisions on how use is restricted during periods of drought in accordance with agreed processes and rules.

During the 2017-18 water crisis, decisions on water use restrictions were not instituted in time which increased the severity of the drought impacts. In May 2016, 20% restrictions compared to initially agreed balance in the reconciliation strategy were imposed by the DWS on domestic and agriculture water use in the Western Cape but the enforcement of these restrictions on agriculture were delayed. One year later, restrictions were gradually increased for agriculture from 30% to 60%, and from 40% to 45% for domestic use. Although restrictions had been decided by the end of 2016, the agriculture restrictions were only enforced and implemented in March 2017, which was too late to have an impact on the 2016/17 irrigation season (Ziervogel, 2019[3]). It has also been alleged by some stakeholders that the restrictions for agriculture during the summers of 2015/16 and 2016/17 were not adequately enforced. As a result, the total use from the WCWSS exceeded the available yield.

In response to the severe restrictions and penalty tariffs for high volume consumers decided by the city during the crisis, many residents and businesses in Cape Town developed alternative supplies including drilling private boreholes. The legal status of these boreholes was poorly defined legally (guidelines were issued by the DWS in 2018) and have led to over-abstraction, illegal resale of water, inadequate water quality compliance and difficulties to get people to register their boreholes through the online registry.[4] Unregulated boreholes are likely to pose a long-term threat to the recharge and sustainability of underground water bodies as well as quality issues due to possible contaminated aquifers in the absence of protected areas. Moreover, the unregulated use of groundwater is competing with legal use granted through water licences. This may lead to a potential overuse of groundwater causing seawater intrusion which further deteriorates water quality making it unusable for many usages. Farmers also looked into micro-solutions to address the drought with the construction of dams on site and the drilling of additional boreholes.

Building upon the drought experience, the city of Cape Town has committed to significantly reduce reliance on rain-fed dams and aims by about 25% when augmentation projects are completed and running at full capacity. A mix of solutions is contemplated comprising augmentation of surface water storage and transfer capacity, groundwater abstraction, desalination, reuse and IAP clearing programmes (City of Cape Town, 2020[22]).

Undermined trust across levels of governments and among stakeholders

Public procurement: "Irregular expenditure" and harmful delays

Since 1994, public procurement processes have been decentralised from the Central National Tender Board to individual ministries and departments. Over the years, the oversight of these processes by the National Treasury and the Department of Public Services and Administration have been weakened while procurement rules have hardened. Nevertheless, in his 2018 report on the DWS (2018[10]), the Auditor-General notes that "irregular expenditure continues to significantly increase year on year. [They are mostly] related to deviations from prescribed procurement processes on the basis of emergency procurement. Although such deviations are allowed, [...] it was often not approved; or, if approved, the reasons for the deviation were not reasonable and/or justifiable". The amount of irregular and wasteful expenditure is reported to reach a total of ZAR 31 billion (USD 2.1 billion) (Minister of Human Settlements, Water and Sanitation, 2020[11]).

In addition, some of the DWS senior management staff vacancies mentioned in section on Capacity gap were linked to integrity issues and resulted from precautionary suspensions linked with allegations of misconduct or corruption. This situation led to the creation of a Stabilisation Committee which is a disciplinary unit dealing with 166 cases, emanating from the Auditor-General's annual reports over a number of years ((Minister of Human Settlements, Water and Sanitation, 2020[11])). The examination of previous cases led to 97 officials being found guilty, 16 being found not guilty and 24 resigning. This widespread situation of public procurement irregularities led to growing mistrust which in turn led to stricter rules and legal provisions.

During the water crisis, the DWS also delayed the enforcement of crucial water management decisions. Whereas the city of Cape Town and the provincial government had both declared a drought disaster during the first trimester of 2017, the DWS waited one more year to do so, thus preventing budgets from being reprioritised and emergency relief funding from being released. The South African Water Caucus asserts that the reason for this delayed decision stems from spiralling debt, mismanagement, maladministration and corruption in the DWS (South Africa Water Caucus, 2017[23]) which illustrated, at the time, the possible capture of the department.

The abovementioned evolution together with the procurement challenges and budgetary constraints faced by the DWS resulted to some extent in underinvestment and low level of operation and maintenance of in DWS-owned infrastructure (Auditor-General, 2018[10]). These issues also led to impactful delays in the appointment of firms and consultants. For instance, in 2016 and 2017, the DWS experienced challenges in the appointment of consultants to update the Reconciliation Strategy for the WCWSS. This, unfortunately, coincided with the severe drought experienced within the WCWSS leading to a lack of information limiting the use of hydrological models.

Taking stock of the situation, the city of Cape Town underlines in its Water Strategy its ambition to optimise procurement processes (Box 3.5) "with particular attention to value for money and the time taken to contract" (City of Cape Town, 2019[16]).

Box 3.5. Public procurement procedures in Cape Town, South Africa

Municipal procurement is regulated by the Municipal Finance Management Act No. 56 of 2003 (MFMA) and its regulations, including the Municipal Supply Chain Management Regulations (2005). These regulations specify the minimum requirements but municipalities are allowed to apply stricter standards. The National Treasury also sets further requirements. The MFMA outlines the competitive procurement processes and unsolicited bids are not encouraged. As stipulated by the National Treasury, for projects worth more than ZAR 30 000 (USD 2 056) but less than ZAR 50 million (including value-added tax), the price contributes 80 points of the total score and the Broad-based Black Economic Empowerment (B-BBEE) status contributes 20 points. For projects above ZAR 50 million (USD 3.4 million), the price contributes 90 points and the B-BBEE status 10. Municipalities can also specify prequalification criteria to limit the competition to certain groups. These groups include companies with higher B-BBEE scores, exempted micro-enterprises (EMEs) and qualifying small enterprises (QSEs).

Companies wishing to do business with the city of Cape Town must first register with city's supplier database and the national Central Supplier Database (CSD). For goods and services less than ZAR 200 000 (USD 13 700), Cape Town publishes Requests for Quotations (RFQs) on its procurement portal. Companies must first register as a supplier and then register on the portal. For goods and services exceeding ZAR 200 000 (including value-added tax), a formal bidding (tender) process is required. Companies must be registered as a supplier and registered on the tender portal where tenders are advertised. Tenders are also advertised in local newspapers. For tenders valued at more than ZAR 10 million (USD 0.7 million), there is a more extensive process, including additional documentation requirements.

Source: GreenCape (2019[13]), *Water: Market Intelligence Report*, https://www.greencape.co.za/assets/Uploads/WATER-MIR-2019-WEB-01-04-2019.pdf.

From a "command and control" to a "collaborate and communicate" approach

Cape Town's 2017-18 water crisis was marked out by several turning points in communication triggering important changes in trust among stakeholders. At the beginning of the crisis, the city of Cape Town introduced several "command and control" measures, using a top-down approach and a "carrots and sticks" policy to address the drought situation. In January 2016, Cape Town first introduced water restrictions without clearly explaining the reasons leading to these restrictions. It also began to launch a "name and shame" media campaign to expose repeat water restriction offenders. "The identities of all customers who pay admission-of-guilt fines or who appear in court regarding contravention of level 3b water restrictions will be made public by the city of Cape Town," (City of Cape Town, 2017[24]) announced the mayor in the media. In 2017 and 2018, further water demand management measures were implemented such as tariff increases[5] and penalties for high volume consumers which appeared as punitive solutions; reduced pressure in distribution networks or instalment of water management devices in households using more than their water allowance. This "command and control" approach and the lack of a pro-active communication on the rationale for such decisions eroded trust and public support. This loss of trust from the citizens led to a questioning of the capacity of the city of Cape Town to address the critical situation. In this context, many Cape Town residents installed rainwater tanks or drilled private boreholes. Although these water supply alternatives reflected the adaptive capacity of residents, they also translated, to some extent, a sense of distrust towards the city and a loss of social cohesion with the search of individual solutions for those who could afford the investment (Sieff, 2018[25]). In the long-term, these solutions can jeopardise groundwater resources sustainability (see section on Data and co-ordination challenges to effectively manage water balance and restrictions). For instance, water-intensive industries that were hit hard by punitive tariffs and restrictions during the drought significantly augmented their supply with groundwater which has had a reverberating impact on municipal revenue and groundwater resources. Discontent grew further when the mayor proposed to levy an additional "drought charge" on certain properties to gradually compensate for the water budget deficit (ZAR 1.7 billion in 2017/18, USD 116.5 million) caused by the drastic consumption reduction. "This levy was perceived as a "punitive tax" for adhering to the city's water preservation campaign" (Visser, 2018[26]).

In addition, in May 2017, a reorganisation of water and sanitation responsibilities within the city administration, in a rather tense political context with the mayor surviving a vote of no-confidence by one vote and imminent municipal elections scheduled in 2019 as well as internal political tensions in the mayor's party, have also contributed to further trust erosion. A Water Resilience Task Team (WRTT) was established in the Directorate of the Mayor and, as such, was politically accountable to the executive mayor. The drought management prerogatives were thus transferred from the Cape Town Water and Sanitation Department to the WRTT. This marked an important breakdown in trust and communication between the mayor and the Water and Sanitation Department.

In January 2018, the city communication changed when the mayor released a press statement (City of Cape Town, 2018[27]) saying: "It is quite unbelievable that a majority of people do not seem to care and are sending all of us headlong towards Day Zero. At this point, we must assume that they will not change their behaviour and that the chance of reaching Day Zero on 21 April 2018 is now very likely".

Although this statement may be perceived as externalising the drought management failure onto citizens, the mayor's message also acknowledged, to some extent, the failure of the "command and control" approach by recognising that Day Zero was inevitable despite all measures undertaken by local public authorities. As pointed out by Ziervogel (2019[3]), "The Mayor's message [...] was also the point where the burden of responsibility shifted from the City of Cape Town, saying they were in charge and could augment water supply, to citizens being responsible for reducing water to avoid a crisis". The overall approach to the crisis progressively shifted from "command and control" to "collaborate and communicate". Throughout this period, several bottom-up initiatives stemming from a variety of stakeholders emerged. For instance, the Water Warriors were created, whose purpose is to collect donated water from the general public and big businesses through volunteer donation stations and distribute it to areas affected by the drought. Virgin Active, a nationwide health and fitness club, invested over ZAR 24 million (USD 1.7 million) towards an extensive range of technological, behavioural and process-related interventions to reduce and save water. The business reduced water usage within its Western Cape branches by 62% and as a result, now use a total of 7 652 kilolitres per month. The payback period of all interventions was 20 months. Transpaco Flexibles, a manufacturer, recycler and distributor of plastics products in the Western Cape, reduced its water use by 85% within a 4-month timeframe, from 87 m^3 per day to 13 m^3 (GreenCape, 2018[28]; 2019[29]).

Collaboration across stakeholders and levels of government took several forms. At the regional level, Provincial Disaster Management Clusters worked for 3 years supporting the city of Cape Town and other municipalities through the drought. Agriculture water from Groenvlei Water Users Association was released to assist the city of Cape Town during a critical period of the drought. At the city level, the Water Resilience Advisory Committee (WRAC) was established in Cape Town in August 2017. This committee meets monthly since its creation and comprises 15 members from academic institutions, businesses, NGOs or provincial and national governments. Building on an important community of practice in Cape Town, the WRAC gathers a variety of stakeholders outside the municipal administration in order to encourage information and knowledge sharing. In its Water Strategy, Cape Town capitalises on this experience to further create a Collaborative Resilience Action Plan – a multi-stakeholder platform to co-ordinate efforts and improve governance and decision-making during any crisis. In addition, the city of Cape Town has set up an Open Data Portal where datasets on basic service and infrastructure, demography, human settlements, finance, economic development, etc. are accessible. However, despite all the efforts and work accomplished, the incorporation of technical information into decision-making is not always optimal and there is still room for improvement in evidence-based decision-making.

Communication also changed with data and knowledge progressively becoming the backbone for information sharing with stakeholders. The Water Dashboard, launched in November 2017 and accessible on the city of Cape Town website, gives weekly updates on dam levels and water consumption in the form of tables and graphs. Furthermore, in January 2018, the Water Outlook was created. As stated by the city of Cape Town itself, "during 2017, information on Cape Town's management of the drought was limited. This caused much suspicion, distrust and significant misinformation. The Water Outlook was [...] developed to provide credible information to stakeholders which was easily digestible and covered the main themes emerging from public enquiries" (City of Cape Town, 2018[30]). It presents an overview of the city's programme to manage water demand, to augment water availability and water provision, as well as the associated costs (Box 3.6).

Box 3.6. The city of Cape Town Water Outlook

The city of Cape Town's Water Outlook describes the responses being considered to increase the security of the water supply going forward to include:

- Managing the dam system optimally.
- Updating hydrological information to confirm the yield of dams and integrated system. This will help develop safe yield rather than over-allocate.
- WCWSS management.
    - Updating the reconciliation strategy.
    - Determining optimal augmentation volumes and timing aligned with reconciliation strategy.
    - Better defining governance responsibilities in the reconciliation strategy.
- Improving catchment management with a focus on clearing alien vegetation that can increase the system yield.
- Reviewing the level of desired supply assurance for the city of Cape Town (currently 1 in 50 years).

Source: Ziervogel, G. (2019[3]), *Understanding the Cape Town Drought: Lessons Learned*, https://www.africancentreforcities.net/wp-content/uploads/2019/02/Ziervogel-2019-Lessons-from-Cape-Town-Drought_A.pdf.

In addition, to these key water-related communication documents, Cape Town also developed guidelines for the safe use of alternative water supply, thus recognising their growing importance, and a guide for the safe use of greywater focusing on recommendations to reduce health and environmental risks. Water-saving materials (downloadable posters, leaflets, presentations, videos, hospitality materials, etc.) were made available on the city of Cape Town website page Think Water. In January 2017, an online map was also launched, with green dots showing houses that were doing well at saving water.

Businesses, including major retailers and shopping centres, also took part in the global communication efforts, especially in early 2018, at the peak of the crisis, by increasing their communication around water saving. Partnerships with companies and non-profit organisations assisted in raising water-saving awaireness and spreading water-saving messages. A retail group invited the city to provide information sessions for their staff and allowed the city to position representatives in their stores to engage with shoppers about saving water. Wesgro, the tourism, trade and investment promotion agency for Cape Town and the Western Cape, established a communication centre comprising about 30 people, which has been reconvened to face the COVID-19 crisis. Taking stock of the growing resistance from Cape Town residents towards tourists and visitors seen as competing water users, Wesgro also issued a data-oriented press release explaining that touristic water consumption was very low (from 1% to 3% of overall domestic consumption) compared to the economic growth it generated. This data and information sharing type of communication succeeded in diffusing citizens' adverse reaction on the issue. Joining efforts with businesses, the city of Cape Town launched a communication campaign in October 2017 entitled "Save like a local", targeted at tourists and visitors. Nevertheless, the water crisis had extensive economic impacts. It resulted in 37 000 job losses in the Western Cape Province and an estimated 50 000 people were consequently pushed below the poverty line. The accommodation sector reported a 10% decline in occupancy rate.

Lessons learned throughout the drought crisis in terms of collaboration and communication were hailed as the key to improve stakeholder engagement and trust. As stated in its 2019 Water Strategy, the city of Cape Town intends to strengthen further long-term collaborative relationships with local water stakeholders by co-producing data and evidence, jointly creating and maintaining collaborative platforms, and conducting regular social surveys to better understand the needs and perceptions of citizens, for instance (Box 3.7). Although these efforts need to be amplified and sustained over time, interesting outcomes have already emerged from collaborative programmes such as the Water Resilience Collaboration Laboratory, thus paving the way to strengthen collaboration and potentially turn it into co-operation.

Box 3.7. Cape Town strategy to building resilience through partnering and collaboration

The city of Cape Town recognises that collaborative relationships need to be built and maintained at many different levels of the Cape Town water system, including between:

- Citizens and the city of Cape Town government.
- Customers and the service provider.
- Citizens and political leadership.
- Officials and politicians.
- City of Cape Town departments.
- Spheres of government.
- Businesses and the city of Cape Town.
- The city of Cape Town and the scientific community.
- The city of Cape Town and other users of the WCWSS.

Collaborative relationships are based on trust and trust is built where there is transparency and mutual accountability, and where stated intentions of all partners are consistently translated into actions. Based on the intensive experiences of engagement during the drought and learning from these, the city of Cape Town will promote and facilitate the building of trust in the following tangible ways:

- **Engaging citizens and civil society**. The city of Cape Town will endeavour to create an enabling environment in order to be responsive to citizen-led water initiatives. The city will continue to work with social partners and collaborative intermediary organisations. It will undertake regular social surveys to better understand the needs and perceptions of citizens, and work with research institutions, NGOs and neighbourhood organisations that have established processes for documenting community water use and needs, perceptions and attitudes.
- **Engaging business**. The city of Cape Town will continue to work with collaborative intermediary organisations such as GreenCape, Wesgro and the WWF to better understand business needs and perceptions and improve communications.
- **Engaging government**. The city of Cape Town will continue to work with collaborative intermediaries such as the Western Cape Economic Development Partnership (EDP) and the

National Treasury's City of Cape Town Support Programme to facilitate productive relationships with other spheres of government including the Western Cape Government and various national government departments.

- **Engaging labour**. The city of Cape Town will continue to work with organised labour as a key partner in service delivery to ensure that the rights of workers are protected.
- **Engaging researchers**. The city of Cape Town will continue to engage with research working groups such as the Freshwater Forum, the Cape Higher Education Consortium, the Water Research Group, the Water Research Commission and the Water Hub to develop and pursue applied research and evidence-based decision-making to assist the city of Cape Town to better fulfil its mandate and implement this strategy. The city of Cape Town will also explore a transdisciplinary research approach and partner with researchers to co-design research agendas and projects for the city.
- **Engaging key customers**. The city of Cape Town will set up a key customers unit to be more responsive to their needs.
- **Engaging international expertise and experience**. The city of Cape Town will enhance existing and develop new knowledge sharing partnerships with national and international bodies able to share relevant knowledge and experience to enable more effective implementation of this strategy. Where appropriate, Cape Town will make use of collaborative intermediates to support this effort. In addition, the city is committed to sharing its own experiences with these institutions in order to contribute to the global community of practice.

Source: City of Cape Town (2019[16]), *Cape Town Water Strategy*, , http://resource.capetown.gov.za/documentcentre/Documents/City%20strategies.

Below-cost recovery charges generating funding gap

Below-cost recovery charges

Below-cost recovery charges at national level

As described in Chapter 2, the DWS is currently regulating water resource management charges, water resource development charges, bulk water and wastewater charges and wastewater discharge charges. Although some generic tariff setting principles are established in the *Pricing Strategy for Raw Water Use Charges* (DWS, 2007[31]) (Table 3.3), no precise method (detailing tariff-setting formula, for instance, and the associated required information to be collected/provided) and no clear tariff-setting process are defined, apart from a yearly stakeholder consultative process on tariff. In addition, the current regulatory capacity in the water sector is insufficient in terms of: the number of skilled staff to implement regulatory requirements; the appropriate tools for regulation in the context of limited staff (3% of DWS staff is in charge of all regulatory tasks); and financial resources. As a result and in the absence of robust economic regulation guidance and means, tariffs and charges are set below-cost recovery level. This situation weakens the DWS' financial capacity to properly maintain, rehabilitate and upgrade its water and sanitation assets.

Table 3.3. Water use charges setting principles

Type of charge	Setting principle
Water resource management charge	Cost recovery
Water resource development charge	Cost plus rate of return
Bulk water tariff	Cost plus rate of return
Bulk wastewater tariff	Cost plus rate of return
Wastewater discharge charge	Cost recovery

Source: DWS, (2007[31])Pricing Strategy for Raw Water Use Charges

It should also be mentioned that there was some reluctance among water service authorities to see water charges increase. Some of them perceived the raw water tariff as an "economic rent" for the DWS which is both the operator and the regulator of raw water infrastructure, resulting in a gamekeeper and poacher problem. There is also a perception among water service authorities that the establishment of CMAs will increase the water resource management charge significantly, thus ultimately increasing the overall water tariff. This triggered resistance to any charge increase despite their current low level.

Below-cost-recovery tariffs at the local level

The city of Cape Town recognises in its Water Strategy (2019[16]) that the water tariff has to change in order to better reflect costs of service provision: "both the structure and level of water and sanitation tariffs will change over time to better reflect actual costs and provide appropriate signals for efficient water use and investment in additional supplies". Currently, the water and sanitation tariff covers operation and maintenance expenditure. The city of Cape Town plans to increase the tariff so that revenues will at least meet actual costs, including the cost of replacing ageing infrastructure. This evolution is needed as, for instance, the current targets for water and sewers network renewal rates range from 0.2% to 0.4% (City of Cape Town, 2019[14]). This means that the network is presently amortised over a maximum period ranging from 250 to 500 years which is not sustainable.

In Cape Town, residents in formal housing use 66% of the city's water while informal settlements account for 4% of the total consumption (Box 3.8). The rest of the consumption concerned industrial and commercial uses. About 1.5 million people cannot afford to pay for water and are eligible for the Free Basic Water Policy. This policy, passed by the South African government in 2001 and that promotes more equal service delivery, mandates that municipalities provide 25 litres per day per person, or 6 m3 per month for a household of 8, at no cost to end-users and accessible within 200 m from their homes. When translating this national policy requirement into its local water policy, Cape Town decided to expand the Free Basic Water volume to 10.5 m^3 per month.

Box 3.8. Water and sanitation in Cape Town informal settlements

According to South Africa's 2011 Census, 20.5% of Cape Town's households live in informal dwellings – with 7% in informal backyard structures and 13.5% in informal settlements. This proportion is expected to rise steadily as more and more people move to the city looking for work. Urban or peri-urban informal settlements are located near urban centres or economic node and are characterised by a lack of formal town planning layout and approvals, a lack of formal tenure and informal housing without building plans and related approvals (Housing Development Agency, 2014[32]).

There are currently 204 recognised informal settlements in Cape Town comprising 437 individual pockets. These pockets can be large blocks of hundreds of homes, small clusters of only a few homes scattered on land in between formal houses or individual homes on plots surrounded by food gardens. There is a wide variation in the number of households in a pocket, ranging from 3 in Chris Hani Park area to nearly 8 000 in Enkanini area. Many of the informal settlements in Cape Town were established before 2000 and are not recognised as permanent, and their residents lack occupation rights and security of tenure. Only 17 pockets (4%) are less than 5 years old; around 286 pockets (65%) were established before the year 2000 and 103 (24%) were established before democracy.

In line with the national government policy, the city of Cape Town provides free basic water and sanitation services to residents in informal settlements with 1 water tap per 25 families within a radius of 200 m and a minimum of 1 toilet per 5 families. As a whole, the city of Cape Town provides and maintains over 10 000 communal standpipes (taps) and over 50 000 toilets which are regularly cleaned. Most informal settlements have full flush (waterborne) toilets and these are generally preferred by both the city and communities. However, it is not always possible to place flush toilets in areas that are vulnerable to flooding, on unstable ground (e.g. former solid waste disposal sites), on private land or so densely settled that there is no room for water infrastructure. Hence, alternative toilets have also been installed comprising, for instance, chemical toilets, portable flush toilets or container toilets. The majority of these non-flush alternatives are cleaned three times a week. From 2006 to 2014, 30 000 toilets have been installed in informal settlements throughout the city of Cape Town.

Source: City of Cape Town, South Africa website, 2020; Housing Development Agency (2014[32]), "Informal settlements: Rapid assessment and categorisation".

In 2020, 270 000 households were receiving free basic water and sanitation which represented a cost of ZAR 681.5 million (USD 46.7 million) or approximately 10% of the yearly operational expenditure (City of Cape Town, 2020[33]) (Figure 3.3). This cost is expected to keep growing due to continued urbanisation and migration flows toward the city. The level of non-revenue water reaches on average 22% (City of Cape Town, 2019[14]). As a result, about 78% of the water produced generates billing. As the invoice collection ratio is 84% in 2019/20 (City of Cape Town, 2020[33]), the revenues from invoicing effectively cashed in represent 66% of the water produced which strongly reduces the financial base of the water and sanitation service (Figure 3.4). As a result, setting cost-reflective tariffs may generate affordability and acceptability issues, especially in a context of increasing block tariff structure.

Figure 3.3. Costs of providing and number of households receiving free basic water and sanitation

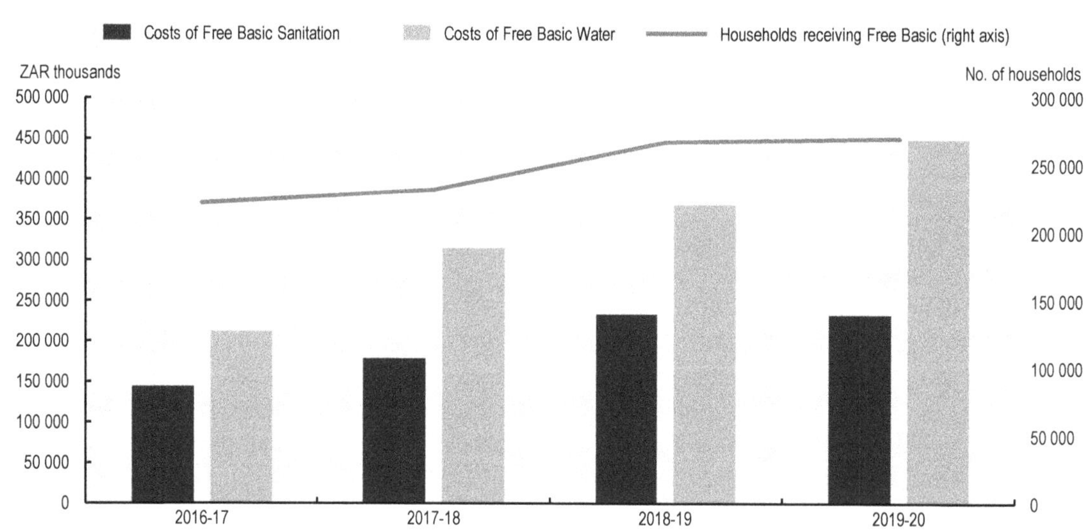

Note: The bars are should be read against the left vertical axis while the line should be read against the right vertical axis.
Source: City of Cape Town (2020[33]), *Budget*.

Figure 3.4. City of Cape Town water balance, 2016

(A) System Input 329 003 715 100%	(B) Authorised 278 188 341 84.6%	(D) Billed 255 971 841	(H) Metered 255 971 841	External Customers	33 556 585	(Q) Revenue Water 255 971 841 77.8%
				Internal Customers 222 415 256: Free Basic	50 064 802	
				Internal Customers 222 415 256: Non-Free Basic	172 350 454	
			(I) Unmetered		0	
		(E) Unbilled 22 216 500	(J) Metered 13 396 500	Informal Settlements	11 049 660	(R) NRW 73 031 874 22.2%
				Formal Metered Unbilled	2 346 840	
			(K) Unmetered 8 820 000	Formal Unmetered	8 820 000	
	(C) Losses (UAW) 50 815 374 15.4%	(F) Apparent Losses 19 509 978	(L) Unauthorised		2 906 686	
			(M) Meter Inaccuracies		16 603 292	
		(G) Real Losses 31 305 396	(N) Mains		20 520 569	
			(O) Storage		403 800	
			(P) Connections		10 381 027	

Source: City of Cape Town (2019[14]), *Departmental Business Plan 2019/2020*, Department of Water and Sanitation.

The city of Cape Town foresees that the current fixed charge, established in 2018, will increase to cover a greater share of fixed costs while ensuring that the tariff remains affordable. The variable share of the water price will gradually be set at the average incremental cost.[6]

Funding gaps

Funding gap at the national level

Funding needs for water resource management

Although water resource management charges and the waste discharge charge exist in South Africa, the waste discharge charge is not implemented and the water resource management charge is set too low to serve as an incentive and effective economic instrument to manage water resources and to collect needed revenues, thus not delivering their economic nor financial function in the end.

According to the Pricing Strategy for Water Use Charges (DWS, 2007[31]), their setting method is based on the actual cost recovery of the activities required "to protect, allocate, conserve, manage and control the water resources and manage water quality".

> *"These costs could include but are not limited to the following activities:*
>
> - *Planning and implementing catchment management strategies.*
> - *Monitoring and assessing water resource availability and use.*
> - *Water use allocations.*
> - *Water quantity management, including flood and drought management, water distribution, control over-abstraction, storage and streamflow reduction activities.*

> - *Water resource protection, resource quality management and water pollution control.*
> - *Water conservation and demand management.*
> - *Institutional development and enabling the public to participate in water resources management decision-making".*

However, despite these generic provisions and principles, no detailed costing method is set forward. The strategy only states that "total budget cost of each activity will be divided by the registered volumes to arrive at a unit charge per activity". As a result, the level of the water resource management charge remains low due to low estimates of activities' funding needs. In the revision of the Pricing Strategy for Water Use Charges dated 2015 (DWS, 2015; not approved[34]), it was provided that in "situations where there is an under-recovery of costs, or where there are limited revenue opportunities in the water management area, to cover the costs of public interest functions, i.e. activities that are in the interest of the broader society, the National Department for Water and Sanitation (DWS) will provide fiscal support to the CMAs". Fiscal resources were hence foreseen to complete water resource development charges to reach full cost recovery. However, this revision was never approved. As a result, the absence of a sound method for setting abstraction and pollution charges in South Africa remains an issue that should be addressed to reap off the benefits of these economic instruments.

In addition, water users should also be charged for the environmental and scarcity costs induced by water abstraction or use, as this is essential for achieving full cost recovery. Indeed, the general principle for setting water charges is to reflect the externalities that water abstraction (or water pollution) by one user causes to third parties and the environment – not only to pay for the activities required "to protect, allocate, conserve, manage and control the water resources and manage water quality" (DWS, 2007[31]) (Box 3.9). In most cases, due to data limitations and practical issues, public authorities are not able to measure environmental and opportunity costs of using water accurately. Still, water users must get an accurate signal about relative water availability and quality across time and space.

Box 3.9. Environmental and opportunity costs

Environmental costs correspond to damage induced by water abstraction or pollution. For example, too much groundwater abstraction may cause saline intrusion in coastal aquifers or reduce river flows. Excessive surface water abstraction may result in reduced environmental flows and ecosystem functioning and require expensive infrastructure in some sectors to allow them to ensure secure water supplies. Note that the same level of pollution can generate different levels of externalities, depending on features of the receiving water body (e.g. dilution capacity, instream water quality levels) and potential uses downstream (recreational, drinking water or others). Industry and public water supply can incur significant increased treatment costs to ensure that the abstracted water meets their quality standards.

Opportunity costs of using water represent the foregone opportunities of alternative water uses. These costs are incurred when one water user or polluter affects the use of the resource by any third party. For example, higher water withdrawal by a city might affect the quantity of water available to downstream irrigators, thus imposing costs on these users. There are also opportunity costs associated with the exclusion of other potential users in areas where water quality is unsuitable for use. Technically the opportunity cost is defined as the value of the water in its highest value alternative use. Opportunity costs are typically higher where water is scarce and competition to access is fierce. They are also higher when water is being used for low-value uses, preventing access for higher-value uses. If property rights are in place and tradeable, the market value of water would reflect opportunity costs.

Source: OECD (2017[35]), *Water Charges in Brazil: The Ways Forward*, https://doi.org/10.1787/9789264285712-en.

Funding needs for water and sanitation investment and operation

Volume 1 of the National Water and Sanitation Master Plan (DWS, 2019[2]) clearly acknowledges that the situation of the water and sanitation sector is currently not financially sustainable. This is confirmed by the outcomes of the Municipal Strategic Self-Assessment (MuSSA)[7] 2019 that shows that one of the top areas of vulnerability of water supply and sanitation (WSS) services is the *financial management* of services. This situation raises important concerns with regard to asset management and the associated negative externalities. A total of 56% of the over 1 150 wastewater treatment plants are in poor and critical condition and need urgent rehabilitation and proper operation. Infrastructure is ageing with 57% of the asset being depreciated and needing renewal. This situation generates water quality issues in areas where effluents are discharged. In this context, the capital funding needs have been assessed to approximately ZAR 90 billion (USD 6.2 billion) per year for the next decade, with about 78% for water supply and 12% for sanitation. This assessment of capital expenditure needs includes the necessary funding to address refurbishment (ZAR 59 billion, USD 4 billion) and renewal (ZAR 332 billion, USD 22.8 billion) backlogs, as well as the development of new infrastructure and an asset replacement value representing 8% of the installed value. A funding gap of ZAR 33.3 billion (USD 2.3 billion) per year (or ZAR 333 billion, USD 23 billion, in total for the coming 10 years) is anticipated (Table 3.4), representing more than one-third of the capital funding needs. In addition, the National Water and Sanitation Master Plan (DWS, 2019[2]) also points out that a yearly funding operational gap of ZAR 5 to 10 billion (USD 0.35 to 0.7 billion).

As stated in the National Water and Sanitation Master Plan (DWS, 2019[2]), several reasons account for this long-lasting insufficient funding situation of the water and sanitation sector in South Africa:

- The low collection rate of fees from municipalities and Water Boards has increased by 14%, from ZAR 13.1 billion (USD 0.9 billion) in September 2018, to ZAR 14.9 billion (USD 1 billion) in September 2019 (DWS), which weakens further the DWS capital expenditure capacity.
- The reduced revenues generated by high non-revenue water which amounts to 36% on average in 2019 at the national level with a maximum of 49% in Limpopo Province (DWS).
- The non-cost-reflective tariffs despite the provisions of the Water Services Act.
- The absence of effective economic regulation in the sector.
- The fiscal constraints that have lowered the national subsidies granted to the sector.
- The capacity constraints.
- The sub-optimal procurement processes that generate recurrent financial mismanagement.

Table 3.4. Capital funding gap assessment for the water and sanitation sector, South Africa

In ZAR billion

	Funding requirement	Funding available	Funding gap
Municipal water infrastructure	278	171	
Regional bulk (potable) infrastructure	101	74	
Regional bulk (non-potable) infrastructure	7	4	
Water resource infrastructure	255	149	
Total water infrastructure	704	434	
Sanitation infrastructure	195	132	
Total WSS infrastructure	**899**	**566**	**333 (37%)**

Source: DWS, (2019[2]), National Water and Sanitation Master Plan

Funding gap at the local level

The city of Cape Town, unlike many other municipalities in South Africa ((DWS, 2019[2])), holds separate water accounts from city accounts since 2018, thus ensuring a clear identification of water money revenues and spending. Nevertheless, Cape Town water and sanitation service is not financially sustainable as revenues collected are low and insufficient to cover operating, maintenance and renewal costs. The existing funding gap is further aggravated by a decreasing invoice collection ratio which dropped from over 90% in 2012/13 to a low of 60% in 2018 (Figure 3.5). The period of the drought also brought along important financial issues with water consumption more than halved. As a result of this sharp reduction, the revenues of the service also decreased dramatically with a ZAR 1.7 billion deficit in 2017 (Visser, 2018[26]). The COVID pandemic and the associated economic crisis are likely to degrade further the collection ratio which had resumed increasing in 2019.

Cape Town water and sanitation asset base is valued at ZAR 75 billion. The operating budget was ranging between ZAR 7 and 8 billion from 2016 to 2018 but rose to ZAR 11 billion since then. In its 2019 Water Strategy, Cape Town plans a ZAR 40 billion investment programme over the next decade (or approximately ZAR 4 billion per year). This represents a sharp 70% increase compared to 2018/19 capital expenditure and even a higher effort compared to the years before. A mix of solutions is being considered to fill the funding gap. They include a WSS tariffs increase, economic and technical efficiency gains, a pooled city of Cape Town financing strategy as well as grants. Indeed, the financial framework for WSS investment funding in South Africa mainly relies on a mix of tariffs, grants and subsidies. National government grants represented 54% of capital spending on municipal WSS services in 2014/15 (DWS, 2015[36]). In addition to investment grants, operating subsidies are also distributed to WSS services and represented 12% of total operating income from water services in municipalities. Overall, the level of grants received by local WSS varies according to the size of the municipality and ranges from 62% for rural towns to 18% for metropolitan areas, like Cape Town (Figure 3.6). Nevertheless, fiscal constraints may reduce the amount of available subsidies, thus aggravating further the existing funding gap for the city of Cape Town water and sanitation service.

Figure 3.5. Billing collection ratio, Cape Town, South Africa

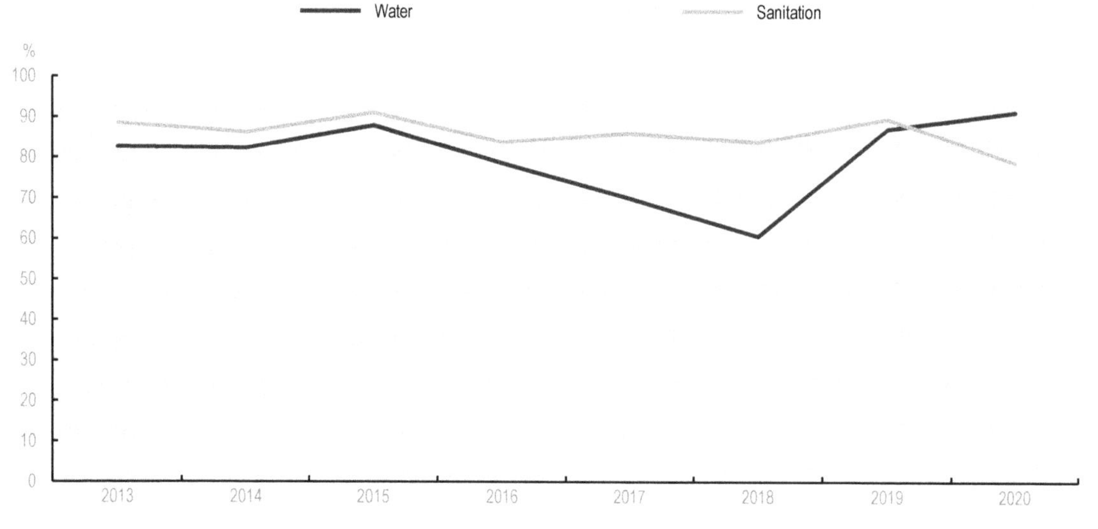

Source: City of Cape Town, (2021[37])

Figure 3.6. Funding sources of WSS services in South Africa

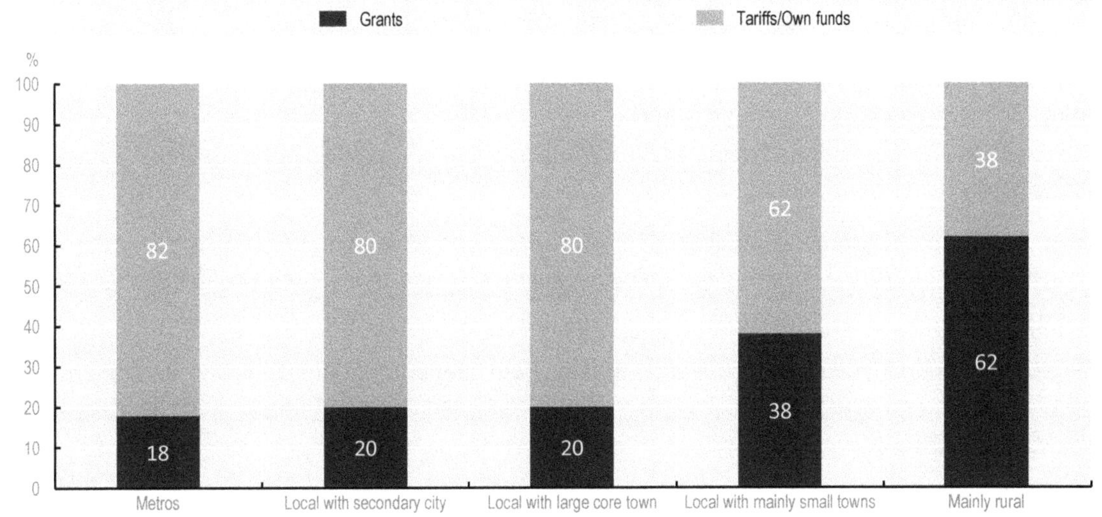

Source: DWS (2015[36]), *Strategic Overview of the Water Sector*, Department of Water and Sanitation.

References

Auditor-General (2018), *Report of the Auditor-general to the Joint Committee of Inquiry into the Functioning of the Department of Water and Sanitation: Challenges Facing the Water and Sanitation Portfolio*, https://www.corruptionwatch.org.za/wp-content/uploads/2020/02/180327AGSA-Challenges_Water_Sanitation.pdf. [10]

Bahl, R. (1992), *Urban Public Finance in Developing Countries*, Oxford University Press. [40]

Centre for Environmental Rights (2012), "Stop treading water: What civil society can do to get water governance in South Africa back on track". [12]

City of Cape Town (2021), *Private communication.* [37]

City of Cape Town (2020), *Budget.* [33]

City of Cape Town (2020), *Water Outlook 2020 Report*, Department of Water and Sanitation. [22]

City of Cape Town (2019), *Cape Town Water Strategy*, Department of Water and Sanitation, http://resource.capetown.gov.za/documentcentre/Documents/City%20strategies%2c%20plans%20and%20frameworks/Cape%20Town%20Water%20Strategy.pdf. [16]

City of Cape Town (2019), *Cape Town's Drought Crisis Communication.* [15]

City of Cape Town (2019), *Departmental Business Plan 2019/2020*, Department of Water and Sanitation. [14]

City of Cape Town (2018), *Day Zero now likely to happen – new emergency measures*, https://resource.capetown.gov.za/documentcentre/Documents/Speeches%20and%20statements/18%20January%2018-%20Day%20Zero%20new%20emergency%20measures.pdf. [27]

City of Cape Town (2018), *Private communication.* [20]

City of Cape Town (2018), *Water Outlook 2018 Report*, Department of Water and Sanitation, https://resource.capetown.gov.za/documentcentre/Documents/City%20research%20reports%20and%20review/Water%20Outlook%202018%20-%20Summary.pdf. [30]

City of Cape Town (2017), *City's water crisis warning on freeway signs goes live*, https://www.capetown.gov.za/Media-and-news/City%E2%80%99s%20water%20crisis%20warning%20on%20freeway%20signs%20goes%20live. [24]

Dassah, M. (2018), "Theoretical analysis of state capture and its manifestation as a governance problem in South Africa", *Journal for Transdisciplinary Research in Southern Africa*, Vol. 14/1, p. a473. [6]

DWS (2019), *National Water and Sanitation Master Plan*, Department of Water and Sanitation, http://www.dwa.gov.za/National%20Water%20and%20Sanitation%20Master%20Plan/DocumentsReports.aspx. [2]

DWS (2015), *Strategic Overview of the Water Sector*, Department of Water and Sanitation. [36]

DWS (2007), *Pricing Strategy for Raw Water Use Charges*, Department of Water and Sanitation. [31]

DWS (2015; not approved), *Draft Revision of the Pricing Strategy for Water Use Charges*. [34]

Galvin, M. and S. Roux (2019), "Dam state capture: Its cascading effect on the Department of Water and Sanitation", *Transformation: Critical Perspectives on Southern Africa*, Vol. 100. [8]

GreenCape (2019), "Water resilient businesses, case study: Reducing water use in health and fitness clubs", https://www.greencape.co.za/library. [29]

GreenCape (2019), *Water: Market Intelligence Report*, https://www.greencape.co.za/assets/Uploads/WATER-MIR-2019-WEB-01-04-2019.pdf. [13]

GreenCape (2018), "Water resilient businesses, case study: Transpaco Flexibles reduce water use by 85% through tech interventions and reuse of process water", https://www.greencape.co.za/library. [28]

Housing Development Agency (2014), "Informal settlements: Rapid assessment and categorisation". [32]

Jonas (2016), *'Mcebisi Jonas opens up on state capture'*. [39]

Martin, M. and H. Solomon (2016), "Understanding the phenomenon of "state capture" in South Africa", *Southern African Peace and Security Studies*, Vol. 5/1. [7]

Minister of Human Settlements, Water and Sanitation (2020), *speech on DWS Budget 2020/21*, https://www.gov.za/speeches/minister-lindiwe-sisulu-delivers-water-and-sanitation-dept-202021-budget-vote-23-jul-22-jul#. [11]

Muller, M. (2018), "Lessons from Cape Town's drought – Don't blame climate change. People and poor planning are behind most urban water shortages", *Nature*, Vol. 559. [17]

Munnik, V. (2020), "The reluctant roll-out of Catchment Management Agencies: Assessing the key risks and consequences of delays in finalising institutional arrangements for decentralised water resource management", Water Research Commission, Pretoria, http://www.wrc.org.za/wp-content/uploads/mdocs/2943_final.pdf. [5]

OECD (2021), *Water Governance in Cape Town, South Africa*. [19]

OECD (2017), *Water Charges in Brazil: The Ways Forward*, OECD Studies on Water, OECD Publishing, Paris, https://doi.org/10.1787/9789264285712-en. [35]

OECD (2015), *OECD Principles on Water Governance*, OECD, Paris, https://www.oecd.org/gov/regional-policy/OECD-Principles-on-Water-Governancebrochure.pdf. [1]

Otto, F. et al. (2018), "Anthropogenic influence on the drivers of the Western Cape drought 2015-2017", *Environmental Research Letters*, Vol. 13, pp. 1-10, https://doi.org/10.1088/1748-9326/aae9f9. [21]

Sieff, K. (2018), "Divided by drought", Washington Post. [25]

South Africa Water Caucus (2017), *Report on the State of the Department of Water and Sanitation*, https://www.fse.org.za/Downloads/SAWCStateofDWSReport.pdf. [23]

The Nature Conservancy (2018), *The Greater Cape Town Water Fund, Assessing the return on Investment for Ecological Infrasytructure Restoration, Business Case*, The Nature Conservancy, https://www.nature.org/content/dam/tnc/nature/en/documents/GCTWF-summary-11.14.18.pdf. [4]

UN (n.d.), *Big Data for Sustainable Development*, United Nations, https://www.un.org/en/sections/issues-depth/big-data-sustainable-development/index.html. [18]

Vienings, L. (2015), *Integrated Water Sector Skills Intervention Map Based on a Sector Skills Gap Analysis*, Water Research Commission, Pretoria. [9]

Visser, W. (2018), "A perfect storm: The ramifications of Cape Town's drought crisis", *Journal for Transdisciplinary Research in Southern Africa*, Vol. 14/1, p. a567, https://doi.org/10.4102/td.v14i1.567. [26]

Whelan (2016), *"State capture' in SA is a buzzword more accurately defined as 'Zuma capture"*. [38]

Ziervogel, G. (2019), *Understanding the Cape Town Drought: Lessons Learned*, https://www.africancentreforcities.net/wp-content/uploads/2019/02/Ziervogel-2019-Lessons-from-Cape-Town-Drought_A.pdf. [3]

Notes

[1] This reconciliation strategy provides a decision support framework to facilitate the reconciliation of predicted future water requirements with available water in the WCWSS over a 25-year planning period.

[2] "State capture can be defined as the actions of individuals or groups both in the public and private sectors, influencing the formation of laws, regulations, decrees and other government policies to their own personal advantage. [...] It is apparent to note that state capture undermines the efficiency of the state, especially where there is a direct relationship between state capture and corruption. This primarily happens when a state is paying more than it is supposed to for outsourced goods and services. State capture also undermines the efficiency of the state. This happens through poor quality services and public goods being delivered by patronage networks but less than capable service providers, through fiscal resources being redirected away from public goods provision for the poor or from value-adding economic endowments towards servicing some or other patronage network; and by weakening state capacity through appointing pliable but less than capable people in key positions, especially in finance procurement and political bearers (Whelan, 2016[38]). Jonas (Jonas, 2016[39]) asserts that the most important element state capture takes away from a state is its legitimacy. This happens through governance systems and rules being flouted with, leading to a lack of transparency and accountability within the structures of the state" (Martin and Solomon, 2016[7]).

[3] NIWIS is the National Integrated Water Information System (http://www.dwa.gov.za/niwis2).

[4] See https://www.capetown.gov.za/City-Connect/Register/Water-and-sanitation/Register-a-borehole.

[5] Special permission was obtained from National Treasury to change the tariff within the year.

[6] The average incremental cost is the average of the future cost incurred in adding additional supplies and can be calculated by dividing the discounted value of future supply costs by the (similarly discounted) amount of additional water to be produced (Bahl, 1992[40]).

[7] Overseen by the DWS, the Municipal Strategic Self-Assessment asks 5 questions that cover 18 key business health attributes.

4 Strengthening water governance in Cape Town: Policy recommendations

This chapter suggests ways forward and policy recommendations to upscale the use and effective implementation of policy and economic instruments to bridge identified governance gaps in Cape Town and South Africa. It suggests in particular, strengthening water resource management and financing at the catchment level, promoting innovative approaches to manage water balance and complete water allocation reform, improving the economic regulation and financial sustainability and efficiency of water and sanitation services, enhancing capacity, as well as strengthening transparency, integrity and engagement.

Key messages

Key water governance challenges identified for Cape Town and South Africa encompass issues related to policy and institutional fragmentation, scale mismatch, policy coherence, capacity, data and information, funding, regulation, integrity, transparency, stakeholder engagement, trade-off management and evaluation (see Chapter 3). Building upon these challenges, policy recommendations were formulated to bridge identified governance gaps (Table 4.1).

Table 4.1. Policy recommendations to bridge governance gaps in Cape Town and South Africa

OECD Principle on Water Governance	Associated governance challenge identified	Policy recommendation
1. Clearly allocate and distinguish roles and responsibilities for water policymaking, policy implementation, operational management and regulation, and foster co-ordination across these responsible authorities	Although roles and responsibilities are defined in a set of acts, multi-level co-ordination issues have occurred for water resource and conservation policy implementation, especially in a context of poorly funded mandates.	- Establish a single catchment management agency (CMA) covering the Western Cape Water Supply System (WCWSS) territory to enhance multi-level and multi-stakeholder co-ordination. - Make better use of abstraction and pollution charges to fund water resources and conservation policies and mandates.
2. Manage water at the appropriate scale(s) within integrated basin governance systems to reflect local conditions and foster co-ordination between the different scales	Co-ordination of policies and stakeholders at the catchment level has proven difficult as CMA instalment process has stalled.	Establish a single CMA covering the WCWSS territory to enhance multi-level and multi-stakeholder co-ordination.
3. Encourage policy coherence through effective cross-sectoral co-ordination, especially between policies for water and the environment, health, energy, agriculture, industry, spatial planning and land use	Challenges occurred with water restriction co-ordination, implementation and enforcement across levels of government and sectors.	Establish a single CMA covering the WCWSS territory to enhance multi-level and multi-stakeholder co-ordination.
4. Adapt the level of capacity of responsible authorities to the complexity of water challenges to be met and to the set of competencies required to carry out their duties	Capacity gaps identified across levels of government encompass important turnover and vacancies, ageing staff and difficulty to attract the adequate number of skilled staff.	Strengthen capacities at all levels of government by including within the updated National Water Strategy at the national level and incorporating into an action plan at the city level a section dedicated to capacity building and development operationalisation for the water sector; by restoring and expanding engineers mentoring programmes; by joining communities of practice to foster peer learning and exchange of good practices across water operators and practitioners.
5. Produce, update and share timely, consistent, comparable and policy-relevant water and water-related data and information, and use it to guide, assess and improve water policy	The planning models used to determine water balance were interpreted according to unjustified assumptions including, for instance, an effective eradication programme for invasive alien plants (IAPs), hydrology systems up-to-date or effective operation of water systems.	- Based on planning data and models, prioritise cost-effective green solutions to augment water yields in the WCWSS. - Routinely use data and existing key performance indicators (KPIs) to guide water and sanitation service management and improvement and to enhance transparency and accountability through their public disclosure.
6. Ensure that governance arrangements help mobilise water finance and allocate financial resources in an efficient, transparent and timely manner	Below-cost recovery charges generate important funding gaps at the national and local levels.	- Improve the efficiency and long-term financial sustainability of water and sanitation services through the adoption of sufficiently cost-reflective tariffs and the implementation of technical and economic efficiency utility turnaround efforts. - Prioritise cost-effective green solutions to augment water yields in the WCWSS as an optimised portfolio of grey and green infrastructure is critical to build and sustain

OECD Principle on Water Governance	Associated governance challenge identified	Policy recommendation
		water security and resilience.
7. Ensure that sound water management regulatory frameworks are effectively implemented and enforced in pursuit of the public interest	Despite the existence of a Pricing Water Strategy, charges and tariffs are set too low.	Strengthen economic water regulation through the establishment of an independent water regulator that pursues equity goals and pays special attention to poor households.
8. Promote the adoption and implementation of innovative water governance practices across responsible authorities, levels of government and relevant stakeholders		Set up innovative open contracting models.
9. Mainstream integrity and transparency practices across water policies, water institutions and water governance frameworks for greater accountability and trust in decision-making	Public procurement was characterised by irregular expenditure and harmful delays.	Strengthen transparency and integrity through a culture of consequences, the uptake of innovative open contracting models and by making the water sector an "island of integrity".
10. Promote stakeholder engagement for informed and outcome-oriented contributions to water policy design and implementation	At the beginning of the water crisis, stakeholder engagement was limited and communication was done on a "command and control" mode before evolving towards a more collaborative approach.	Strengthen further stakeholder engagement by promoting fair and equitable access to engagement opportunities to ensure a balanced and representative process.
11. Encourage water governance frameworks that help manage trade-offs across water users, rural and urban areas, and generations	During the crisis, water allocation from the Western Cape Water Supply System exceeded its yield, thus triggering the need to revisit water balances and requirements.	Manage water allocation trade-offs between equity and efficiency.
12. Promote regular monitoring and evaluation of water policy and governance where appropriate, share the results with the public and make adjustments when needed	The yearly updates of the Reconciliation Strategy Status and of the Blue and Green Drop reports were not consistently and timeously performed.	Better assess and monitor the performance of the service through the existing KPIs that can be used as steering and managing tools to measure change and evaluate improvement against specific goals.

Strengthen integrated water management at the catchment level

Establish a single catchment management agency (CMA) covering the Western Cape Water Supply System territory

The National Water Act mandates the decentralisation of water resources management through CMAs. However, the rollout process of CMAs has been stalled for more than a decade, thus hampering decentralisation of water resource management at the catchment level. This situation has resulted in challenges with regard to co-ordination across levels of governments and sectors throughout the Western Cape territory. As such, resuming and completing the establishment of CMAs is crucial to overcome the current lack of co-ordination and further strengthen the integration of water resource management for the Western Cape.

Indeed, catchment organisations are important tools for co-ordinating water policy at the territorial level, as suggested by the Principle 2 of the OECD Principles on Water Governance (OECD, 2015[1]), which calls for "managing water at the appropriate scale(s) within integrated basin governance systems to reflect local conditions and foster co-ordination between the different scales". They can be useful to manage water at the appropriate scale through integrated basin governance to reflect local conditions and foster multi-level co-operation for the management of water resources; to encourage sound hydrological cycle management and promote adaptive and mitigation strategies. Finally, they can help manage water risks, thus supporting and reinforcing water security.

In a study dated 2020, the Water Research Commission (WRC) published a report listing priority actions to pave the way for CMA rollout resumption and completion (Box 4.1).

Box 4.1. Priority actions to deal with delays in CMA establishment

1. Support the National Department for Water and Sanitation (DWS) in committing to a clear strategy for establishment, which includes negotiation with key stakeholders and a clear communication strategy empowering officials on the ground in their interactions with stakeholders.
2. Document and present in clear (non-specialist) language the achievements and experiences of the two existing CMAs as an argument for establishing CMAs and practical guidelines emerging from experience.
3. Develop a clear and mutual understanding with the trade unions involved, about the public nature of CMAs, as well as details of the transition to CMAs of certain DWS functions, as it will affect their members. Moreover, their support will help implement CMAs.
4. Work with stakeholders who have been part of CMA establishment processes, especially in catchment management fora, and win back their trust.
5. Make sure that CMAs are oriented towards and willing to effect transformation in Water Use Allocation as well as institutions managing water, such as Irrigation Boards and Water User Associations, and that powerful local actors are not in a position to dominate CMA decision-making.
6. Understand the concerns of the National Treasury about funding CMAs and support the DWS in presenting a clear case to the National Treasury. This should include the need for funding based on water use charges as well as direct fiscal support for public interest functions.

Source: Munnik, V. (2020[2]), "The reluctant roll-out of Catchment Management Agencies: Assessing the key risks and consequences of delays in finalising institutional arrangements for decentralised water resource management", http://www.wrc.org.za/wp-content/uploads/mdocs/2943_final.pdf.

Furthermore, to avoid potential territorial conflicts between catchments in the Western Cape, stakeholders have argued that a single CMA covering the entire Western Cape Water Supply System (WCWSS) territory could be favoured compared to two or three CMAs. This would provide a single and integrated co-ordination institution acting at the most relevant scale for water resource management in the Western Cape. In September and October 2020, the National DWS issued a Gazette Notice proposing to amend and expand the Breede-Gouritz Water Management Area (WMA) to include the Berg-Olifant WMA, thus creating a single CMA covering both catchments. This proposal marks a positive evolution after many delays and uncertainties with regard to CMAs rollout. For instance, the 2017 DWS review of institutional arrangements for water resource management culminated with the announcement of a proposal to establish a single national entity, the National Water Resource Management Agency (DWS, 2017[3]). The business case for this entity stated that the CMAs established or in the process of being established would be converted into regional units of the National Water Resource Management Agency. This proposal illustrated the reluctance from the national government to proceed with decentralisation and the attempt of "repurposing"[1] over public institutions.

Along with the possible creation of the Breede-Olifant CMA, the progressive delegation of powers and functions (see below) should also be resumed and completed. Currently, the Breede-Gouritz CMA is endowed with initial functions focusing mainly on co-ordination missions at the catchment level, as stated in the National Water Act (NWA) (see Chapter 3). However, in addition to these initial functions, which limit CMAs' reach and effectiveness, complementary powers and functions may be delegated by the National DWS, as stated in Schedule 3 of the NWA (see Chapter 3). Box 4.2 provides international examples of substantive functions carried out by basin organisations, including strong multi-level consultation mecanisms.

Box 4.2. A range of situations for river basin governance in Europe

In the **European Union**, the Water Framework Directive gives high importance to the participation of stakeholders and society in general, but this is done at a consultative level. This type of consultation and open debate is particularly relevant at the beginning of the preparation of the river basin plans, when an extensive public consultation process is mandatory to identify the so-called "significant questions". The resulting plan must respond to those significant questions largely identified by the water users and civil society. Meanwhile, the government of each member country has to designate the "competent authority" that is responsible for water management at the basin level. Representatives of water users and civil society in state councils and basin committees should be selected to guarantee genuine and recognised representativeness and should keep close links with the sector that they represent in order to share information and convey consensual positions of the sector on the most relevant matters.

In **Spain**, "*confederaciónes hidráulicas*", which are part of the Ministry of Environment of the central government, manage the river basins that are shared by more than one autonomous region. In each basin there is a river basin council in which the governments of the autonomous regions participate. The river basin councils are consultative bodies and river basin plans prepared by the "*confederaciónes hidráulicas*" are discussed and previously approved by these councils, and finally adopted by the Council of Ministers following consultation of the National Water Council. All executive powers stay in the hands of the "*confederaciónes hidráulicas*", which means in the hands of the Ministry of Environment.

In **Portugal**, the 2005 Water Law created hydrographical region administrations that are regional public institutes with full executive powers dependent from the Ministry of the Environment and in close articulation with the national agency responsible for water. There are corresponding hydrographical region councils of a consultative nature that help to identify key issues and need to be consulted at various predefined situations. The river basin plans require prior approval of the councils and then they are approved by the Council of Ministers; central authorities are also responsible for all matters related to the conventions regulating transboundary basins, although some measures can be delegated to the hydrographical region administrations.

In the **Netherlands**, water boards are an autonomous level of the organisation of the state in political terms. To give them democratic legitimacy, there are general elections for water boards, and there are even some political parties specialising in this level of public authority. However, in administrative and financial terms, they are submitted to the rules and to the inspection of the provinces and the central government and heavily controlled by them. They are a level of government in the Dutch Constitution and enjoy specific taxation powers and a governance framework (functional democracies).

In **Germany**, the *Länder* are basically responsible for water management and have to build consensus about shared river basins, namely in the process of preparing river basin plans. In some cases, like in the Rurh River basin, there are users' associations with delegated powers promoting a consistent basin approach. There is no dominion of the Länder, and the *Bundenstag* and the federal government produce legislation that all *Länder* have to obey. The federal government is also responsible for international conventions on transboundary rivers (such as the Rhine, the Danube, the Odra or the Elbe).

Source: OECD, (2015[4]), *Water Resources Governance in Brazil*, https://doi.org/10.1787/9789264238121-en

The priority action listed in the National Water and Sanitation Master Plan (DWS, 2019[5]) to "establish financially sustainable CMAs across the country, and transfer staff and budget and delegated functions, including licensing of water use and monitoring and evaluation of water resources" seems to point in the direction of delegating complementary functions to CMAs. However, this priority action was to be completed by 2020, which is still not the case. As a result, uncertainties remain with regard to the pace of the reform and its possible form and outcomes.

These uncertainties also exist with regard to the origin of the Breede-Olifant CMA staff. Currently, in the two established CMAs, a majority of the staff members worked previously for the National DWS. Incentivising and securing staff movement from the DWS to the CMA is an important step to ensure that skilled and experienced staff joins the Breede-Olifant CMA to come. In 2018, one-third of senior management posts remained unfilled and one-quarter of professionally qualified posts. In its 2018 annual report, the Breed-Gouritz CMA recognises that "the South African labour market is characterised by skills shortage which poses major challenges to many organisations and the water sector and the Breed-Gouritz CMA are no exceptions to this situation. These challenges manifest especially during the acquisition of skilled talent that require registration with professional bodies like Professional Engineers, Hydrologists, Geohydrologist, Freshwater Ecologist, Industrial Technicians among others. The skills shortage is a serious impediment to the entire recruitment value chain especially in the core functions of the business" (Breede-Gouritz Catchment Management Agency, 2019[6]).

Make better use of abstraction and pollution charges

Although water resource management charges and waste discharge charge exist in South Africa, the waste discharge charge is not implemented and the water resource management charge is set too low to serve as an incentive and effective economic instrument to manage water resources and to collect needed revenues for the financial sustainability of the sector, thus not delivering their economic nor financial function in the end.

Despite the provisions embedded into the *Pricing Strategy for Water Use Charges* (DWS, 2007[7]), stating that these charges should be set so as to fully recover costs associated with activities required "to protect, allocate, conserve, manage and control the water resources and manage water quality", no detailed costing method is set forward. Furthermore, the recovery of environmental and opportunity costs are not clearly indicated. This absence of a sound method should be addressed to reap the benefits of these economic instruments. To design an effective charging scheme, some key elements should be considered such as the alignment of these economic instruments with other water policy objectives, the link between water charges and the licence system, the incentives it provides to improve water resources quantity and quality, or the flexibility and adaptability of this charging scheme (Box 4.3).

Box 4.3. Charging for water abstraction and discharges – A checklist

How will the charges scheme link with permitting systems?

- How will your charging scheme fit in with other mechanisms to manage water resources, in particular, the use of permits to set limits and conditions on abstraction and discharges? And will your permitting and compliance monitoring systems ensure that charges are calculated fairly and accurately?
- Ideally, the locations of all abstractions and discharges would be identified and would all be controlled (or nearly all if a risk-based approach is taken) through permits backed up by routine compliance monitoring and enforcement where necessary. The permits would then form the basis for the approach taken in the charging scheme and the specific charge related to each

user. All abstractions would have a means of measurement designed to ensure compliance with volumetric limits. Other permit conditions, such as restrictions on abstraction at low flows, would also have a means of ensuring compliance. Discharges should also have a volumetric limit and means of measurement, as well as emission limits to protect the environment and human health for the parameters in the discharge. There should be an agreed basis for monitoring the quality of the discharge at a frequency that meant that the results were statistically significant, auditable and appropriate to the type of process involved.

Designing the charging scheme

- How will you structure the charges so that they align with the policy objectives? For both abstractions and discharges, will you use the volume authorised on the permit or the actual volumes abstracted or discharged? The latter requires more effort to oversee: the water user or your inspector will need to record and report the volumes, there must be a means of measurement of certified accuracy in place (e.g. a calibrated meter) because otherwise, you could be over- or under-charging. Your billing system must also be capable of calculating different charges according to the volume at the billing frequency that you choose.
- Do you want to impose a separate administrative charge to cover the costs of managing and carrying out the technical determination of applications for new permits or revisions to existing ones?
- Do you want your abstraction charges to send signals about the degree of water stress and incentivise reduced consumption? And what do you mean by "water stress" or "water scarcity": if it is stress as a result of excessive abstraction, will you rely on charges alone to achieve a sustainable balance with the available resource or will you also take other measures to reduce abstraction (e.g. by buying out entitlements or by forcible reductions in authorised volumes)? If scarcity is more dynamic, such as from low rainfall and the risk of drought, what will trigger the charging response? And how will you ensure that charge payers are aware of what is happening on a dynamic basis and, where possible, have access to advice about how to reduce their consumption?
- For discharges, what signals do you want to send to polluters and how costly do you want to make the act of pollution? If you want to incentivise a reduction in pollution load from toxic substances, do the permits specify limits on, for example, pesticides, hydrocarbons, metals, cyanides etc.? And how will you reflect this in the charges scheme through a sliding scale from cooling water through to discharges from chemical works and mining operations? If you want to see improved water quality to protect human health and support target ecosystems, can you use charges to help achieve this faster than through the use of progressively tighter limits in environmental quality standards-based permits?
- Do you want to send signals about the value of effluent as a resource? In other words, where, when and in what volumes effluent discharges are made is important to other water users (providing that the quality is within permitted limits) and, although these matters can be specified in permits, do you want to reward discharges that benefit resources? Similarly, do you want to penalise abstractions through higher charges where the net return is low because the water has evaporated, been incorporated in a product, lost through leakage or taken up by growing crops?
- How will you ensure that your charging schemes are flexible and adaptable to changes in water demand, environmental stress, climate change and droughts? And what feedback mechanism will you build in to allow for periodic reviews of its effectiveness?

Source: OECD (2017[8]), *Water Charges in Brazil: The Ways Forward*, https://doi.org/10.1787/9789264285712-en.

A review of international experience in setting and governing economic instruments for water resources management shows that water abstraction charges are commonly managed at the subnational level. In South Africa, they are differentiated for each WMA. The level of the water charge is usually differentiated by the type of user (domestic, industry, agriculture), like in South Africa, but also by water source (groundwater or surface water) with higher charges often imposed on groundwater than on surface water. Moreover, specific rates are sometimes applied to special zones, specific aquifers or rivers that are facing higher water stress or scarcity (Box 4.4).

Box 4.4. Water resources charges in Portugal

In Portugal, the Water Resources Tax (*Taxa de Recursos Hídricos*, TRH) implements the basic idea that the user of water resources must compensate the cost generated to the community and/or restore the benefit the community grants ("polluter pays" and "user pays" principles). The TRH is due on a yearly basis and the debtor entity is the user of water resources. The TRH compensates: i) the advantage resulting from the privative use of public water; ii) the environmental costs related to the activities likely to cause a significant impact on water resources; and iii) the administrative costs regarding planning, management, supervision and water quality and quantity assurance.

The structure of the TRH is the following:

$$TRH = A + E + I + O + U$$

in which:

- A is the amount paid for the abstracted water in m^3.
- E is the amount paid for the discharged effluent, including chemical oxygen demand and biochemical oxygen demand expressed in kg.
- I is the amount paid for the gravel and sand taken from the bed and margins of the river course expressed in m^3.
- O is the amount paid for the occupation of the "public water domain" by any sort of infrastructure or construction, expressed in m^2.
- U is the amount paid for the use of water, expressed in m^3, subject to public planning and management.

Although the parcels A and U relate both to abstracted water (in cubic metres), A corresponds to the appropriation for a privative use of the water itself as a public asset, while U compensates for the planning and management of the river basin. This distinction has an interesting consequence: if the source of water is private (basically groundwater), only TRH = U is considered because there is no appropriation of public water; if the source of water is public (basically all surface water, except spring water occurring in private land while it stays inside that private property), the water charge is given by TRH = A+U, which pays for the public water (A) and for planning and management activities (U).

This approach circumvented the need of declaring all water as public because it was found out that such a measure would cause an enormous reaction from farmers who are used to look at water in wells as part of their properties that actually determines to a large extent the value of the land. However, the fact that groundwater is considered "private" does not mean that it is not subject to "public discipline", namely because the use that is made in one property may interfere with the availability in neighbouring properties. Therefore, although it is considered "private" water, it is subject to licensing procedures but there is no reason to pay for "A" corresponding to the appropriation of a public asset.

Recently, a new parcel "S" was added to the water charges, aiming at promoting the sustainability of water services in the hinterland and in mountainous areas where the cost of water services is much higher than in the more flat and more affluent coastal areas.

According to the original Decree-Law No. 97/2008, revised in 2017 (Decree-Law No. 46/2017), typical values per cubic meter for the component A are EUR 0.0032 of water used for irrigation and fish farming, EUR 0.00002 for hydropower production, EUR 0.0027 for cooling thermoelectric stations and EUR 0.015 for domestic supply. These values can be aggravated by up to 20% in scarcity-affected areas of southern Portugal. The discharge of 1 kg of BOD is charged EUR 0.37 and 1 kg of total nitrogen and total phosphorus are charged EUR 0.17 and EUR 0.21 respectively. The extraction of 1 m^3 of gravel or sand is charged EUR 2.5. The occupation of the public domain varies from EUR 0.002/m^2 (hydropower production and fish farming) to EUR 10/m^2 (permanent beach occupation for commercial uses). The new parcel S was introduced in 2017 with a value of EUR 0.004/m^3. These values may seem quite low but it should be taken into account that they are applied to hundreds of millions of cubic meters or thousands of square meters.

These values may be multiplied by some aggravating or dis-aggravating factors, including a scarcity factor. Indeed, the water charge for the abstraction of public water for private uses includes the use of a shortage coefficient which varies across the river basin region. It is calculated by multiplying the base value of the respective use by the volume of water drawn, diverted or used expressed in cubic meters and by the applicable shortage coefficient. The coefficient of shortage is applied differently by river basin region:

- 1 for PTRH1, PTRH2 and PTRH3 (including Ave, Cávado, Douro, Leça, Lima and Minho Basins)
- 1.1 for PTRH4 and PTRH5 (including Lis, Mondego, Oeste and Vouga Creeks and Tejo Basin)
- 1.2 for PTRH6, PTRH7 and PTRH8 (comprehending Algarve, Mira and Sado Creeks and Guadiana Basin).

This component is applicable to the following sectors: agriculture, fish farming, aquaculture, hydraulic energy production, thermal energy production, public water supply systems and other cases. Although it cannot be claimed that the shortage coefficients used in Portugal measure in an accurate way the water resource cost, they constitute a first attempt for charging water scarcity.

Of note: since 2008, water supply and sanitation service providers include abstraction charges in the retail tariffs, dependent on the actual use and the type of user. The proceedings are earmarked to a water protection fund (50%) or finance Basin Water Authorities (40%) and the National Water Authority in charge of water resources management (10%).

Source: OECD (2017[8]), *Water Charges in Brazil: The Ways Forward*, https://doi.org/10.1787/9789264285712-en.

Charges are volumetric in most cases – like in South Africa, with the user paying a unitary rate per cubic metre abstracted. Alternative structures include, for example, fixed charges per hectare for non-metered agricultural abstraction or a price per megawatt-hour for energy production. For groundwater abstraction, increasing block tariff structures are sometimes in place.

Pollution charges are usually calculated based on pollution volume and content, and differentiated according to the sector (e.g. industries or agriculture) (Box 4.5). More countries have adopted pollution charges compared with abstraction charges. However, examples of pollution charges for diffuse source pollution remain limited. The heterogeneous impacts and damage costs of diffuse water pollution make their management more difficult than point source pollution. Additional reasons for the slow uptake of pollution charges in the management of diffuse water pollution may include: political resistance from polluters; limited data on the costs of environmental degradation; difficulties in measuring diffuse sources of pollution and attributing them to landowners.

Pollution charges are typically collected at the local level and since charges are often earmarked for environmental funds and water protection (treatment, monitoring, enforcement, etc.), the money usually remains at the local level. There is a large variation in how and for which pollutants water pollution charges are implemented in different countries or regions.

Box 4.5. Differentiating pollution charges per user and pollutants in France

In France, water pollution charges are differentiated according to water users, such as households, agriculture and industry – although they can be the same between users. Charges for pollution with domestic origin are based on the water consumption of the household. Table 4.2 compiles the pollution charge for domestic users for the Adour-Garonne River Basin (one of the six river basins in France) and Table 4.3 those for non-domestic users.

Table 4.2. Pollution charge for domestic users in the Adour-Garonne River Basin, France

Year	2013	2014	2015	2016	2017	2018	Maximum limit set by law
Pollution charge (EUR/m^3)	0.3	0.305	0.31	0.315	0.32	0.33	0.5

These charges contrast with those for livestock and pollution with non-domestic origin in agriculture and industry, which are based respectively on number of livestock (above a certain level) and discharged pollutants. In the following table, we report the pollution charge for non-domestic users for the Adour-Garonne River Basin.

Table 4.3. Pollution charge for non-domestic users in the Adour-Garonne River Basin, France

Main pollutant elements	Pollution charges (in EUR per unit)						Maximum limit set by law
	2013	2014	2015	2016	2017	2018	
Total dissolved solids (per kg)	0.119	0.122	0.124	0.127	0.129	0.132	0.3
Chemical oxygen demand (COD per kg)	0.074	0.076	0.077	0.079	0.081	0.082	0.2
Biochemical oxygen demand in 5 days (per kg)	0.149	0.152	0.155	0.158	0.161	0.164	0.4
Nitrogen (per kg)	0.3	0.305	0.31	0.315	0.32	0.33	0.7
Nitrates, nitrites (per kg)	0	0	0	0	0	0	0.3
Phosphorus (per Kkg)	0.4	0.41	0.42	0.43	0.44	0.44	0.2
Metox (per kg)	0.7	0.71	0.73	0.74	0.76	0.77	3.6
Metox for groundwater (per kg)	6	6	6	6	6	6	6
Toxicity high (per kiloequitox)	6.7	6.8	7	7.1	7.2	7.4	18
Toxicity high in groundwater (per kiloequitox)	30	30	30	30	30	30	30
Dangerous substances for the environment in surface water (per kg)				3	4	5	10
Dangerous substances for the environment in groundwater (per kg)				3	4	5	16.6
Dissolved salts (m^3 [siemens/centimetre])	0	0	0	0	0	0	0.15
Heated water in sea, except in winter (per megathermie)	1.26	1.29	1.31	1.34	1.37	1.4	8.5
Heated water in river, except in winter (per megathermie)	1.26	1.29	1.31	1.34	1.37	1.4	8.5

Source: OECD (2017[8]), *Water Charges in Brazil: The Ways Forward*, https://doi.org/10.1787/9789264285712-en.

Promote innovative approaches to manage water balance and complete water allocation reform

Prioritise cost-effective green solutions to augment water yields in the WCWSS

During the water crisis, water use from the WCWSS exceeded the system yield. This situation calls for a review of water requirements among users, which is currently being done through the revision and update of the WCWSS Reconciliation Strategy. For the long-term planning of WCWSS water resources, the level of assurance of supply for the domestic and industrial sectors is set at 97%. This level is used to determine the yield of the dams. In the case of irrigation, the WCWSS long-term assurance of supply reaches 91% which is higher than in other catchments because of the type of crops. As stated in the updated Reconciliation Strategy, agriculture will be curtailed first and more frequently than domestic and industrial users and the current curtailment rules may, therefore, need to be reviewed. Many types of water balance review mechanisms are possible, allowing for temporary or regulated water allocation transfer among water users. In a context of increasing water scarcity and high marginal costs of new water production, these mechanisms can generate economic benefits while addressing equity and redress concerns (see next section on effectively redressing past inequities). Box 4.6 provides the example of the water resource management model implemented in the state of Ceará (Brazil) that includes negotiation mechanisms to review water balance among users to promote an efficient use of water.

Box 4.6. The water resources management model of Ceará, Brazil

The experience of the state of Ceará is characterised by the search for a specific model adapted to the Brazilian semi-arid region. Progress achieved, with the support of World Bank loans, can be largely characterised as follows:

- Management of water stored in dams, given scarcity problems derived from multi-annual seasonality of precipitation and high evaporation that occur in semi-arid regions.
- Allocation of water to multiple uses, based on socially negotiated decisions in users' collegiate structures (principally users' associations of the reservoirs), based on established relationships between water height and stored volume that provide reliable projections of water availability in the short and medium terms.
- Transport of raw water over long distances, over the limits of watersheds, reaching the major demand sites, especially the Metropolitan Region of Fortaleza, where the largest demands for industrial and domestic consumption are concentrated.
- Collection of charges for the services of non-treated water storage, transport and distribution provided to the industrial users and to the concessionaires of domestic supply (those charges are formally different from the charges associated with the abstraction of non-treated water).
- Adoption of mechanisms of negotiation among water users, allowing for changes in water allocation in order to increase the efficiency of water use (sectors with higher added value may pay for subsidising the reduction or suspension of activities of users with less added value – particularly irrigation with high demand).
- Promotion of local associations of small users in order to facilitate the negotiation processes for water allocation.

- A single state agency, the COGERH, created as a mixed economic enterprise acting in all the state territory and beyond the limits of the river basins, interconnecting reservoirs and systems for water transfer, being responsible for the operation and maintenance of the entire system.
- A Secretariat for Water Resources that keeps all the competences of the state, notably those concerning the granting of permits and the systematic inspection of compliance.
- An agency for the construction of water-related public works (SOHIDRA), and another one for the collection of hydro-meteorological data (FUNCEME).
- A total collection of Brasilian Real 57 million in 2012, with a large part used to cover the operational costs of the raw water storage and transport systems.

Ceará water management is oriented towards the process of conciliation of conflicts among the multiple uses of water in a Brazilian semi-arid region, both for rural uses (family-based agriculture and large irrigation schemes), and metropolitan use in Fortaleza (urban and industrial consumption). Therefore it addresses both the bulk and retail dimensions of water supply, from a regional point of view and based on large infrastructures held by the state, and formulates new projects to satisfy expanding needs, according to the profiles of water users and uses. An additional merit of the system is the consistency of available data for supporting the processes of negotiation, which are crucial to reallocating water among users and generating higher added value. The real operation and maintenance costs of dams, canals, conduits and other equipment are fully covered by the charges that are collected for the non-treated water supplied, always rigorously metered. Hence, Ceará's water resources management system relies on governance, governability, financial consistency, in addition to a regional development strategy.

Source: OECD, (2015[4]), *Water Resources Governance in Brazil,* https://doi.org/10.1787/9789264238121-en

In the 2019 WCWSS Reconciliation Strategy update, five water balance scenarios were developed to compare future water demand with current and future available yield depending on investment options (Figure 4-1). The water augmentation options include alien vegetation clearing, water conservation and demand management, groundwater development, desalination, water reuse and surface water augmentation.

Figure 4-1. Impact of augmentation options on the water balance of the WCWSS

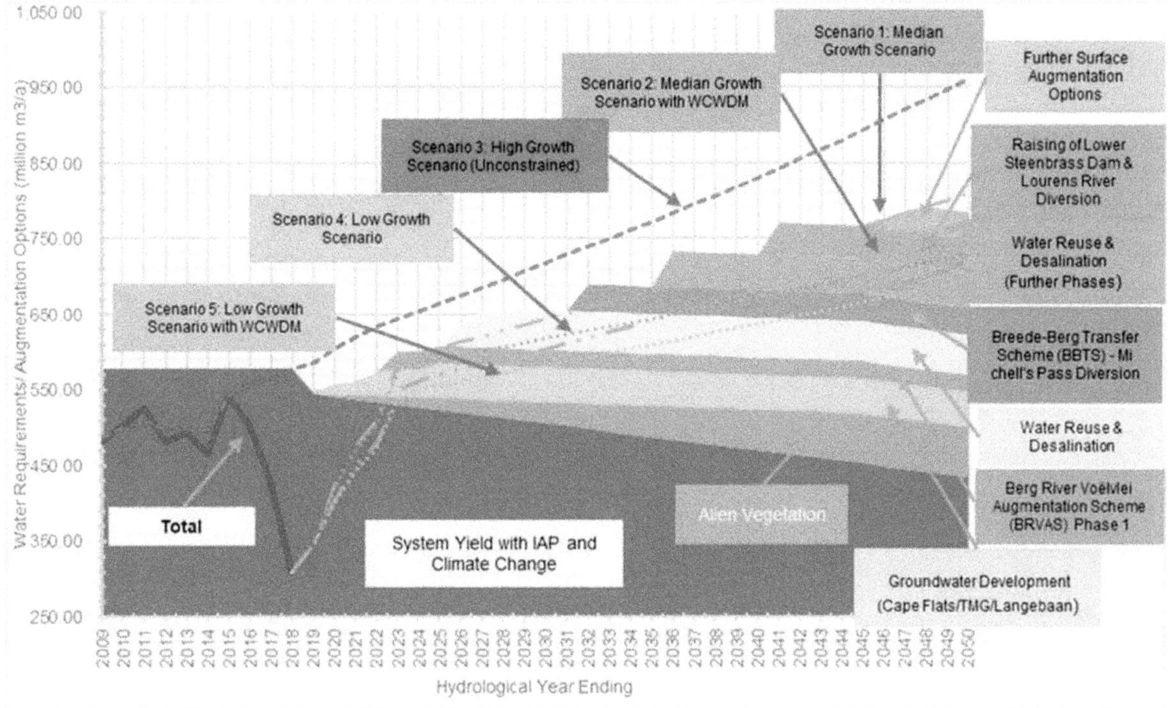

Source: DWS, (forthcoming[9]),Western Cape Water Supply System Reconciliation Strategy, Status Report 2019

These options include a mix of grey and green infrastructure[2] with water conservation and demand management being the most effective solution to increase the system yield (Table 4.4).

At the city level, the 2019 Water Strategy (City of Cape Town, 2019[10]) also relies on a mix of grey and green solutions for its augmentation programme. Furthermore, it recognises that nature-based solutions are among the most cost-effective solutions to increase water yields (Box 4.7). As such, they have been prioritised along with water demand management and improvements of the management and effectiveness of the integrated surface water systems (Table 4.5). In addition, nature-based solutions such as IAPs clearing allow the creation of an important number of jobs which generates additional positive externalities in Cape Town and its surrounding areas where the unemployment rate reaches 29% (Statistics South Africa, 2020[11]).

Table 4.4. Updated water reconciliation options for the Western Cape Water Supply System

Type of committed intervention	Additional yield (million m^3/year)
Water conservation and demand management	60
Groundwater	45.64
Reuse	34.68
Desalination	18.25
Surface water resources	23
Total	**181.56**

Source: DWS, (forthcoming[9]),Western Cape Water Supply System Reconciliation Strategy, Status Report 2019

Table 4.5. Committed new water programme over ten years, provisional yields and costs, Cape Town, South Africa

Intervention	Effective yield (Mm³/year)	Total capital expenditure (ZAR million)	Operation cost (ZAR/m³)
Demand management	26	410	3
Alien vegetation clearing	20	372	~1-2
Management of WCWSS	10		~0.2-0.5
Cape Flats Aquifer Strandfontein Wellfield	1.8	378	6.5
Cape Flats Aquifer Hanover Park Wellfield	1.5	158	8.5
Cape Flats Aquifer Strandfontein North and East Wellfield	5.5	772	6.5
Cape Flats Aquifer Philippi Wellfield	2.2	434	8.5
Cape Flats Aquifer Mitchells Plain Wellfield	7.3	673	8.5
Atlantis Aquifer	5.8	314	8.5
Table Mountain Group Phase 1	9.1	468	5.5
Table Mountain Group Phase 2	5.5	523	5.5
Table Mountain Group Phase 3	4.4	376	2.2
Berg River augmentation	15		4.62
Water reuse Phase 1	26	1 882	5.7
Desalination Phase 1	18	1 800	9
Total new supply	**158.1**	**8 560**	

Source: City of Cape Town, (2019[10]) Water Strategy; City of Cape Town, (2020[12]) Water Outlook 2020 Report

Box 4.7. Reaping off the benefits from green infrastructure in the water sector

Green infrastructures are defined as "a strategically planned network of natural and semi-natural areas with other environmental features designed and managed to deliver a wide range of ecosystem services. It incorporates green spaces (or blue if aquatic ecosystems are concerned) and other physical features in terrestrial (including coastal) and marine areas" (European Commission, 2013[13]). They are increasingly recognised as part of the answer to water challenges in OECD countries, especially when cities compete with other users (e.g. agriculture and thermal energy) to access the water they need and when water management is considered in relation to land use and other policies.

The United Nations Environment Programme (2014[14]) lists green infrastructures for water resource management, some of which are useful in an urban context. Colin Green (OECD, 2013[15]) adds demand management and local processing of black or grey water to this list. Technologies related to sludge recycling, wastewater-energy generation and water cycle energy efficiency could also be considered. Energy efficiency translates water utilities' objective of minimising and translating costs into opportunities to generate additional revenues. Energy-related technologies have ancillary benefits in terms of energy and climate policies. Green infrastructures provide solutions to all four risks that determine urban water security: droughts, floods, pollution and ecosystem resilience. Most of the technologies inventoried in Table 4.6 are mature. Some have been in use for centuries, e.g. Venice has relied on rainwater harvesting since its infancy and Paris adopted in the 19th century a three-pipe system supplying non-potable water to uses that did not require potable water.

Table 4.6. Green Infrastructure solutions for water resource management

	Urban water management issue							
	Water supply and sanitation (including drought)	Water quality regulation			Moderation of extreme events (floods)			Protection of ecosystems
		Water purification	Biological control	Water temperature control	Reverine flood control	Urban stormwater runoff	Coastal flood (storm) control	
Green infrastructure solution								
Demand management	X							X
Local processing of black or grey water	X	X	X					
Wetlands restoration/conservation	X	X	X	X	X			X
Constructing wetlands	X	X	X	X	X			X
Water harvesting						X		
Green spaces	X	X		X		X		X
Permeable pavements	X	X				X		X
Green roofs						X		X
Protecting/restoring mangroves, coastal marshes, dunes, reefs							X	X
Corresponding grey infrastructure (primary service level)								
Dams, groundwater pumping	X			X				
Dams, levees				X	X			
Water distribution systems	X							
Water treatment plant		X	X					
Urban stormwater infrastructure						X		
Sea walls							X	

The benefits of green infrastructures are increasingly well-documented. The Nature Conservancy (McDonald, 2014[16]) has computed that if cities invested in watershed conservation, 700 million people could receive better-quality water and water utilities could save USD 890 million a year in water treatment costs. Watershed conservation may be particularly relevant to low-income cities that cannot afford the capital and operation and maintenance (O&M) costs of built infrastructures.

Source: Adapted from UNEP (2014[14]), *Green Infrastructure Guide for Water Management: Ecosystem-based Management Approaches for Water-related Infrastructure Projects*, United Nations Environment Programme; OECD (2013[15]), *Barriers to and Incentives for, the Adoption of Green Water Infrastructure*, OECD, Paris; OECD (2015[17]), *Water and Cities: Ensuring Sustainable Futures*, http://dx.doi.org/10.1787/9789264230149-en.

An optimised portfolio of grey and green infrastructure appears critical to build and sustain water security and resilience. The population growth and urbanisation of African cities require increased investment in water resource management. So far investments have primarily targeted “grey” infrastructure, including reservoirs, distribution pipes and treatment plants. The connection between urban water security and upstream catchment, as shown by a study from The Nature Conservancy (The Nature Conservancy, 2016[18]), underlines the pressing need to expand and develop water source protection through "green" infrastructure and land management. The example of Nakivubo wetland in Kampala is also advocating for green infrastructure investment as being among the most cost-effective solutions for water resources management (Box 4.8).

Box 4.8. Lessons from Kampala's Nakivubo Wetland, Uganda

The Nakivubo Wetland, one of several large wetland systems that are found within and around the city of Kampala, is severely degraded. Polluted water from the city passes through the wetland before entering Inner Murchison Bay.

In the late 1990s, it was ascertained that the water treatment service performed by the wetland yielded a significant cost saving for the nearby Ggaba Water Treatment Works. However, as the city has continued to grow, pollution flows into the wetland have increased significantly, while the size and assimilative capacity of the wetland have decreased. As a result, the nearby water treatment works has been upgraded twice and new treatment works have been sited far from the city.

Fisheries in Inner Murchison Bay have also all but collapsed and the wetland itself has become the site of slum development. These concerns, as well as the increasing shortage of public open space areas in the city that are available for recreation, have led to the city's consideration of the rehabilitation of the Nakivubo Wetland, both to restore its functioning and to create the opportunity for a recreational area with associated possibilities for economic development. In this study, a sequential set of interventions was identified to restore the wetland to a level where economic benefits could be realised. This "treatment train" included improved sanitation infrastructure and measures, extending and upgrading the wastewater treatment works, wetland rehabilitation, conservation measures and investment in recreational facilities. Excluding some of the required sanitation work which is already underway, the proposed fix would incur an initial cost of USD 53 million, with ongoing maintenance and operating costs of USD 3.6 million per year. Benefits of the project would include water treatment cost savings of USD 1 million (limited because of sunk costs) and recreational benefits exceeding USD 22 million per year. The net present value of the project over 15 years would be in the order of USD 80 million (- USD 24 to USD 220 million) and the internal rate of return would be in the range of 20% (4% to 34%), depending on assumptions.

The restoration would also enhance the feasibility of creating a waterfront development next to the wetland. Nevertheless, the initial capital costs are high, and such a project may well not be undertaken due to financial constraints and political intractability. There are important lessons to be learned from this study. Considerable environmental, economic and fiscal costs have been incurred by allowing the built environment to encroach on and largely eradicate a crucial part of the city's natural capital endowment. A green urban planning paradigm would have yielded the sustained flow of benefits outlined above. It is now too costly and, from a political point of view, impractical to restore the wetland to a state where these benefits can be achieved. This lesson holds for the many additional wetland areas that could become engulfed as Kampala continues to grow. Most wetlands within the existing urban area have already been effectively lost. Without proactive interventions, the wetlands outside of the present urban core will also be destroyed and the cumulative impacts on Murchison Bay and any economic activities around the bay, including the viability of future waterfront development, could be significant. One of the main challenges in achieving such interventions will be institutional. Greater Kampala extends well beyond the boundaries of the Kampala Capital City Authority (KCCA), which originally encompassed the entire city. Unless the KCCA area is adjusted accordingly (as has been done in other countries), the problems that will arise in a growing city will be in areas under multiple other jurisdictions. Recreational benefits would exceed USD 22 million per year.

Source: Turpie, J. et al. (2016[19]), "A preliminary investigation of the potential costs and benefits of rehabilitation of the Nakivubo Wetland, Kampala", in *Promoting Green Urban Development in Africa*, World Bank, Washington.

Furthermore, a way forward could be to explore augmentation solutions that are designed according to circular economy principles, i.e. making efficient use of natural resources as primary materials and optimising their reuse; planning and carrying out activities in a way to close, slow and narrow loops across value chains; and designing and building infrastructure to avoid linear lock-in to avoid material waste. The circular economy is expected to generate positive impacts on the environment through reducing atmospheric emissions, increasing the share of renewable energy and recyclable resources, as well as reducing the use of raw materials, water, land and energy (Box 4.9).

Box 4.9. Water and the circular economy

The circular economy is a new socio-economic paradigm promoting a shift towards a restorative and regenerative economy. The growing interest in the circular economy is due to three main factors: i) restrictions on access to resources, due to current megatrends such as demographic growth, urbanisation and climate change; ii) technological development, through which the circular economy is more attractive and viable for businesses and operators; iii) socio-economic opportunities emerging from moving from a linear approach of "take, make and dispose" to a circular system, including better access to services and job creation.

The water sector has been applying circular principles for a long time. Managing water in a circular way implies: reducing the use of water in the production cycles; ensuring more sustainable water flows; reusing water for specific purposes taking into account the effects on health and the environment; and generating energy and recovering of a wide variety of materials from wastewater treatment. For example, activities consist of generating biofuels from sewage sludge to provide energy; using wastewater biosolids as an organic fertiliser to preserve soil, while improving water quality through the recovery of nutrients (nitrogen and phosphorus) from wastewater effluents; or using wastewater sludge for the manufacture of construction materials forming part of aggregates, bricks, cement, mortars or concrete.

According to the results of the OECD Survey on the Circular Economy in Cities and Regions, a total of 66% of circular economy initiatives focus on the water and sanitation sector, after the waste sector (78%). Water can be treated for reuse in recharging aquifers, supplying agricultural systems as well as for refrigeration in industrial processes, irrigation of parks and gardens, street washing and even for drinking water. For example, in Singapore, in 2003, the Public Utilities Board (PUB), Singapore's national water agency, introduced NEWater, high-grade reclaimed water produced from treated used water, which exceeds the drinking water standards set by the World Health Organization and the US Environmental Protection Agency. NEWater is used primarily for non-potable industrial purposes at wafer fabrication parks, industrial states and commercial buildings.

There are also examples of circular wastewater facilities. In the city of Granada (Spain), the public water utility company transformed the concept of a wastewater treatment plant into a biofactory by producing energy and new materials. In 2019, the biofactory almost reached its 100% energy self-sufficiency goal while 18.91 million m^3 of treated water were reused for irrigation and for the maintenance of the minimum ecological flow of the local Genil River. In addition, from the 16 525 metric tonnes of fresh sludge material produced in the biofactory in 2019, 14.3% was reused for compost and 85.7% for direct application in the agricultural sector. A similar example exists in Santiago del Chile (Chile) where three biofactories – La Farfana, La Florida and Mapocho-Trebal – located in the metropolitan region currently treat 100% of the wastewater of Greater Santiago. The biofactories allow a clean portion of water to be returned to the Mapocho River and the rest to the farmers on the metropolitan region.

Many cities and regions in the OECD area incorporate water into their circular economy strategies. For example, Amsterdam focuses on closing local nutrient cycles. It combines water reuse techniques with educational programmes and procurement tools; the Barcelona Metropolitan Area prioritises the creation of a water cluster and provided funds for research and development (R&D) in the sector. It promotes the creation of the water cluster with different stakeholders and adopts an intersectoral approach, in relation to the interplay of the water sector with others, such as food and design. Water-related initiatives in Flanders consist of supporting companies in closing water loops and facilitating demonstration projects. The Partnership Circular Flanders created different spaces for stakeholder collaboration with a strong technical innovation approach. In Rotterdam, actions concentrate in the health sector through filtering wastewater, while Paris is advancing in wastewater-energy recovery to heat and cool public buildings and using technology to monitor water consumption in green public spaces.

The transition to a circular economy does not come without obstacles. Matching the biological and technical cycles of cities and regions and the various ways in which resources can be repurposed and reused, from water to energy, is a complex task for integrated master plans, which reflect interests and motivations within a very complex urban society. In developing and emerging economies, enabling conditions and the right investments could leapfrog developed countries in digital and materials innovation aimed at sustainable production and consumption patterns.

Source: OECD (2020[20]), *The Circular Economy in Cities and Regions: Synthesis Report*, https://doi.org/10.1787/10ac6ae4-en.

Manage water allocation trade-offs between equity and efficiency

Beyond the review of the water balance and requirements within the WCWSS, many water stakeholders recognise the need to revisit the water allocation regime to face growing pressures on water resources and redress inequities in water use distribution.

Provision for the Ecological Reserve

The National Water Act (NWA) in its Section 3 requires that water reserves be determined for water resources, i.e. the quantity, quality and reliability of water needed to sustain both human use and aquatic ecosystems, so as to meet the requirements for economic development without seriously impacting on the long-term integrity of ecosystems. The reserve is one of a range of measures aimed at the ecological protection of water resources and the provision of basic human needs. South Africa's ambitious approach to the protection of the environment through the concept of a priority allocation to an environmental reserve, embedded within the Water Act of 1998, was heralded at the time as international best practice. However, although environmental flows should be included in the water regime, this is not always the case in practice. Box 4.10 provide specific examples of how certain countries are dealing with in-stream flows and concretely implementing an environmental reserve.

Box 4.10. Options for treatment of in-stream flows within a water allocation regime

When designing an allocation regime and setting a long-term abstraction limit, it is important to decide whether or not to include some or all entitlements in this limit. The most common approach is to set aside the amount needed for environmental needs, non-consumptive uses, and transfers to other systems (including downstream obligations) as a prior right and then to allocate the remainder to take water for consumptive purposes.

An alternative approach, being tested in Australia, is to assign some water to the environment as an entitlement to a share of all inflows and define this entitlement separately from the arrangements used to ensure that base flows, for example, are maintained. In the Murray-Darling Basin, a Commonwealth Environmental Water Holder has been established and by 2019 is expected to hold around one third of the Basin's water entitlements. Under this new arrangement, it is not possible for the government to allocate water to consumptive users without making a pro rata allocation to the Commonwealth EnvironmentalWater Holder.

Australia is moving to this approach in order to put environmental water on the same footing as all other water users. Under this arrangement, allocations are made in proportion to the number of entitlements held in the interests of the environment, no matter how dry or wet it is. As a result, administrators are not able to transfer environmental water to other users.

In the United States, non-governmental groups have been buying water to ensure that the environment is looked after. A well-known example is the OregonWater Trust, which became a programme of The Freshwater Trust in 2008.

Source: OECD, (2015[21]), *Water Resources Allocation: Sharing Risks and Opportunities*, https://doi.org/10.1787/9789264229631-en

Failure to provide adequate environmental flows can lead to a wide range of negative and often unexpected impacts (Box 4.11). Freshwater systems provide a wide range of ecosystem services and those services depend on particular flow regimes. A study by Turpie et al. (2017[22]) valued ecosystem services in South Africa at an estimated ZAR 275 billion (USD 18.9 billion) per annum. This includes many services beyond traditional "conservation" objectives and can include services such as:

- Increasing water yield.
- Supporting food security.
- Improving water quality.
- Reducing flood damage.
- Reducing fire risk from the growth of invasive alien vegetation.
- Storing carbon and helping us to cope with climate change.
- Providing jobs for semi-skilled and unskilled people.
- Tourism and ecotourism.
- Rural economies and SMME development.

Further, international experience shows it is extremely difficult to recover water for the environment once it has been allocated for consumptive use. This highlights the importance of reserving appropriate flows for environmental purposes from the outset (Box 4.12).

Box 4.11. Impacts of failing to consider environmental flows

Freshwater systems provide a wide range of ecosystem services. Changes to the natural flow regime can affect the ability of a river to provide these services. Poor water allocation practices can mean that many of the services that rivers provide – for free – can be lost, with significant impact on dependent human communities. Examples from the international experience include:

- **Heightened flood risk** – such as in Yellow River, China, where overallocation resulted in the build-up of sediment and changes to river morphology. This led to the river being perched above the floodplain and created a significant increase in the risk of flooding. Dedicated flows, representing around 35% of the mean annual flow, are now provided as part of the allocation regime to improve sediment movement as part of efforts to reduce the risk of flooding.
- **Saltwater encroachment and related environmental declines** – such as in the Indus River, Pakistan, where overallocation and massively reduced flows at the river mouth led to saltwater intruding around 64 kilometres inland, resulting in the loss of approximately 1.2 million acres of farmland.
- **The outbreak of pest species** – such as in the Orange River, South Africa, where hydropower development resulted in more stable base flows, thus creating a habitat for blackflies. This led to blackflies reaching pest proportions, with significant impacts on cattle production.
- **Declines in fish and other aquatic populations** – such as in the Yangtze River, China, where changes to the downstream flow regime as a result of the construction of the Three Gorges Dam have caused a decline in juvenile fish stocks of the 4 major carp species of up to 95%, with subsequent effects on fisheries production.

Source: Speed, R. et al. (2011[23]), "Policy measures, mechanisms, and framework for addressing environmental flows", International Water Centre, Brisbane.

Box 4.12. The definition of e-flows: Results from the OECD survey on water allocation

A significant majority (76%) of countries responding to the OECD survey on water allocation indicated that minimum environmental flows are defined. A wide range of methodologies to do so was reported. For example, in Israel, in some places, a minimum quota of water has been set aside and must be allocated to ecosystems. In Slovenia, the ecologically acceptable flow is set depending on the type of water use and type of ecological needs. In England and Wales, environmental flow indicators are used as an indicator of the flows required by the environment. In Portugal, minimum environmental flows are determined on a case-by-case basis. In China, the warning-level river flow against the drying out of a downstream river course shall not fall below 200 cm3/sec at Xiaheyan hydrological stations. In the Murray-Darling basin, Australia, the Basin Plan limits water use at environmentally sustainable levels by determining long-term sustainable diversion limits for both surface and groundwater resource. A key component of the Basin Plan is the environmental watering plan, which co-ordinates all environmental watering across the basin.

Of the examples indicating that minimum environmental flows/sustainable diversion limits are taken into account, 82% take freshwater biodiversity into account in the definition of e-flows and 64% take terrestrial biodiversity into account. For example, in France, the minimum biological flow and the reserve flow required are based on the observation of ecological needs.

Source: OECD (2015[21]), *Water Resources Allocation: Sharing Risks and Opportunities*, http://dx.doi.org/10.1787/9789264229631-en.

Effectively redressing past inequities

Replacing the previous Water Act 1956 that was racially discriminating for water allocation, the 1998 National Water Act abolished riparian rights, although pre-existing water use is recognised, provided it was legal in the two years prior to its promulgation. The NWA also removed the notion of private owner and declared water as a national resource owned by all South Africans. As such, the NWA provisions aimed to redress past inequities through redistribution of formal water use rights, primarily through the process of "compulsory licensing", which allows the DWS to review all water uses in an area that is or is soon likely to be under water stress or where it is necessary to review prevailing water use to achieve equity of access to water. This is done by converting existing lawful water use into licences.

Although it provided a significant step forward, the NWA did not detail how redistribution should be carried out in practice, which is why the situation did not evolve much in the absence of a practice-oriented policy to guide allocation reform. As a result, in 2008, the DWS launched a Water Allocation Reform Strategy (WARS) aiming to redress persisting inequities through a number of mechanisms including the provision of financial support to resource-poor farmers or the processing of licences and/or general authorisations to support the uptake of water by historically disadvantaged people. The WARS set ambitious targets to reach:

- 30% of allocable water allocated to previously disadvantaged individuals by 2014, at least 50% of which should be in the hands of women.
- 60% of allocable water allocated to black people by 2024.

More recently, in 2013, the National Water Resources Strategy and National Water Policy Review prioritise equity criteria in (re)allocation decision-making. However, despite prioritising equity outcomes, once again, these have not been clearly defined, nor have the complex trade-offs of reallocation been considered in sufficient details to support decision-makers. As explained by Rawlins (2019[24]), "there is a clear disjuncture between legal and policy objectives defining priorities for both new allocations and reallocations. Initial allocations are assessed on a first-come, first-served basis. If a water use licence meets the required criteria, it cannot be declined in favour of an application not yet submitted, even though it may produce a more socially, economically or environmentally favourable outcome". This partly explains the slow rollout of compulsory licensing, with only 3% of average water availability reallocated through this process (Kidd, 2016[25]). As a result, existing lawful uses which were intended to serve as a transitionary measure to enable the implementation of a new system to reallocate water rights, tend to be anything but transitional. This situation applies to both South Africa as a whole and the Western Cape region.

If the completion of the water resource management decentralisation is soon achieved, a way forward could be to delegate complementary powers and regulatory functions to CMAs so that they are legally entitled "to manage and monitor permitted water use within its water management area" and "to make rules and regulate water use" (DWS, 1998[26]). With these clear and coherent mandates, CMAs would have in their hands policy instruments as well as economic instruments (through the water resource development charge) to implement water (re)allocation at the catchment level. They would thus have the necessary tools to respond to water allocation long-term environmental, economic and social objectives while ensuring the involvement of water stakeholders.

Improve the financial sustainability of water and sanitation services

Strengthen economic water regulation

Since 2015, the DWS contemplated a pricing strategy review and an economic regulator reform. However, both projects stalled and remain incomplete as of today. In the course of the Pricing and Economic Regulations Reforms (PERR) project, the DWS conducted extensive work and consultation regarding three possible economic regulation institutional arrangements: an internal branch within the DWS, a government component and a national public entity. "Based on the assessment criteria and external stakeholder preferences established during the consultation process, the preferred institutional option for the economic regulator is the establishment of an external regulator, as a national public entity. This option allows for the greatest separation of roles between DWS as a regulated body, and the economic regulator. It also allows for the necessary freedom in terms of the recruitment and appointment of the highly skilled technical staff that will be required to perform this function effectively. It builds on the relatively successful National Energy Regulator of South Africa model" (DWS, 2013[27]). However, in a contradictory PERR presentation (DWS, 2013[28]), the preferred option is stated to be a National Government Component, outside the DWS. More confusion is added when looking at the figure illustrating the five-pillar turnaround strategy as displayed in the National Water and Sanitation Master Plan (DWS, 2019[5]), where the economic regulator seems to sit under the DWS authority (Figure 4-2).

In the 2018/19 Budget Vote speech (DWS, 2018[29]) to the National Assembly, the minister reiterated the project of installing a National Water Resources and Services Regulator. The Annual Performance Plan 2019/20 to 2021/22 of the DWS also reiterates the objective of establishing an independent regulator endowed with regulatory functions including licensing, water pricing, regulatory performance management, consumer protection and infrastructure investment. However, the process still needs to be completed, and the National Water and Sanitation Master Plan does not set any timeframe nor a deadline for the completion of this long-lasting reform.

Figure 4-2. Possible future institutional arrangements for the water sector as presented by the DWS in the National Water and Sanitation Master Plan and to be set up by 2020

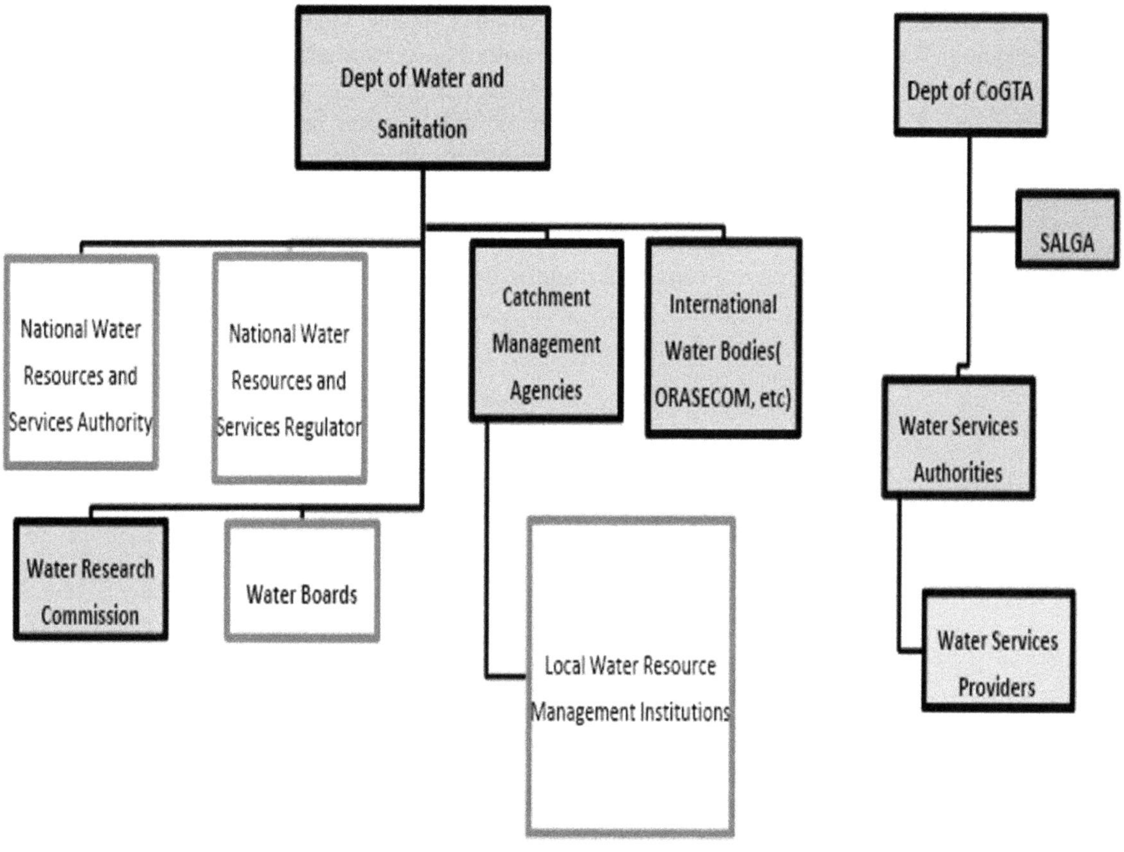

Source: DWS (2019[5]), *National Water and Sanitation Master Plan*, http://www.dwa.gov.za/National%20Water%20and%20Sanitation%20Master%20Plan/DocumentsReports.aspx.

The OECD Principle 7 of Water Governance (OECD, 2015[1]) underlines the importance to ensure that sound water management regulatory frameworks are effectively implemented and enforced in pursuit of the public interest. In a fragmented and politicised sector such as water and sanitation services, improving the regulatory environment and limiting political interference requires establishing a regulatory authority that enjoys a certain degree of independence:

- *De jure* independence, through explicit reference in the law.
- *De facto* independence through a mix of governance features and operational modalities, involving independent decision-making, i.e. decisions that are taken without being subject to government assessment; staffing based on technical grounds rather than political criteria; protection of the board and top management from political interferences; and a budget which does not depend primarily on the government (Box 4.13 and Box 4.14).

Box 4.13. Ensuring *de jure* and *de facto* independence of water regulators

A majority of water regulators surveyed by the OECD are legally independent regulatory bodies. Exceptions include Romania, where the regulator is an authority subordinated to a minister. In Flanders, Belgium, the regulator is a sub-entity of a governmental agency and has mainly an advisory role. In the case of Indonesia, the regulatory body is independent but has a purely advisory capacity. In Estonia, the regulatory duties for water supply and sanitation (WSS) have been vested in the competition authority (Figure 4-3).

Figure 4-3. Legal status of surveyed regulatory agencies

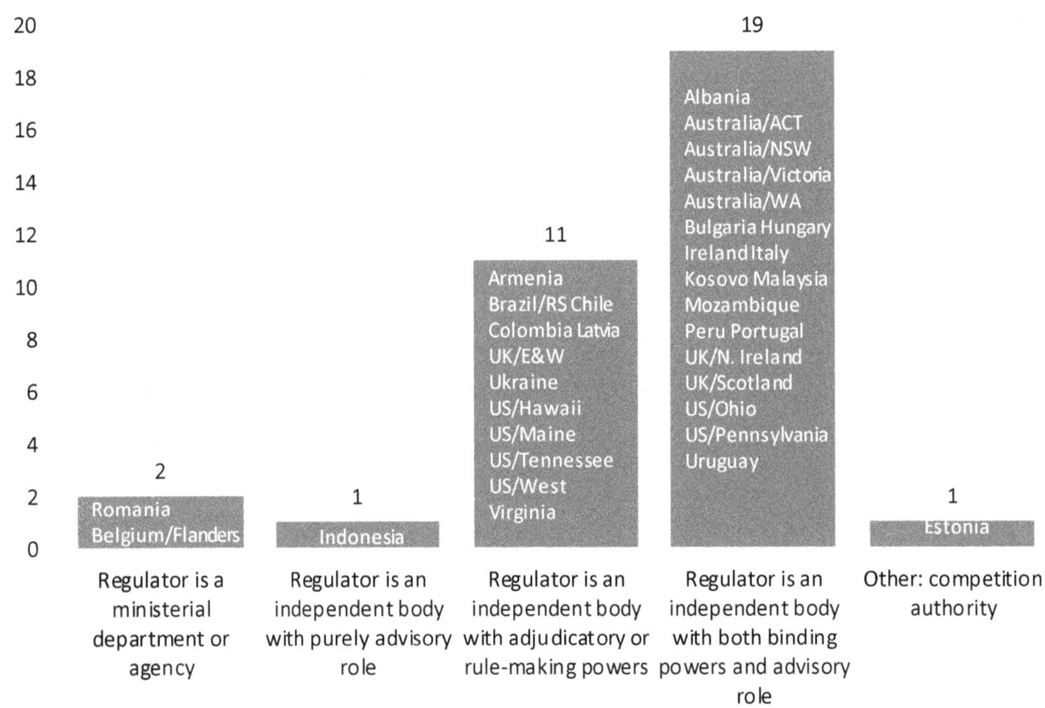

Source: OECD, (2015[30]) *The Governance of Water Regulators*, https://doi.org/10.1787/9789264231092-en
Note: 34 regulators surveyed

De jure independence through explicit reference in the law is achieved for 22 regulators.

De facto independence of regulators is ensured through a mix of governance features and operational modalities:

- Decisions taken without being subject to government assessment (28 regulators).
- Staffing based on technical grounds rather than political criteria (28 regulators).
- Protection of the board and top management from political interferences (26 regulators).
- Budget which does not depend primarily on the government (23 regulators).

In 13 cases, the regulator combines both *de jure* and all *de facto* conditions, achieving, at least on paper, the organisation most likely to ensure independence (Figure 4-4).

Figure 4-4. Ensuring independence from political influence

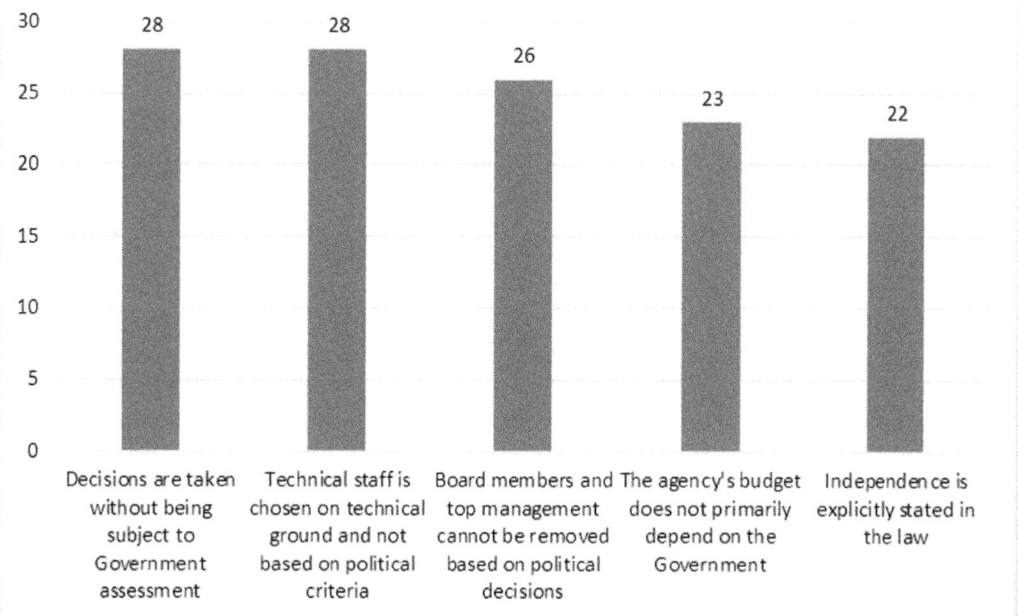

Source: OECD (2015[30]), *The Governance of Water Regulators*, https://doi.org/10.1787/9789264231092-en.
Note: 33 regulators surveyed

Box 4.14. Guidance to establish an independent regulator

The OECD has produced guidance on how to establish and implement independence with regulators (2017[31]) which identifies five key dimensions of independence (Figure 4-5).

Figure 4-5. The five dimensions of independence of regulators

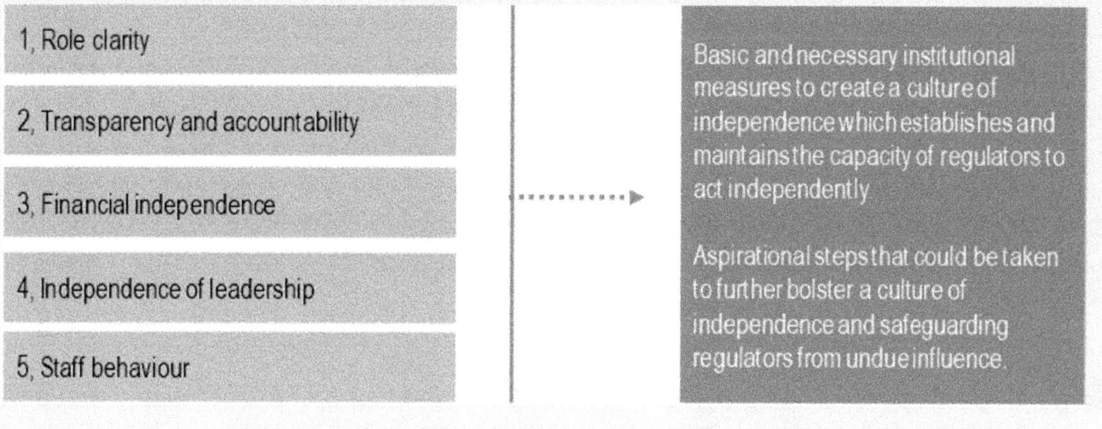

Each of the five dimensions includes practical guidelines that can be considered as the basic and necessary institutional measures to create a culture of independence which establishes and maintains the capacity of regulators to act independently, based on an analysis of regulators' institutional processes and practices within the OECD Network of Economic Regulators. The guidelines also include a set of aspirational steps that could be taken to bolster a culture of independence and safeguarding regulators from undue influence.

Source: OECD (2017[31]), *Creating a Culture of Independence: Practical Guidance against Undue Influence*, https://doi.org/10.1787/9789264274198-en.

In addition to preventing the abuse of monopolistic power, regulatory authorities can be created with the purpose to fulfil many other missions, which include, for instance, the protection of consumers' rights, in particular, ensuring the provision of goods and services of proper quality and in sufficient amount at economically reasonable prices (Box 4.15). Regulatory authorities should pursue equity goals and pay special attention to poor households. To fulfil these goals, regulatory arrangements should promote water and sanitation access expansion, pro-poor tariff level and structure that foster service access, a flexible approach to service quality or mechanisms to address complaints from all customers including marginalised ones.

Box 4.15. Missions of the National Commission for the State Regulation of Energy and Utilities in Ukraine

The reasons to create the National Commission for the State Regulation of Energy and Utilities of Ukraine are clearly defined in its statute:

- Balance interests of economic entities, consumers and the state.
- Ensure the transparency and openness of activity on the markets of natural monopolies and adjacent markets in the sphere of heat supply and centralised water supply and sewerage.
- Protect the rights of consumers, in particular, ensuring the provision of goods and services of proper quality and in sufficient amount at economically reasonable prices, stimulating improvement of their quality and meeting the demand on them.
- Shape price and tariff policy and ensure its transparency for markets.
- Ensure the self-repayment of activity of subjects of natural monopolies and economic entities on adjacent markets.
- Provide equal possibilities for consumers to access goods (services) on markets, which are in the state of natural monopoly.
- Limit the influence of subjects of natural monopolies on state policy and stimulate competition on adjacent markets in the sphere of heat supply and centralised water supply and sewerage, recycling and disposal of waste to ensure the effective functioning of the respective spheres.

Source: OECD (2015[30]), *The Governance of Water Regulators*, https://doi.org/10.1787/9789264231092-en.

In Kenya, the water and sanitation regulator, WASREB, has developed a Pro-poor Water and Sanitation Services Guideline that supports utilities to expand service in the underserved low-income areas (WASREB, 2015[32]). In addition, each regulated utility reports yearly on a number of pro-poor performance indicators that include water coverage in low-income areas, level of services in low-income areas, or compliance to standards for water kiosks. Utilities are then ranked according to a weighted score based on those indicators and their yearly evolution is monitored and disclosed publicly.

In Zambia, 60% of the urban population live in low-income or peri-urban areas with the highest population growth and the lowest water and sanitation service coverage (NWASCO, n.d.[33]). Utilities lack the financial means to extend services to these areas where mostly underprivileged and poor people live. To address this situation, the Government of Zambia established a Devolution Trust Fund (DTF) through the water regulator, the National Water Supply and Sanitation Council (NWASCO), in 2001. The DTF is a basket financing instrument with the aim to assist the water supply and sewerage utilities to extend public water distribution systems and onsite sanitation in low-income areas. In comparison to the rehabilitation and construction of water systems with networks and household connections, projects funded by the DTF need relatively small amounts of funds but have a great impact on the living conditions of the urban poor.

Quality standards are a key determinant of service costs and hence, of tariff levels. Keeping tariffs affordable while ensuring an appropriate level of cost recovery can be achieved through the adaptation of service quality standards to local needs. Quality regulation, therefore, needs to be flexible and consider the trade-offs between quality and price, so that quality standards and requirements can be adapted to the circumstances in different service areas. Initiatives, such as flow limiters, the use of plastic-bodied water meters, ground tanks and semi-pressure water service levels, were first introduced to South Africa by the water service of eThekwini (Box 4.16).

Box 4.16. Adapting quality standards in eThekwini, South Africa

In eThekwini (South Africa), Durban Metro Water Services experimented alternative service standards in order to meet the needs of customers in poor areas. Varying quality standards were proposed to customers so that they could choose between a range of options with differentiated price/quality characteristics. For example, eThekwini Metro Water Services developed semi-pressurised water systems with the provision of a roof tank as an alternative to a full pressurised system (which may be unaffordable). In such a system, water is reticulated using small diameter piping, which is laid along the major access routes or tracks located within the informal area. At appropriate intervals, connections are made to this reticulation and a manifold, which allows approximately 20 houses to connect to the water main, is installed. Each consumer receives a 200-litre water tank that is serviced by a water bailiff every day. This system results in a low level of unaccounted for water because of the low pressure and effective customer demand management. Overall water consumption through such a service delivery system is estimated to be up to 50% less than conventional systems to communities of similar profile. The approach nevertheless provides sufficient water to households to maintain a basic level of hygiene and health. In areas where this system could not be installed, standpipes/water dispensers are provided to supply informal communities as an interim measure. Furthermore, water sachets or tankered water are supplied in the case of prolonged service interruptions. Finally, water boreholes are available where there is no water reticulation.

Source: World Bank (2006[34]), "Taking account of the poor in water sector regulation", *Water Supply & Sanitation Working Notes*, No. 11; eThekwini (2019[35]), *Water and Sanitation Service Level Standards, 13th edition, July 2019/2020.*

Consumer representation and protection is a critical function of regulators particularly in a sector where access to services is vital to fulfilling basic human needs. In Zambia, NWASCO, which regulates the water and sanitation sector, has a very lean structure with offices in Lusaka only. However, in wanting to ensure that NWASCO is present on the ground for first-hand information and addressing consumer complaints, Water Watch Groups (WWGs) have been established, comprising customers from the service areas. The

WWGs have delegated power and duties from NWASCO. Membership to the WWG is voluntary and does not attract any remuneration for the services provided. NWASCO, however, endeavours to provide WWGs with stationery, transport and other necessary logistics to enhance their smooth operations. Due to poor service delivery and the increasing number of unresolved complaints, many people were willing to serve as volunteers. The Lusaka WWG was the first to be established as a pilot project in 2002. The demand for WWGs has increased with more people appreciating the added value and impact on the ground. Consequently, in towns where there are no WWGs, people are requesting to be recognised as WWGs. However, due to the demand of monitoring as well as the cost involved, NWASCO has been cautious with the establishing rate of WWGs. Currently, there are 8 WWGs across the country.

The WWGs functions include the representation of consumers' interests, the follow-up of unresolved consumer complaints, the improvement of the communication between consumers and providers, the arbitration in conflicts between consumers and service providers, the collection of information on providers' performance, NWASCO information on regulations effectiveness and the proposition of possible adjustments, poor consumer information with regard to their rights and obligations, and consumer information with regards to the role and functions of NAWSCO. To fulfil these functions, WWGs hold public meetings with consumers and meetings to review/validate complaints. They engage in outreach and publicity programmes via awareness meetings, television and radio broadcasts. They submit periodic reports to NWASCO including feedback from consumers. They participate in workshops, conferences, etc. They assist in the recruitment and training of new WWGs.

In addition to the above-mentioned regulatory examples on equity goals, regulation ultimately ought to be effective to balance a range of economic, social and environmental interest and manage the associated trade-offs. In recognising the need for the development of such an effective WSS regulatory framework, six regulators from the Eastern and Southern African region established formal co-operation on water regulation issues (Table 4.7). The ESAWAS Regulators Association was thus created in 2007 as an informal gathering of regulators to share experiences and knowledge, and was later formalised in 2010.

Once South Africa has defined and implemented its regulatory arrangement in the water sector, a way forward could be to engage in communities of practice, be they regional or international, to take part in benchmarks, share and learn about good practices. Joining the ESAWAS Regulators Association, whose objectives include capacity building and information sharing at the international, national and regional levels and regional regulatory co-operation to identify and encourage the adoption of best practices to improve the effectiveness of WSS regulation, could serve that purpose.

Table 4.7. Overview of the Eastern and Southern Africa Water and Sanitation Regulators association members

Regulator	Operational since	Number of urban water utilities regulated
National Water Supply and Sanitation Council (NWASCO), Zambia)	2000	18
Water Regulatory Council (CRA), Mozambique	2000	15
Water Services Regulatory Board (WASREB), Kenya	2003	103
Rwanda Utilities Regulatory Authority (RURA) Rwanda	2003	1
Energy and Water Utilities Regulatory Authority (EWURA), Tanzania	2006	130
Lesotho Electricity and Water Authority (LEWA-Lesotho)	2013	1

Source: ESAWAS Regulators Association (2015[36]), *Regional Benchmark of Large Water Supply and Sanitation Utilities, 2013/2014 Report*.

Improve the efficiency and financial sustainability of water and sanitation services

As is the case in many countries, the revenues from water and sanitation tariffs do not cover the operation, maintenance and renewal costs of the water sector in South Africa. This is partly a consequence of the real costs not being reflected in the price of water. Nevertheless, the financial sustainability of water and sanitation services crucially depend on revenues raised through tariffs, in addition to subsidies (Box 4.17).

Box 4.17. Setting tariffs: A trade-off between financial sustainability, economic efficiency, environmental conservation and social fairness

Setting the right tariffs for domestic water use is a challenging task. In many cases, utilities do not know the cost of the service and operate inefficiently, which adds costs to the provision of services. In addition, from a political standpoint, charging below cost can be seen as paying off. However, it is in general counterproductive. When tariffs are set below cost recovery, the provider must either rely on government subsidies or cut back on service, maintenance and investment. Generally, tariffs that are below the costs (at least of operation and maintenance) result in poor service, asset deterioration and an inability to invest to meet growing demand. There are four main objectives embedded in the design of water and sanitation tariffs: i) financial sustainability; ii) economic efficiency; iii) environmental conservation; and iv) social fairness. In order to accommodate these objectives, three dimensions of tariff policy are relevant: tariff levels, tariff structure and the tariff setting and revision process.

Financial sustainability: Water tariffs are a key element of long-term financial sustainability of water operators and of systems. Low levels of tariffs, coupled with inadequate compensation from other sources of revenue – typically taxes (and international transfers in developing countries) – over the long run lead to a vicious circle of bad maintenance and deterioration of services that affect users' willingness to pay and might, in turn, induce a decrease in bill collection rate and further reduction of revenue for the sector.

Economic efficiency: Prices provide important signals to providers and users that drive economic efficiency, i.e. that allow allocating water with priority to uses with the highest value to society and service provision at the cheapest costs.

Environmental conservation: Appropriate pricing of water supply and sanitation services contributes to environmental conservation when it is used to manage demand and discourage "excessive" uses of water. To this effect, increasing block tariffs are typically used.

Social fairness: Social fairness generally implies that the water tariff treats similar customers equally and that customers in different situations are not treated the same. Social fairness accommodates affordability concerns, i.e. poor households are able to obtain adequate supplies of clean water. In practice, however, the debate on whether tariffs are the appropriate tool to address affordability concerns is lively. Increasing block tariffs, the traditional policy tool used to achieve social objectives, have raised many criticisms as they may not be appropriate if poor households consume more water than richer ones and if the poor are not connected to the water systems. Cross-subsidies have shown limitations over time when shifts in the balance between subsidised and subsidisers were not anticipated. Targeted subsidies for water consumption have also been criticised, pointing out that precise targeting requires good administrative capacity. Subsidies supporting connections to water networks have proved more helpful for the poor than subsidies to water consumption.

Figure 4-6 Four policy objectives for tariff setting and their components

Environmental sustainability	Financial sustainability
Discourage depletion of critical natural capital • Guarantee the preservation of ecological functions of water natural capital • Minimise the use of "supply side" solutions to water scarcity • Use efficiency - Encourage water saving - Discourage wasteful water use • Minimise the alteration of natural flow patterns	***Guarantee long-term reproduction of physical assets*** • Compensate the resources that are used as inputs in water-related activities • Cash flow should guarantee the conservation of value of physical assets • Cost efficiency: minimise lifecycle costs of services, *i.e.* the creation of physical capital and operation and maintenance costs • Cost recovery should be for efficient costs only
Economic efficiency	Social concerns
Water is allocated to the most beneficial uses and economic resources are not wasted • Allocation efficiency: - Allocate water with priority to uses with highest value to society as a whole - Compare costs of water management and water-related services with their value, *i.e.* do not misallocate economic resources • Regulation should ensure optimal risk allocation among stakeholders (including users and taxpayers)	***Adequate access to affordable water at fair and equitable conditions*** • Identify "water needs" and allocate water in a way that is not skewed by concentration of power • Structure tariffs so that lower-income users can have access to and afford to use WSS services • Achieve an equitable way to share the cost of managing water resources

Source: OECD, (2010[37]), *Pricing Water Resources and Water and Sanitation Services*, https://doi.org/10.1787/22245081.

As explained in Chapter 3, in Cape Town, revenues from water and sanitation invoices effectively cashed in represent 66% of the water produced, which strongly reduces the financial base of the service. Overall, subsidies represent approximately 18% of the funding sources of the city of Cape Town water and sanitation service. However, in a context of pandemic crisis, fiscal constraints may reduce the amount of available subsidies both at the national and local levels, thus jeopardising further the financial situation of water and sanitation services across South Africa. As a result, Cape Town water services must improve their technical and economic efficiency and undertake utility turnaround efforts.

Indeed, service providers should not only approach cost recovery through increases in tariff levels but should also in priority seek efficiency gains, as there exist many areas for improvement (staff efficiency, collection ratio, metering level, energy costs, etc.). Moreover, thorough assessment and monitoring of all costs will help set up tariff calculations and levels that are sufficiently cost-reflective to drive long-term financial sustainability.

Over the past five years, a customer service turnaround project supported by the United States Agency for International Development (USAID) was implemented in the Cape Town water and sanitation service. During the drought crisis, Cape Town residents were made very aware of their water usage and reviewed more closely their bills and rates. This led to a significant increase in customer enquiries and a backlog of unresolved customer issues. In response to the customer problems and the loss of revenues (due to lower collection ratio) during the drought, the USAID project contributed to reform the Water and Sanitation

Department customer service system, which improved public trust in the department as well as revenue collection (Box 4.18).

Box 4.18. Customer service reform for water and sanitation service providers: The Cape Town experience

Like many other municipal water companies or utilities, Cape Town's water problems are compounded by a fragmented organisational structure. The city's water system is managed by many different work units:

- The Department of Water and Sanitation (meter reading, service request resolution, debt management, field operations, billing system, data management, etc.).
- The Executive Director of Area Management at the City Contact Centre.
- The city's Chief Financial Officer and Revenue Department (customer billings and certain debt management activities).
- The Executive Director of Corporate Services at the city's Information and Technology Department.

The city's Water and Sanitation Department has consolidated water and sanitation customer service operations into one organisation. This will improve the efficiency and teamwork among the various operating units involved in water management. The new Customer Service Branch will have a single manager who reports directly to the Executive Director of Water and Sanitation. Six work units will exist within the organisation, including the four business areas outlined above. In addition, there will be a business analysis group responsible for information and technology, as well as a finance and administration unit.

Based on a diagnosis, an action plan was developed, centred on four major work units where issues were identified either as causes or results of deficient customer service and operational inefficiencies: i) metering and meter reading; ii) customer billing; iii) collections and debt management; and iv) customer care and call centres (Figure 4-7). These four business domains make up 95% of the customer relationship management reform effort and directly or indirectly impact revenue flows.

Figure 4-7. Customer relationship management business areas

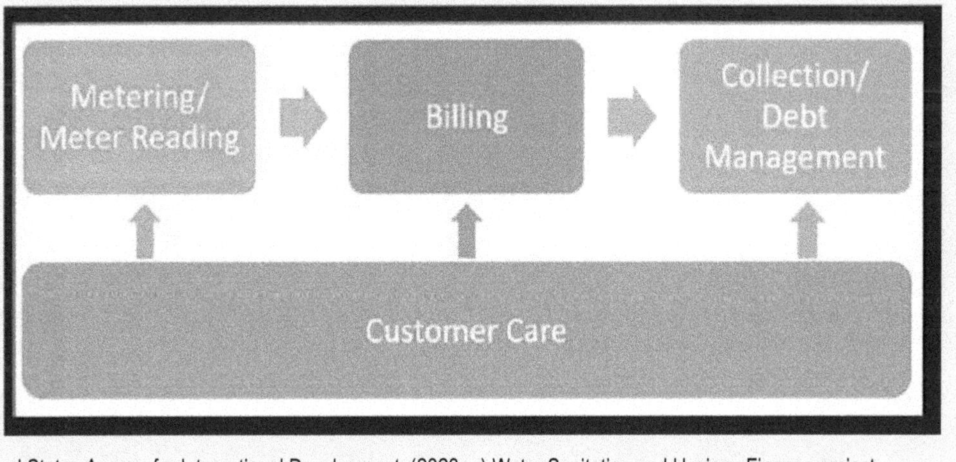

Source: United States Agency for International Development, (2020[38]) Water Sanitation and Hygiene Finance project

Furthermore, the French Development Agency (AFD) recently announced a transversal programme aiming at supporting the financial sustainability of the city of Cape Town water service. This 18-month programme, starting late 2020 and named Long-Term Technical Assistance to the City of Cape Town for the Financial Sustainability of Water and Sanitation Services will target:

- The development of an investment plan with capital expenditure level meeting the city's growing needs and sustaining the service by continually upgrading and/or replacing assets.
- The cost-effective total spending, with incremental and ongoing improvements in service performance and efficiency.
- The development of a sound and sustainable revenue model comprising a mix of tariffs, grants and other revenue. This objective includes effective data management, accurate billing, low levels of estimated readings, good meter management and up-to-date records. This is planned to be achieved through a comprehensive metering system upgrade (670 000 meters) to yield significant revenue increases and customer service improvements.
- The implementation of a tariff model able to generate sufficient tariff revenues.
- The improvement of cash collection.
- The development of a sustainable, equitable and well-targeted subsidy scheme to promote affordability.

In addition to these ongoing programmes aiming to improve the efficiency and financial sustainability of Cape Town water service, complementary actions can be implemented to better assess and monitor the performance of the service. Key performance indicators (KPIs) are widely and commonly used in the water and sanitation sectors around the world as steering and managing tools to measure change and monitor improvement against specific goals (Box 4.19). The city of Cape Town Water and Sanitation Department has set up 36 KPIs to assess and monitor the service quality. They are part of a broader corporate monitoring and appraisal system at the city level. For each of these 36 KPIs a target value is defined each year and KPI monitoring is shared monthly with the Water and Waste Portfolio Committee, the Executive Mayor and the Mayoral Committee, and the City Council. However, the yearly result achieved for each KPI is not publicly available.

Box 4.19. Selected examples of water performance indicators

In **Peru**, 35 performance indicators are grouped into two high-level areas: provision of services and business management. Every high level has three sub-levels and two sub-levels respectively (Table 4.8).

Table 4.8. Performance indicators in Peru

Provision of services			Business management	
Quality of service delivery	Billing	Affordability	Sustainability of services	Business efficiency
Presence of residual chlorine	Average rate	Potable water coverage	Working relationship	Non-revenue water
Presence of thermotolerant coliform	Average billing	Sewerage coverage	Replacement of fixed assets	Micrometering
Turbidity	Unit consumption measured		Maintenance costs of infrastructure	Active connections billed by metering
Continuity	Unit volume billed		Current liquidity	Default ratio
Pressure			Indebtedness	Operating cost per unit volume produced
Total density claims			Interest coverage	Operating cost per unit volume billed
Wastewater treatment			Operating margin	Produced water obtained from underground sources
			Return on assets (ROA)	Produced volume per unit
			Return on equity (ROE)	Staff costs per unit volume billed
				Sales and services costs per unit volume billed
				Density of breaks in the distribution networks potable water
				Density of sewer blockages

Some of these performance indicators are used to set the management goals of the water companies. The main management goals are related to increasing coverage and improvement of the service quality such as:

- Household potable water connections.
- Household sewer connections.
- Annual increase in new water meters.
- Water unbilled.
- Pressure.
- Continuity.
- Wastewater treatment.
- Update of technical and commercial cadastre.
- Density of breaks in the distribution networks potable water.

- Density of sewer blockages.

The tariff increases authorised by the regulator are subject to compliance of these management goals.

In **Portugal**, the indicators are grouped into three high-level areas: protection of user interests, operator sustainability and environmental sustainability (Table 4.9). ERSAR, the regulator, has created a technical guide which establishes all of the definitions for the data and indicators, and the methodologies to collect the information. For each of the 16 indicators per service, there are reference brackets that define if the service is good, average or unsatisfactory. The process, from the collection, in office validation and onsite auditing of all the information provided, until the disclosure of the information to the general public, follows an annual cycle.

Table 4.9. Categories of performance indicators in Portugal

Drinking Water and Wastewater Services indicators		
Protection of user interests	Operator sustainability	Environmental sustainability
Accessibility of services to users	Economic sustainability	Efficient use of environmental resources
Quality of service provided to users	Infrastructure sustainability	Efficiency in pollution prevention
	Physical productivity of human resources	

Source: OECD (2015[30]), *The Governance of Water Regulators*, https://doi.org/10.1787/9789264231092-en.

Many urban water utilities in Africa routinely use data and KPIs to guide their water and sanitation services management policies (Table 4.10). These data and information are also publicly communicated in their annual report available on the organisation's website. These data encompass: water quality and quantity; water demand and supply; economic, environmental and social sustainability of the service; and human resources management. As such, KPIs are not only a powerful steering tool but also a successful exercise of transparency and accountability.

Table 4.10. Summary of the National Water and Sewerage Company performance, Uganda, 2018-19

Category	Fiscal year 2018/19	Fiscal year 2017/18
Economic sustainability		
Turnover (Uganda Shilling thousands)	442 000 000	388 000 000
Operating expenditure (Uganda Shilling thousands)	346 000 000	296 000 000
Operating profits (Uganda Shilling thousands)	96 000 000	92 000 000
Investment made (Uganda Shilling thousands)	302 000 000	258 000 000
Asset base (Uganda Shilling thousands)	3 100 000 000	1 700 000 000
Number of towns	253	236
Environmental and ecological sustainability		
Number of towns using solar pumps	25	22
Number of towns using electrolysis instead of chlorination	25	25
Volume of sewerage treated and discharged (million litres)	100	95
Expenditure on energy (Uganda Shilling billions)	66	57
Social sustainability		
Domestic customers served	535 532	479 729
Commercial/industrial customers served	88 340	78 761
Institutional/government customers served	17 368	17 368
Public Stand Post consumers served	17 186	13 728

Category	Fiscal year 2018/19	Fiscal year 2017/18
Total number of customers served	659 157	587 863
Water mains extension (kilometres)	2 727	2 171
Sewer mains extension (kilometres)	59	24
Number of customer complaints received	166 698	147 708
Number of customer complaints handled	163 557	138 567
Resolution rate of complaints (%)	98	94
Number of staff employed	3 778	3 443
Staff costs (Uganda Shilling thousands)	137 265 190	112 000 000
New water connections	69 215	50 341
New sewer connections	368	272
Corporate social responsibility		
Amount spent on donations (Uganda Shilling thousands)	914 000	1 300 000
Number of beneficiaries of donations	5 000 000	3 000 000
Amount paid in taxes (Uganda Shilling thousands)	40 000 000	38 000 000
Human resource sustainability		
Number of staff recruited	355	310
Number of employees over 55 years	119	117
Total number of staff + board	3 778	3 443
Gender composition (staff + board) (%)	Female 30 Male 70	Female 29 Male 71
Amount spent in long time awards (Uganda Shilling thousands)	57 000	120 000
Amount spent on research and training (Uganda Shilling thousands)	750 000	700 000
Number of interns trained	1 700	1 500

Source: NWSC (2019[39]), *Integrated Annual Report 2018-2019*, National Water and Sewerage Corporation.

Furthermore, the ESAWAS started in 2013 a benchmarking exercise among large water and sanitation utilities located in Eastern and Southern African countries. To do so, a set of ten common KPIs was identified along with associated Minimum Service Level guidelines (Table 4.11). Adopting these ten KPIs and taking part in this regional benchmark could be an opportunity for Cape Town water service to be compared with peers and learn from good practices. Such an approach also allows to identify the service main strength and weakness areas, thus forming a basis for decision-making in order to craft measures to improve utility effectiveness (Table 4.12).

Table 4.11. The Eastern and Southern Africa Water and Sanitation Regulators Association benchmarking KPIs

Indicator	Definition	Calculation	Boundaries	Weight
Quality of service				
Water coverage	Percentage of the total population with access to improved water supply: individual household connection, kiosk, public stand posts, communal/shared tap	[Total Population Served/Total Population in the Service Area]	75-90	10
Sewerage coverage	Percentage of the total population with access to sewerage services (no septic tanks)	[Total Population Served/Total Population in the Service Area]	40-70	5

Indicator	Definition	Calculation	Boundaries	Weight
Water quality - Residual Chlorine - Bacteriological	Percentage of water samples undertaken meeting quality requirements	[Percentage of Tests Compliant in Relation to Applicable National Standards]	90-95	15
Hours of supply	Aggregated average hours of supply (per town/zone/area, etc.) in the reporting period	[Sum of Weighted Averages per Town]	16-20	10
		Economic efficiency		
Operation and maintenance cost coverage by billing	Level of costs covered by billed amounts	[Billed Amount/Operation and Maintenance Costs]	1-1.5	10
Collection efficiency	Collected amounts from the billing (%)	[Collected Amount/Billed Amount]x100	85-95	15
Staff cost	Personnel cost as a proportion of operation and maintenance cost (%)	[Personnel Cost/Operation and Maintenance Costs]*100	30-35	5
		Operational sustainability		
Staff per 1 000 connections	Staff per 1 000 water and sewerage connections	[Total Number of Staff x 1 000]/[No. of Water + Sewerage Connections]	5-8	5
Non-revenue water	Water that does not produce revenue in a given period (%)	[System Input Volume (Imported + Produced) – Billed Volume]/System Input Volume	30-35	15
Metering ratio	Proportion of metered customers from the total (%)	[Functional Metered Connections]/Total Connections]x100	85-95	10

Source: ESAWAS Regulators Association (2015[36]), *Regional Benchmark of Large Water Supply and Sanitation Utilities, 2013/2014 Report.*

Table 4.12. Summary of utilities performance in Kenya, Zambia, Tanzania, Mozambique, Lesotho and Rwanda, 2014

	Indicator	NCWSC	LWSC	DAWASCO	AdeM	WASCO	WASAC
Quality of service	Water coverage (%)	76.9	86.2	57	64	60	80.2
	Sewerage coverage (%)	45.9	20.1	7.8	-	5.5	-
	Water quality (%)	89.2	93.8	72	90.4	92	94.5
	Hours of supply	18	18	8	16	18	12
Economic efficiency	Operation and maintenance cost coverage by billing	1.07	0.98	0.77	1.13	0.99	1.23
	Collection efficiency	0.89	1.02	0.95	0.94	0.88	0.77
	Staff cost (%)	50.5	56.7	16.5	32.2	46.67	29.6
Operational sustainability	Staff per 1 000 connections	5	6.86	5.62	3.72	6.12	5.58
	Non-revenue water (%)	38.9	42.2	55.5	45.8	28.8	41
	Metering ratio (%)	94.3	71.8	98	74	100	100

Note: Nairobi City Water and Sewerage Company (NCW&SC), Kenya; Lusaka Water and Sewerage Company (LWSC), Zambia; Dar Es Salaam Water and Sewerage Corporation (DAWASCO), Tanzania; Águas da Região de Maputo (AdeM), Mozambique; Water and Sewerage Company (WASCO), Lesotho; Water and Sanitation Corporation (WASAC), Rwanda.
Colour legend: Green: Good performance; Pink: acceptable performance; Orange: poor performance.
Source: ESAWAS Regulators Association (2015[36]), *Regional Benchmark of Large Water Supply and Sanitation Utilities, 2013/2014 Report.*

Strengthen capacities at all levels of government

The capacity gap is another important challenge for the water sector in South Africa, especially since it often has a spill-over effect on the information gap which can, in turn, generate an accountability gap. Institutional strengthening and capacity building at all levels is crucial for effective governance of water policies in response to the challenges of the 21st century. For instance, such capacity building is a prerequisite for effective channelling of financial resources to make investment projects happen, or to prioritise investments according to their cost-benefit for the society, or to implement utility efficiency turnaround.

The National Water and Sanitation Master Plan acknowledges that "an effective water sector requires human resources capacity for different functions at different institutions – both in terms of numbers to meet the demand for specific skills; and competencies in terms of skills, qualifications and experience" (DWS, 2019[5]). It also refers to a skills gap analysis conducted by the Water Research Commission (WRC) in 2015[3] looking at numbers of staff and their skills relative to required skills. This analysis showed significant skills gaps in all water sector institutions, including DWS, CMAs, Water Boards and Water Services Authorities. This gap is further recalled by the Engineering Council of South Africa in a report dated 2015 stating that South Africa has 1 engineer per 2 600 people, compared with international standards of 1 engineer per 40 people.

Although there are robust but generic overarching principles and strategies in the field of capacity development (Skills Development Levies Act, National Qualifications Framework Act, National Skills Development Strategy III and National Development Plan), it seems that the operationalisation of skills development remains a vivid challenge in the South African water sector. The National Water and Sanitation Master Plan (DWS, 2019[5]) foresees a water and sanitation sector skills capacity needs analysis (including a mapping throughout the water value chain), and the elaboration of a skills and institutional capacity development strategy for the sector. However, these documents have not been produced yet.

Peer-learning and exchange of practices across water operators and practitioners could be supported and promoted, for instance, by the Energy and Water Sector Education and Training Authority (EWSETA) which is the responsible institution for co-ordinating and facilitating skills development and capacity building in the water sector. In order to fulfil its missions, this institution has developed a six-year plan (from 2015 to 2020) which includes detailed strategic objectives linked to four different programmes and associated with performance indicators. The evaluation and monitoring of the strategic plan are done yearly through a performance report. However, the data reported are not disaggregated enough to distinguish results and achievements between energy, renewable energy, gas and water services sectors.

A possible way to start addressing the capacity gap is to include within the updated National Water Strategy at the national level, and into an action plan at the city level, a section dedicated to capacity building and development operationalisation for the water sector. As stated in OECD Principle 4 of Water Governance (OECD, 2015[1]), the level of capacity of responsible water institutions should be adapted to the complexity of water challenges which have to be addressed. Countries and cities can identify, as part of their national and local development plans, training needs for water resources and management. They should also provide the required working conditions to retain trained personnel. Levels of governments must assess their own capacity to equip their water specialists so that they are enabled to implement the full range of activities for integrated water resources management. Information, education and communication support programmes must also be an integral part of the development process (Box 4.20).

Furthermore, the 2015 WRC study points out an interesting outcome regarding the characteristics of the capacity gap that the water sector is facing. This research work performs an assessment of whether the higher education system in South Africa was producing enough qualified people to fill the capacity gaps. Data from the Department of Higher Education and Training's management information system showed that the number of civil engineering graduates had doubled from 2010 to 2014 from approximately 1 000 to

2 000 graduates per year. The graduation numbers of other relevant engineering and science qualifications that can apply to the water sector also increased dramatically over the same period. These findings tend to show that the capacity issue rather lies in the percentage of graduates that enter the water sector as opposed to other sectors and that enter the public sector as opposed to the private sector, as noticed by the report. Trying to answer these questions, the study underlines that, "while many institutions offer generic engineering, science and technology qualifications that could be applied in the sector, only two public universities (Venda and University of the North) have specific water-related courses and qualifications" (Vienings and Lima, 2015[40]).

Box 4.20. OECD Water Governance Principle 4 on Capacity Building

Adapt the level of capacity of responsible authorities to the complexity of water challenges to be met and to the set of competencies required to carry out their duties, through:

1. Identifying and addressing capacity gaps to implement integrated water resources management, notably for planning, rule-making, project management, finance, budgeting, data collection and monitoring, risk management and evaluation.
2. Matching the level of technical, financial and institutional capacity in water governance systems to the nature of problems and needs.
3. Encouraging adaptive and evolving assignment of competencies upon demonstration of capacity, where appropriate.
4. Promoting the hiring of public officials and water professionals that uses merit-based, transparent processes and are independent of political cycles.
5. Promoting education and training of water professionals to strengthen the capacity of water institutions as well as stakeholders at large and to foster co-operation and knowledge-sharing.

Source: OECD (2015[1]), *OECD Principles on Water Governance*, https://www.oecd.org/gov/regional-policy/OECD-Principles-on-Water-Governancebrochure.pdf.

A way forward, as highlighted by the Engineering Council of South Africa, could be to restore and expand mentoring programmes to attract and accompany graduates towards a professional level. These programmes used to foster a culture of training engineering graduates toward registration. They used to be performed by bodies that were adequately staffed with qualified professionals who could plan training programmes, supervise work experience and mentor candidates. This could be resumed through induction of graduates to observe the work of competent engineers and perform specific processes under close supervision. Such consolidating skills and learning programmes could help increase the conversion rate of candidates to registered professionals. Bearing in mind that 61% of registration candidates are black whereas 74% of registered professionals are white, the bridging capacity gap needs to be addressed through targeted transformation and equity measures. In addition, implementing such programmes poses multifaceted problems which include organisational commitment of water institutions to perform induction programmes, adequate supply of supervisors and mentors, and technical bursaries.

At the utility level, skills and capacity gaps can be addressed through a dedicated action plan. In Namibia, the national water utility has developed a human resources strategy. It is a long-term plan setting objectives to be achieved in the field of human resource development in the organisation. It encompasses the following three dimensions:

- "Human resources development" that include training and development activities, as well as induction, internal and external bursaries, job attachments or internships.

- "Talent management" that include graduate development programmes, understudy programmes, succession management programmes.
- "Human resources development centre" that include internal and external vocational training courses, monitoring and evaluation, or student support.

In Uganda, the National Water and Sewerage Corporation develops a 5-year Strategic Direction which is regularly monitored in publicly available reports. This strategic document lists key deliverables in four Strategic Priority Areas. The 4th Strategic Priority Area is dedicated to productivity and capacity development and comprises the following "strategic focus areas": skills development, R&D, business re-engineering and staff productivity. For each of these "strategic focus areas", deliverables are defined along with a corresponding timeframe.

Strengthen transparency, integrity and engagement

Strengthen transparency and integrity

Culture of consequences

Transparency and integrity efforts have to be supported by a culture of consequences. When procurement rules are broken with impunity and illegal directives from political heads are not questioned, the absence of consequences gives an incentive to continue. Enforcement mechanisms that provide appropriate responses to all suspected violations of public integrity standards by public officials should be implemented. This is key for public infrastructure investment, especially large-scale projects that are particularly vulnerable to corruption and mismanagement. Budget overruns, delays and white elephants are common. Yet, public infrastructure also presents an opportunity for the government to showcase integrity and enhance citizens' trust. Governments can capitalise on such major events and investments by applying the OECD *Integrity Framework for Public Infrastructure* (OECD, 2016[41]) and demonstrate that infrastructure projects can be productive, transparent and free from corruption.

The OECD *Integrity Framework for Public Infrastructure* aims to assist governments and private sector actors in mitigating corruption risks in public investment by identifying corruption entry points over the entire public investment cycle (Figure 4-8). The framework identifies tools and mechanisms to promote integrity in public investment, including measures for promoting ethical standards, managing conflict of interest, strengthening monitoring and controls, and increasing transparency. The instrument can be applied at the national and subnational levels and across sectors.

Innovative open contracting models

Municipal procurement is regulated by the Municipal Finance Management Act No. 56 of 2003 (MFMA) and its regulations, including the Municipal Supply Chain Management Regulations (2005). These regulations specify the minimum requirements but municipalities are allowed to apply stricter standards. Another recommendation would be to make greater use of open contracting models. Allowing free access, through an online portal, for all stakeholders, including potential domestic and foreign suppliers, civil society and the general public, to public procurement information notably related to the public procurement system (e.g. institutional frameworks, laws and regulations), specific procurements (e.g. procurement forecasts, calls for tender, award announcements) and the performance of the public procurement system (e.g. benchmarks, monitoring results) are key measures to enhance the transparency of public procurement systems. Monitoring and analysing public procurement information is also essential to foster greater accountability of the contracting authority. This can be done through various innovative tools (Box 4.21).

Figure 4-8. Steps to mitigate integrity risks during the public investment cycle

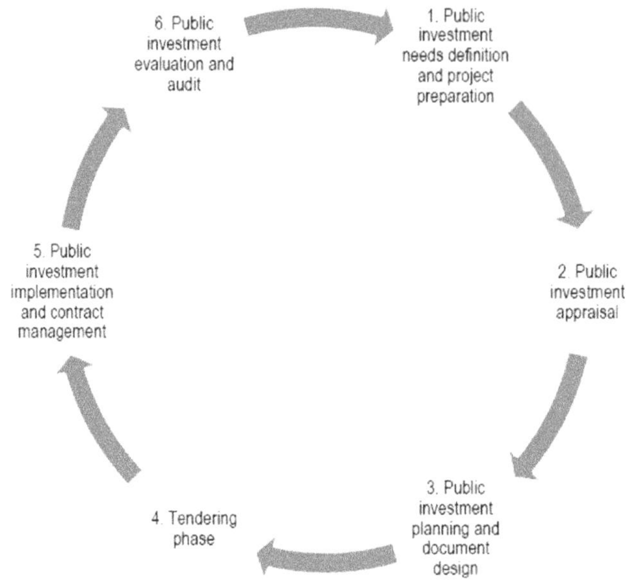

Source: OECD (2016[41]), *Integrity Framework for Public Infrastructure*, https://www.oecd.org/corruption/ethics/Integrity-Framework-For-Public-Infrastructure-Brochure.pdf.

Box 4.21. Innovative tools to enhance public procurement

Integrity pacts are mutual commitments between public and contracting parties to refrain from corruption and guarantee transparency during a procurement process. An independent third party, usually a civil society organisation (CSO), is given access to documents and procedures and ensures adherence to the integrity pact.

E-procurement envisages moving away from a paper-based procurement system so that the process takes place on a publicly available platform. At the very least it requires the publication of procurement information on an e-procurement platform.

Open contracting data standards prescribe standards for what information should be published and how. The use of this standard ensures that there is uniformity and standardisation of data which improves data quality and allows for comparison and analysis.

Red flag monitoring uses algorithms to analyse data and pick up anomalies. A set of procurement norms are built into the software and when a procurement practice violates a norm, the system generates a red flag notification. Members of civil society are then able to investigate this further in order to determine whether the deviation amounts to corruption or non-compliance with procurement law.

Source: Corruption Watch/WIN (2020[42]), *Money Down the Drain: Corruption in South Africa's Water Sector*, Corruption Watch and the Water Integrity Network.

Water sector as an "island of integrity"

As suggested by Corruption Watch and the Water Integrity Network report *Corruption in South Africa's Water Sector* (2020[42]), designating the water sector as "an island of integrity" could also be a way forward. This phrase refers to institutions that are successful at reducing corruption despite being in a context of endemic corruption. Although there is no formal definition of "islands of integrity", it could take the form of "an anti-corruption forum" gathering "key stakeholders including law enforcement agencies, relevant government departments and agencies, representatives of the private sector, regulators and civil sector organisations active in water and in combating corruption. Reports of corruption and gross irregularities could be submitted to the forum and allocated to the agency best placed to address them. The involvement of the Auditor-General of South Africa and other Chapter 9 institutions[4] would further strengthen the forum" (Corruption Watch/WIN, 2020[42]).

Strengthen engagement

Engaging stakeholders and promoting accountability are also key aspects to prevent political interference and its adverse effects. In a rapidly changing and connected world where climate change, population growth, urban development, rising water need for energy and food, natural disasters and water shortage are likely to damage societies and the environment, stakeholders must be empowered to act together to shape water governance. Stakeholders that compose the water sector play a crucial role in determining the outcome of a given policy or project. They can initiate and support it but they can also oppose efforts, attempt to block them or divert them to serve their own aims. Stakeholder engagement provides opportunities to share objectives, experiences and responsibilities and to be more supportive of solutions that will be reached while voicing and addressing concerns and interests. As such, stakeholder engagement is a means for groups and individuals to share tasks and responsibilities in a sector where they often contribute to challenges as well as solutions (Box 4.22). In Lusaka, for instance, the Lusaka Water Security Initiative, a multi-stakeholder collaboration system comprising the public sector, the private sector, civil society and international actors, was set up through a memorandum of understanding (MoU) to foster dialogue, knowledge sharing and awareness-raising, planning and project development among stakeholders (Box 4.23).

Box 4.22. Stakeholder engagement in the Portuguese water sector

Currently, the institutional framework in Portugal includes the regulatory authority (ERSAR), the environmental and water resources authority (Portuguese Environment Agency), the public health authority (Directorate-General for Health), the consumer protection authority (Directorate-General for the Consumer), the competition authority (Competition Authority) and the financial support management authority.

The success of the Portuguese public policy owes much to the good articulation between the aforementioned state-level bodies and the municipalities, but also to the participation of other stakeholders. The Portuguese National Water Council is the consultation body, independent from the government, where public administration bodies, municipalities, operators, consumers, non-governmental organisations, experts, research centres, universities and representatives from business associations engage to discuss the Portuguese public policies for water. This forum contributes to the coherence between the sector and regional interests and is a relevant platform to promote discussion over public policy and the national water plans. In the case of water services, two other consultative bodies are in place – the Consultative Council and the Tariff Council – both within the regulatory framework. The inclusion of all relevant stakeholders in policymaking is part of a co-operative environment, which highlights and explains the existence of a broad consensus in the Portuguese water sector and in the Portuguese society about the fundamentals of the public policy for water.

Source: ERSAR (2017[43]), *The Portuguese Public Policy for Water Services (1993-2016).*

Box 4.23. Lusaka Water Security Initiative (LuWSI): A successful stakeholder engagement

LuWSI is a multi-stakeholder collaboration system between the public sector, private sector, civil society and international actors working towards the vision of water security for the residents and businesses of Lusaka. LuWSI partners engage in dialogue and leadership, analysis and knowledge generation, advocacy and awareness-raising, planning and project development. The initiative was founded in 2016 and currently has over 20 partners from all sectors. LuWSI is not, as of yet, a registered legal entity but rather a voluntary partnership of partners, bound together through an MoU.

The organisational structure of LuWSI is made up of:

- A steering board – LuWSI's overall decision-making body.
- A Knowledge and Advocacy Committee and a Projects and Collaboration Committee.
- A secretariat – LuWSI's administrative body.
- Project teams – implementing bodies for individual projects under LuWSI.

LuWSI is committed to its vision "Water security for all to support a healthy and prosperous city". Water security is key to economic growth, human well-being and sustaining a green city. All LuWSI partners are committed to working together to make this vision a reality.

LuWSI mission is to strengthen multi-stakeholder collaboration to safeguard Lusaka's water resources while enhancing the sustainable and timely access to water and sanitation for all. Co-operation is crucial if the complex issue of water security is to be addressed sustainably. Water security is everybody's business and every organisation and individual can contribute to improving the water situation in Lusaka.

Core functions

- Assess, prioritise and monitor water security threats and solutions.
- Create awareness, education and advocacy for change.
- Develop and implement projects; mobilise new actors and resources.
- Strengthen capacity for multi-stakeholder collaboration.

LuWSI has five Water Security Action Areas, which were prioritised by its partners in 2016 during a series of strategy development workshops. These action areas are the focus of LuWSI's projects and their partners' activities:

- Groundwater pollution prevention.
- Sustainable groundwater exploitation.
- Healthy Kafue River.
- Access to water supply and sanitation.
- Urban flood risk management.

Source: LuWSI (n.d.[44]), *Homepage*, https://www.luwsi.org/ (accessed on 2 February 2021).

Critical aspects of governance should guide stakeholder engagement frameworks. Fair and equitable access to engagement opportunities is key to ensure a balanced and representative process that takes into account diverse ideas and opinions. Being transparent and open about the ways to identify stakeholders, choose engagement mechanisms and define the objectives pursued can help to raise interest among stakeholders and to develop an understanding of and support for the final decisions. It is not sufficient to provide platforms for stakeholders to share their ideas as decision-makers must also clearly demonstrate how these ideas are taken into account. Procedural transparency and timely disclosure of information, including alternative solutions, are therefore critical to ensure the legitimacy of decision-making processes and their outcomes. Engagement processes may bring together groups with opposing views who fear that their views will not be taken into account. Showing participants what the intention of the process is and how their input will be considered is important to ensure productive discussions and exchange of opinions. It is also important that decision-makers be able to trust the quality and value of input from non-technical experts (Table 4.13).

Table 4.13. Key OECD principles on stakeholder engagement for inclusive water governance

Inclusiveness and equity	Principle 1: Map all stakeholders who have a stake in the outcome or that are likely to be affected, as well as their responsibility, core motivations and interactions
Clarity of goals, transparency and accountability	Principle 2: Define the ultimate line of decision-making, the objectives of stakeholder engagement and the expected use of inputs
Capacity and information	Principle 3: Allocate proper financial and human resources and share needed information for result-oriented stakeholder engagement
Efficiency and effectiveness	Principle 4: Regularly assess the process and outcomes of stakeholder engagement to learn, adjust and improve accordingly
Institutionalisation, structuring and integration	Principle 5: Embed engagement processes in clear legal and policy frameworks, organisational structures/principles and responsible authorities
Adaptiveness	Principle 6: Customise the type and level of engagement as needed and keep the process flexible to changing circumstances

Source: OCDE, (2015[45])Stakeholder Engagement for Inclusive Water Governance,http://dx.doi.org/10.1787/9789264231122-en http://dx.doi.org/10.1787/9789264231122-en

Crises, change or emergency-driven situations also have an impact on stakeholder engagement. Crises shed light on the weaknesses of governments to properly assess the risks and call upon them to set up preventive measures to mitigate their impacts. As such, they are often windows of opportunity for new ideas to emerge and create a social and political environment with a potential for developing partnerships as was the case with the creation of the Water Resilience Advisory Committee (WRAC) in Cape Town.

References

Breede-Gouritz Catchment Management Agency (2019), *Annual Report 2018/2019*, https://breedegouritzcma.co.za/pdfs/annual_reports/bgcma_gov_annual-report-2018.pdf. [6]

City of Cape Town (2020), *Water Outlook 2020 Report*, Department of Water and Sanitation. [12]

City of Cape Town (2019), *Cape Town Water Strategy*, Department of Water and Sanitation, http://resource.capetown.gov.za/documentcentre/Documents/City%20strategies%2c%20plans%20and%20frameworks/Cape%20Town%20Water%20Strategy.pdf. [10]

Corruption Watch/WIN (2020), *Money Down the Drain: Corruption in South Africa's Water Sector*, Corruption Watch and the Water Integrity Network. [42]

DWS (2019), *National Water and Sanitation Master Plan*, Department of Water and Sanitation, http://www.dwa.gov.za/National%20Water%20and%20Sanitation%20Master%20Plan/DocumentsReports.aspx. [5]

DWS (2018), *Budget Policy Speech. Budget Vote 36, 2018/2019 financial year.* [29]

DWS (2017), *Business Case for the Establishment of a Single Catchment Management Agency*, Department of Water and Sanitation. [3]

DWS (2013), *Economic Regulator: Options and Models Report, Recommendations*, https://www.dws.gov.za/Projects/PERR/documents/2013/Economic%20Regulator%20-%20Institutional%20Models%20%2015%20May%202013.pptx. [28]

DWS (2013), *Institutional and financial models for the Economic Regulator*, https://www.dws.gov.za/Projects/PERR/documents/2013/Economic%20Regulator%20Options%20and%20Models%20Report%20(30%20Apr).docx. [27]

DWS (2007), *Pricing Strategy for Raw Water Use Charges*, Department of Water and Sanitation. [7]

DWS (1998), *National Water Act.* [26]

DWS (forthcoming), *Western Cape Water Supply System, Reconciliation Strategy, Status Report 2019.* [9]

ERSAR (2017), *The Portuguese Public Policy for Water Services (1993-2016).* [43]

ESAWAS Regulators Association (2015), *Regional Benchmark of Large Water Supply and Sanitation Utilities, 2013/2014 Report.* [36]

eThekwini (2019), *Water and Sanitation Service Level Standards, 13th edition, July 2019/2020.* [35]

European Commission (2013), *Building a Green Infrastrcuture for Europe*, https://ec.europa.eu/environment/nature/ecosystems/docs/green_infrastructure_broc.pdf. [13]

Kidd, M. (2016), "Compulsory licensing under South Africa's National Water Act", *Water International*, Vol. 41/6, pp. 916–927. [25]

LuWSI (n.d.), *Homepage*, Lusaka Water Security Initiative, https://www.luwsi.org/ (accessed on 2 February 2021). [44]

McDonald, R. (2014), *Urban Water Blueprint: Mapping conservation solutions to the global water challenge*, The Nature Conservancy, https://www.nature.org/content/dam/tnc/nature/en/documents/Urban_Water_Blueprint.pdf. [16]

Munnik, V. (2020), "The reluctant roll-out of Catchment Management Agencies: Assessing the key risks and consequences of delays in finalising institutional arrangements for decentralised water resource management", Water Research Commission, Pretoria, http://www.wrc.org.za/wp-content/uploads/mdocs/2943_final.pdf. [2]

NWASCO (n.d.), *Pro Poor Regulation*, http://www.nwasco.org.zm/index.php/regulatory-tools/pro-poor-regulation. [33]

NWSC (2019), *Integrated Annual Report 2018-2019*, National Water and Sewerage Corporation. [39]

OECD (2020), *The Circular Economy in Cities and Regions: Synthesis Report*, OECD Urban Studies, OECD Publishing, Paris, https://doi.org/10.1787/10ac6ae4-en. [20]

OECD (2017), *Creating a Culture of Independence: Practical Guidance against Undue Influence*, The Governance of Regulators, OECD Publishing, Paris, https://doi.org/10.1787/9789264274198-en. [31]

OECD (2017), *Water Charges in Brazil: The Ways Forward*, OECD Studies on Water, OECD Publishing, Paris, https://doi.org/10.1787/9789264285712-en. [8]

OECD (2016), *Integrity Framework for Public Infrastructure*, OECD Publishing, Paris, https://www.oecd.org/corruption/ethics/Integrity-Framework-For-Public-Infrastructure-Brochure.pdf. [41]

OECD (2015), *OECD Principles on Water Governance*, OECD, Paris, https://www.oecd.org/gov/regional-policy/OECD-Principles-on-Water-Governancebrochure.pdf. [1]

OECD (2015), *Stakeholder Engagement for Inclusive Water Governance*, OECD Studies on Water, OECD Publishing, Paris, https://dx.doi.org/10.1787/9789264231122-en. [45]

OECD (2015), *Stakeholder Engagement for Inclusive Water Governance*, OECD Studies on Water, OECD Publishing, Paris, https://dx.doi.org/10.1787/9789264231122-en. [46]

OECD (2015), *The Governance of Water Regulators*, OECD Studies on Water, OECD Publishing, Paris, https://doi.org/10.1787/9789264231092-en. [30]

OECD (2015), *Water and Cities: Ensuring Sustainable Futures*, OECD Studies on Water, OECD Publishing, paris, http://dx.doi.org/10.1787/9789264230149-en. [17]

OECD (2015), *Water Resources Allocation: Sharing Risks and Opportunities*, OECD Studies on Water, OECD Publishing, Paris, https://doi.org/10.1787/9789264229631-en. [21]

OECD (2015), *Water Resources Governance in Brazil*, OECD Studies on Water, OECD Publishing, Paris, https://doi.org/10.1787/9789264238121-en. [4]

OECD (2013), *Barriers to and Incentives for, the Adoption of Green Water Infrastructure*, OECD, Paris. [15]

OECD (2010), *Pricing Water Resources and Water and Sanitation Services*, https://doi.org/10.1787/22245081. [37]

Rawlins, J. (2019), "Political economy of water reallocation in South Africa: Insights from the Western Cape water crisis". [24]

Speed, R. et al. (2011), "Policy measures, mechanisms, and framework for addressing environmental flows", International Water Centre, Brisbane. [23]

Statistics South Africa (2020), *Statistics South Africa*, http://www.statssa.gov.za/. [11]

The Nature Conservancy (2016), *Sub-Saharan Africa's Urban Water Blueprint: Securing Water Through Water Funds and Other Investments in Ecological Infrastructure*, https://s3.amazonaws.com/tnc-craft/library/Sub-Saharan-Africa-UWB.-2016.pdf?mtime=20180129061945. [18]

Turpie, J. et al. (2016), "A preliminary investigation of the potential costs and benefits of rehabilitation of the Nakivubo Wetland, Kampala", in *Promoting Green Urban Development in Africa*, World Bank, Washington. [19]

Turpie, J. et al. (2017), “Mapping and valuation of South Africa’s ecosystem services: A local perspective”. [22]

UNEP (2014), *Green Infrastructure Guide for Water Management: Ecosystem-based Management Approaches for Water-related Infrastructure Projects*, United Nations Environment Programme. [14]

United States Agency for International Development (2020), *Water Sanitation Hygiene Finance project*. [38]

Vienings, A. and M. Lima (2015), *Integrated Water Sector Skills Intervention Map Based on a Sector Skills Gap Analysis*, Water Research Commission, Pretoria. [40]

WASREB (2015), *Tariff Guidelines*, http://www.wasreb.go.ke/ regulatory-tools/tariff-guidelines. [32]

World Bank (2006), “Taking account of the poor in water sector regulation”, *Water Supply & Sanitation Working Notes*, No. 11. [34]

Notes

[1] This concept refers to “the organised process of reconfiguring the way in which a given state institution is structured, governed, managed and funded so that it serves a purpose different to its formal mandate” (OECD, 2015[46]).

[2] Green infrastructure (GI) is a nature-based solution that encompasses all actions that rely on ecosystems and the services they provide to respond to various societal challenges such as climate change, food security or disaster risk.

[3] Integrated Water Sector Skills Intervention Map based on a sector skills gap analysis report to the Water Research Commission by A. Vienings (Water Concepts) and M. Lima (Onyxx Human Capital) (co-project leaders) (2015[40]).

[4] Chapter 9 Institutions refer to a group of organisations established in the South African Constitution to guard democracy. The institutions are the Public Protector, the South African Human Rights Commission, the Commission for the Promotion and Protection of the Rights of Cultural, Religious and Linguistic Communities, the Commission for Gender Equality, the Auditor-General, the Independent Electoral Commission, and an independent authority to regulate broadcasting.

Annex A. List of stakeholders

List of stakeholders consulted during the water policy dialogue process:

Organisation	Persons
Aurecon consultancy	James Cullis, Lloyd Fisher-Jeffes, Mike Shand
Berg River Main Irrigation Board	Billy Bourbon-Leftley, Enright Willie
Breede-Gouritz Catchment Management Agency	Samantha Braid, Elkerine Rossouw
CapeNature	Gail Cleaver-Christie, Jeanne Gouws, Andrew Turner
Cape Town Water Fund	Mark Botha, consultant for the Cape Town Water Fund
City of CapeTown	Siyabulela Bashe, Conrad Frehse, Christa Hugo, Mpharu Hloyi, Michael Killick, Simon Maytham, Mogamat Mallick, Nokuzola Mhlungu, Rajan Moodley, Floris Mostert, Sarah Rushmere, Bertus Saayman, Daniel Sullivan, Michael Webster, Barry Wood
Council for Scientific and Industrial Research	David Lemaitre
Drakenstein Municipality	Andre Kowalewski
Good, South African political party	Mark Rountree
GreenCape	Claire Pengelly
Independent consultants	Rolfe Eberhard, consultant for the City of Cape Town Peter Flower, Jessica Wilson
International Water Management Institute	William Rex
National Business Institute	Mmaphefo Thwala
Nature Conservancy	Louise Stafford
Oxford University	David Grey
Peer-reviewers	Caroline Figuères, Neil McLeod, Koen Verbist
Regional Office of the National Department for Water and Sanitation	Derril Daniels, Rashid Khan, Melissa Lintnaar-Strauss, Bila-Mupariwa Ntombizanele, Bertrand van Zyl
Saldanha Bay Municipality	David Wright
South Africa National Department for Water and Sanitation	Eustathia Bofilatos, Fanus Fourie, Livhuwani Mabuda, Patrick Mlilo, Menard Mugumo, Mashudu Murovhi, Beason Mwaka
South Africa National Treasury	Shingirai Chimuti, Yasmin Coovadia, Anthea Stephens from the City Support Programme
South African National Biodiversity Institute	Alex Marsh
South African Faith Communities for Environment Institute	Bishop Geoff Davies
Stellenbosch University Water Institute	Leanne Seeliger
Swartland Municipality	Louis Zikman
United States Agency for International Development	Chris Serjak from the WASH-FIN project, implemented by Tetra Tech on behalf of the United States Agency for International Development
University of Cape Town	Gina Ziervogel (African Climate and Development Initiative) Kirsty Carden & Kevin Winter (Future Water Research Institute)
Water Globe Consultants	Gisela Kaiser
Water Research Commission	Jay Bhagwan, John Dini, Dhesigen Naidoo
Wesgro, tourism, trade and investment promotion agency for Cape Town and the Western Cape	Tim Harris
The Wildlife and Environment Society of South Africa	Taryn van Neel
Western Cape Economic Development Partnership	Andrew Boraine, Amanda Gcanga, Selwyn Willoughby
Western Cape Government	Helen Davies, Peter Keuck, Wilna Kloppers, Karen Shippey, Francis Steyn
World Bank	Chris Heymans, Nicholas Kudakwashe Tandi, Erwin de Nys, Markus Wishart, Winston Yu
World Wildlife Fund – South Africa	Caroline Gelderblom, Morné du Plessis, Klaudia Schacht

www.ingramcontent.com/pod-product-compliance
Ingram Content Group UK Ltd.
Pitfield, Milton Keynes, MK11 3LW, UK
UKHW051505290926
15471UKWH00008B/1431

9 789264 679351